Chakaura

AWAKENING THE MUSE

Sacred Journey of a
Modern-Day Mystic

Michèle C. St.Amour

Chakaura: Awakening the Muse
Copyright © 2016 by Michèle C. St.Amour

All rights reserved. No part of this publication may be reproduced, distributed, or transmitted in any form or by any means, including photocopying, recording, or other electronic or mechanical methods, without the prior written permission of the author, except in the case of brief quotations embodied in critical reviews and certain other non-commercial uses permitted by copyright law.

Cover art: Josée Duquette
Editor: Patricia Waldygo

Chakaura Publishing
16 Ole Colonial Rd
Grenville-sur-la-rouge, QC
Canada   J0V 1B0
www.chakaurapublishing.com

ISBN
978-1-77302-263-5 (Hardcover)
978-1-77302-261-1 (Paperback)
978-1-77302-262-8 (eBook)

To everyone who believed in me . . .

Contents

Prologue ix

Chapter 1: The Prophecy 1

Chapter 2: Miracles of Miracles 13

Chapter 3: A Visit from a Spirit Elder—Wonders Never Cease 25

Chapter 4: Chakaura™—The Prophecy Begins 31

Chapter 5: Angelina's Story Begins to Unravel 41

Chapter 6: Journeying into the Akashic 45

Chapter 7: Some Things Are Best Kept to Oneself 53

Chapter 8: The Beginning of the End 63

Chapter 9: The Forgotten Self 69

Chapter 10: Angelina's Purpose 81

Chapter 11: The Lecture—Grounding 89

Chapter 12: New Beginnings 97

Chapter 13: The Quest 107

Chapter 14: Cycles of Life—Endings, Birth, Beginnings 115

Chapter 15: Angelina's Awakening 129

Chapter 16: Dark Night of the Soul—A Gift 137

Chapter 17: Seeking Answers 143

Chapter 18: Meeting Cheyenne 153

Chapter 19: To Explain the Inexplicable 167

Chapter 20: WolfWoman 175

Chapter 21: A Trine Experience—The Power of Three 183

Chapter 22: The Sacred: Initiation 193

Chapter 23: The White Place—A World Beyond 203

Chapter 24: Another Reality 219

Chapter 25: Memories Surface—Laughter and Longing 231

Chapter 26: Other Worlds, Other Realities, Other Truths 245

Chapter 27: Bridging the Worlds—Two Worlds Become One 265

Chapter 28: Endings and New Beginnings 279

Chapter 29: And So the Mysteries of the Subtle Worlds Unravel 293

Chapter 30: At a Crossroads 303

Giving Thanks 321

About the Author 323

About Chakaura™ 325

Chakaura
AWAKENING THE MUSE

Prologue

It has begun...

The beginning of the end, of yet another dream cycle...

Teacher initiated the process with these words:

In order to move forward, you must now release your past.
You will do this by writing of it.
All that comes to you, all that needs to be shared and released,
is now to be written,
so that others may be guided by the Light.
It is why you came.

Once this is accomplished, you will then release it to the
heavens and the earth, with the method you have been taught
and that you teach to those seeking to know the higher worlds.
From that moment on, you will be released from your past, to
move forward into your future destiny, into a new age of Being.

Lightness of spirit is the key to Becoming!
You cannot bring the past with you, for
its weight now clips your wings.

Let go and let Be!
This is our way!

Oshtalo, my dear. It is time to make your way home!

I hung my head to acknowledge Teacher's counsel. As usual, Teacher was right, and I had it within me to see this. The monumental task, though, of what Teacher had asked seemed at this time beyond me. Yet I had faith that as in the past, the Powers that governed would support and provide.

Faith, dear! Faith.
The virtue that raises one is faith!

Prologue

Chapter 1

The Prophecy

As waves come with water and flames with fire, so the universal waves with us."

—*Osho*

My name is Angelina, and I come from a family of seers. Destiny chose me for this role from birth. You cannot read a few books or take a couple of courses and expect to be a seer or a healer. It never happens that way. From a young age, I just knew instinctively what this life had in store for me.

My latest vision had me a bit flushed and annoyed at the magnitude of the information I had to process. I spent a few hours mentally replaying this prophetic revelation. The vision had come upon me like a drug. My body hummed and throbbed with sensations of energy, and I gradually fell into a deep, altered state of consciousness.

This revelation would define the rest of my life in ways I could not imagine.

I sank into darkness, numb to my senses as I floated out to a vast universe of the mind. I hovered in space, looking down on our wondrous planet. I thought, *What a beautiful sight!*

I gazed upon the Atlantic Ocean separating the two continents of the East and the West. As I glided ever eastward, Australia came into view. The colours were so bright and pure. The water reflected a blue from the heavens never seen, except in images of Earth from satellites.

Curiously, a consciousness apart from my own watched a likeness of myself drifting in space above the Earth. Of course, I had travelled in the guise of my Higher Self (HS). Though it resembled my present person, it had qualities and characteristics I had yet to evolve to. I had two levels of awareness, thinking simultaneously. I remember wondering, *Who is this silent observer I know so intimately, watching from a distance?*

As I continued to review scenes from this latest prophetic vision, invisible forces directed my gaze toward the Asian countries.

I recognized China and its surroundings, and a holograph suddenly appeared in mid-air. An inner voice explained the scenes playing out as the "Coming." A bombardment of images—tidal waves and tornadoes—portrayed a time of purification. Water surged, pounded, and swallowed up villages and landmarks alike. People of obvious Asian bloodlines screamed and ran in fear, as a wall of water rolled and thundered toward them, to eventually swallow them up. I could smell the saltwater and hear the soul screams of thousands as they took their last breaths and departed.

I closed my eyes to the shock and horror. After a few moments, silence surrounded me and became so loud, it jerked my attention back to myself. Seconds passed that seemed like minutes. I opened my eyes, and the holographic screen had dissipated. I once again peered at the amazing spectra of Earth.

Next, the invisible forces gently guided my vision westward, to my left. I looked down on the landmass of Africa. Another holographic screen appeared, showing scenes of deserts and sandstorms. People, young and old, wrapped in colourful clothing the sand had dulled to a faded rainbow of patterns, braved battering whirlwinds of scorching sand. Through empathy, I felt their fear and heard their screams of terror. Once again, thousands suffered and departed abruptly, due to nature's power. Mother Earth was having her say, using the force of her elements to cleanse herself: first with water, then with fire and air. The three elements of creation, the Holy Trinity of life, naturally sought balance after being so disrespected and abused.

Suddenly, the inner voice brought me back to the utter quietness of this outer space odyssey, to direct my attention to North America. My approach slower, I glided down nearer to the mass of land. Suspended, I could clearly see the entire eastern seaboard of the United States and Canada. As I marvelled at the size and breadth of our Western world, a great thundering sound drew my gaze toward the Atlantic Ocean. In moments, a tsunami of enormous proportions came rolling in and crashed onto land, literally eating up the East Coast seaboard.

Stunned at the destruction and violence, I watched the land tremble from the collision with the tsunami's wall of water. The Earth shook in anger against what had been done to her vitals. The huge tidal wave reached far inland. Much of the whole coastline remained underwater for hundreds of miles, to recede only in weeks. This cataclysm triggered a massive earthquake on the West Coast, in the area we call California, resulting in landslides with untold damage and loss.

An all-permeating silence reigned once again, as the waters covered the east and the west side of the continent, where land and cities had thrived. Not yet emotionally affected by what I witnessed, I felt calmed by the eerie silence. The implications of these natural disasters had not yet entered my awareness.

The inner voice now directed me to close my eyes and transported me back down to Earth in North America. My body landed gently on a solid base. I opened my eyes as the sounds of chaos assailed my ears.

I stood amongst burning skyscrapers, overturned cars, and smouldering rumble. It reminded me of a scene I once saw in a movie depicting the end of time. Intuitively, I knew this was a city in the Eastern United States, either before or after the floods. I've learned that prophecy does not always occur in the sequence of linear time but often jumps from one probability to another.

I looked around, and people with determined expressions seemed to be heading toward a destination. Gathering things together for a journey, young and old alike had banded in unity to survive this latest attempt by Mother Nature to cleanse her wounds.

The inner voice whispered, *"Pay attention,"* as a figure with long white hair appeared, walking northward with a steady, authoritative gait. Everyone instinctively followed this striking figure, who exuded an aura of strength, power, courage, wisdom, and knowing. I peered intensely at the person's back. Abruptly, the white-haired figure turned toward me and looked me straight in the eyes.

Shocked, I knew deep down that these people couldn't possibly be aware of my role in this vision. How could this person see me, if I were only dreaming and not part of the reality I observed? Doubt entered my mind, as my gaze locked with the penetrating eyes of the white-haired figure, and then a timeless moment of understanding passed between our Selves.

We stood there, unmoving, communicating in a language as ancient as life itself. I wondered whether this person, who seemed oddly familiar, was a man or a woman.

The inner voice rose in a mysterious, evocative tone: *"Remember who you are and where you hence come from!"*

I suddenly understood that here lay my future. Somewhere in this person my future beckoned, though it may have been symbolic.

I approached the Wise One. I came to call them that, because I would meet more of them in the days to come. The first thing that caught my attention was the individual's youthfulness, so contrary to the white hair. I would see this in future encounters with other Wise Ones. Their hair—thick, vibrant, and extremely long—symbolised vitality and wisdom in many cultures.

Everyone—including other Wise Ones—deferred to this particular person, who seemed to be a leader. Many followed this Wise One's footsteps, heading north out of the city. An unspoken understanding of where they were all going and why guided them.

One day, after weeks of travel, we heard a voice say, *"Go to the mountains."* I later realized this message was strangely also meant for me.

As day followed night, I accompanied the group, a ghost in their midst. More people joined us, as the Wise One guided the group to a safe place on what we learned was sacred ground, far north in the mountainous areas.

Often, my mind connected with the Wise Ones', as one consciousness. In those moments, they showed me scenes in my mind's eye, of many other like-minded groups with similar leaders heading north from all over the United States.

Everyone regarded my Wise One, the main leader, with great respect. This white-haired Wise One, who seemed neither man nor woman but a perfect combination of both, communicated telepathically with other Wise Ones travelling from all over the country.

The clear telepathic communication among the Wise Ones amazed me. This was necessary, given the complete breakdown of the technological grid from catastrophic events. This Wise One's impressive telepathic skills could not be intercepted or broken, unless others of like abilities existed—doubtful in a world this chaotic.

A darkness stalked us, and we felt an urgency to arrive at our mountainous haven.

** * ***

We crossed an important boundary and continued to travel northward.

All of the various groups at last arrived at their intended destinations, with no mishaps. In other countries around the world, Wise Ones such as ours had transported survivors to safe areas. I observed this by viewing multiple timelines from my dreaming point. These groups appeared as lights shining in a world gone awry.

They went on to build homes, as they waited for "the time of the prophecy," as told to them by the Wise Ones. These mountains hid our group well from the turmoil down below, the result of so many catastrophic events unconsciously triggered by man and his greed and ignorance. Despite so many signs of the coming apocalypse, most people simply paid no heed.

Wise Ones had come to these sacred mountains prior to Mother Nature's shaking of the Earth, to prepare the necessities and create a sacred space for those destined to be here now. A time of purification had begun, which some called the 6th extinction, similar to past times, when the Earth cleansed for many days and nights.

Forced to move beyond the materialism and greed of the current collective consciousness, the survivors shifted to a new awareness, born of a courage to change. The cycle of unsustainable materialism had ended, and it was about time, because the planet had suffered all of the pilfering and purposeful destruction it could take. A new cycle, a new era, and a new human species arose from this latest apocalypse. I recalled that the word *apocalypse*, from the ancient Greek, meant "uncovering": it speaks of lifting a veil or a revelation.

If this does not wake us up, then nothing will, I thought.

In the next few years, the settlers learned to reconnect and live off the Earth in peace and harmony, guided by the Wise Ones, their leaders. These Wise Ones, with an illuminated air, time and again spoke of things to come. The survivors felt secure, as an invisible energetic shield upheld by the Wise Ones surrounded them. This place embraced the pure of heart, protecting and nurturing them through this time of cleansing.

The survivors were taught that this particular area had an unusual sacredness, for it was the gateway to the cosmic soul of Mother Earth. Important energies grounded the area, so new concepts and ideas could be easily assimilated. The actual camp, the centre of Mother Earth's All-Seeing Eye, opened the doorway of her cosmic energies. Hence, the shields and the energies sourced possessed a divine purity not found anywhere else. For many years, this place, with its unique energies, drew individuals from around the world, in readiness for this sacred time of initiation.

The Wise Ones trained the survivors in daily regimens of special techniques, gradually shifting the survivors into greater conscious awareness. This new understanding obviously had a positive effect, as evidenced by everyone's laughter and happiness. So many questions arose in my mind, as I observed the daily rituals and self-discipline everyone developed.

The inner voice answered my silent questions, as I observed the future unfolding.

> *To become wise means to become free of fear, as you embrace joy in living naturally. You must become knowledgeable of how the state of your inner world determines your outer one. Observe, and in time all will be revealed to you. You must simply remember.*

I knew deep down that my life, intricately tied to this vision, had a symbolism inherently woven into it. The voice continued,

> *The fast approaching day of ascension demands these people be initiated into the mysteries of higher worlds. The Wise Ones agreed to prepare and attune the survivors to Earth's new higher vibration. If the survivors of the apocalypse wish to live on through the last changeling event, discipline and daily practice are necessary to transform them to resonate with the ascended frequency.*

These words made such sense to me. The voice added,

> *These practices, ancient spiritual rites, shift people into higher states of consciousness by bringing their energy up. The techniques originate from knowledge of the science of transformation, grounded in the laws of creation.*

As the voice faded away, I returned to watching the scene before me. By now, I knew with certainty that the Wise Ones were very aware of my presence. Many times, I found myself locked in eye contact with one or another of them, as silent communication passed between us. To the rest of the people, the survivors, my presence remained generally invisible and unnoticed.

Day by day, everyone followed the guidance of the Wise Ones. The new settlers became vibrantly healthy and grew to recognize their innate state as being pure energy. As such, they could access "things miraculous," as they became proficient in the techniques taught to them. They continued to live normal social lives, yet with knowledge to better understand and manage their inner worlds. The fearful feelings of judgment, envy, want, hate, and guilt plaguing them in the past became rare with the wise guidance they received in managing relationships and communicate in healthier, more positive ways. The years unfolded, and this new culture attained a level of awareness only ever found in monasteries and spiritual initiate schools.

The Time of Ascension

One summer morning, the people arose and intuitively knew the time of reckoning had arrived. Calm and prepared, they made their way to the valley below, the basin of a circular area surrounded by mountains with a small lake in its crest. Everyone, including the Wise Ones, had dressed in his or her finest and patiently waited for the momentous culmination of ascension, the "changeling" moment.

I hesitantly followed, sensing a remnant of old fears rising from people, including myself, for at this point I felt as if I were part of this community.

As I wondered about this upcoming challenge, the inner voice answered.

> The body's survival mechanism is triggered in moments of transformation. Only the brave of heart find the courage not to lose control and give in to their fears in moments of great stress. This same process occurs upon physical death. Now you will better understand why the Wise Ones made it so important for the settlers to practice daily to develop very specific spiritual muscles. Observe in these next moments how these "energy muscles" instinctively come into full force during the changeling process. Pay close attention to these teachings, for you must remember and bring them to the world, if people wish to survive the fast-approaching time of purification. It is your destiny! Remember!

Through resonance and empathy, I felt how people naturally prepared themselves with a power not witnessed until now. Their Higher Selves' intuitive readiness for the upcoming shift became a testimony to the people's years of daily disciplined training. I instinctively knew this state of being, although I had no recollection of ever learning about it.

The voice continued,

The laws of physics govern your primary nature, that being energy. If transformation is not managed with wisdom and proper support, people can do themselves irreparable harm, for it generates a great electrical surge. If not properly grounded, people will short-circuit their nervous systems. So few in your time know of this.

As I pondered these words of wisdom, the voice piped up again.

When life transitions are mismanaged, people suffer all sorts of nervous system issues. In fact, most diseases become a by-product of unsupported cycles of change. People of your time can be so self-destructive. They have lost their conscious connection to nature—their source of power—hence, they are no longer grounded, which explains their propensity to destroy the very hand that feeds them, Mother Earth!

* * *

My gaze went to the valley below, as the sun rose. I felt the excitement of everyone present. Suddenly, an electric static filled the air, as a huge mushroom of white shimmering energy exploded on the horizon. It hung there, suspended, for what seemed like minutes and then came toward us in a massive wave of iridescent energy. Everyone tensed, as a last surge of fear of the unknown ran through us.

The voice echoed in my mind: *"Brace yourself, but do not fight the process. Allow it to flow through you, and all will be well."*

In that fateful moment, we thought death would be the outcome of this event. With courage born of faith, we braced ourselves to face this death, as a wall of energy hit us. A flash passed through us like a forceful wind, and the sudden uncontrollable fear we all shared instantly dissipated, grounded by the tremendous energy muscles we had developed over the years. In that moment, we understood the need for, and the seriousness of, the techniques taught to us. I later realized our fearful ideas had been based on our innocence about how these things worked.

Our sudden dread of dying was in fact our survival instinct surging—a very natural reaction to change.

As the flash of light passed through us, we experienced an amazing metamorphosis. Instinct born of daily practice unconsciously triggered the tools taught to us by the Wise Ones. We'd woken up from a dream. All pain and apprehension left us, and only a sense of deep love and contentment prevailed. Our physical bodies, now airy, confined us no longer. I remember at first thinking I must be dead, and this experience of dying had not been what I envisioned: a liberation of sorts. But no sooner did this thought surface than I quashed it with the reality that I still had a physical body, and everything around me remained the same, only more luminous and healthy looking. Everything lived and sparkled with a new sense of life. I noticed those closest to me thinking these same thoughts, and I wondered at the clarity of telepathic communication we now experienced.

We had ascended and transformed ourselves into a dimension of higher energy frequencies of this new world, enabling us to live in peace and harmony for the future survival of mankind. This new beginning ended an old way of being so fraught with suffering. A new age, a new era as prophesied.

I asked when this would unfold, and dates appeared, years away, followed by a year of culmination, all within my lifetime. With the dates flashing in my mind, I slowly regained normal consciousness. My attention returned to my physical body, as I once again became aware of lying inert on the sofa in my sacred room where my vision had begun. The inner voice spoke:

> And so it will be if man does not soon awaken to his destructive ways. You are called now to reawaken and fulfil your destiny, as contracted by your soul bloodline. We will support your awakening and guide you through the many initiations you will be asked to face, and then guide others through, before the tide will turn. Your will shall be served as ordained by the Powers That Be.
>
> We are once again in service to the One. Awaken and remember; the time of resurrection is upon you. Prepare

yourself for the next phase of your present incarnation. Know we are here. Your time of slumber is now over.

Awaken . . . awaken . . . awaken, Angelina, and go to the mountains!

Oshnawega, sweet child; it is time to come home.

My awareness, no longer split into numerous pieces, came to settle within this earthly self in my present timeline. My body felt stiff and vibrated at a higher energy frequency than I was normally used to. It dawned on me that this was no ordinary prophetic vision. Possibly my whole reason for being and the future of mankind depended on many things I had been shown.

Overwhelmed, I got up and began typing out as many details as I could recall, in the hope more would be revealed.

Chapter 2

Miracles of Miracles

"Just as a candle cannot burn without fire, men cannot live without a spiritual life."

—*The Buddha*

Present Day

Today, the last class before the Christmas holidays, the students look forward to the festivities. Simple pinecone and evergreen decorations adorn the Great Hall, dressing the entire institute in splendour.

I take a moment to absorb the beauty and symmetry of this place, feeling proud of how everything came together so smoothly and gracefully over the years. I first envisioned this institute as empowering people through various self-discovery programs. Our centre's philosophy encourages a natural, uncomplicated way of life and understanding the subtle natural energies that mould people's decisions and experiences.

Hubby, the present love of my life, and I were synchronistically guided to these mountains. When I think back to how it all came to be, the turning point occurred one morning when Hubby and I decided to leave the flatlands. This occurred years ago, but the memory is still fresh.

We were talking in the kitchen of the old red brick house, where my previous husband and I had raised the kids.

"Hubby," I said, "this might sound strange, but I think we should look for land up to the north. I had a dream three days ago . . . and in it, a mountain's silhouette appeared on a horizon. Then yesterday when I drove into town, I looked up to see the exact same silhouette as in my dream. You know as well as I do that coincidences do not exist —there is only synchronicity."

He watched me silently, listening. He was like that. He would simply wait until I finished telling my story before commenting or giving his opinion. At times, I found it disconcerting, for I couldn't read him as easily as I did others. He had the shields of a warrior and not much made it through. By now, he knew of my seer "ways," but they still made him uncomfortable at times, being so foreign to his nature. He understood energy, but the world of the subtle mind, where dreams and prophecies dwell, sourced from the sacred feminine, was less familiar.

Getting no response from him, I said, "That's not all I saw in my dream."

I looked at him, waiting. His silence had me squirming in my seat.

"You know I do believe in the axiom 'Ask and you shall receive?'"

He nodded.

I decided to grab the bull by the horns. "Because of what I've been shown in visions and dreams, this is what I want, and I will accept no less!"

At that, his eyebrows went up. "You want?"

I answered, "That's right! I want!" He would not deter me. I was on a mission, and so be it!

"This is what I've sent out to be manifested. That we have mountains on our land with all the acreage we need and priced within our budget." I stopped for breath.

He took advantage of this to mention, "You do realize, Angelina, that the market value of land is three times that price?"

I ignored his sarcasm. "The land will also have a natural spring for our water source. And a plateau facing south to build our dream house with a solar system. And last but not least, it should overlook a lake."

No sooner did those words leave my mouth than Hubby threw his hands up in the air and blurted out, "Well, we might as well give up now, Angelina, for if you think that 'your demands' will ever be met, then, Houston, we have a problem! There is no way in hell God, the Creator, or whatever or whoever you send these demands to will grant this! You're asking for the impossible!"

Not letting his reaction deter me in the least, I calmly answered, "You'll see."

For deep down I knew this feeling, and it never led me astray. We would find this land, and it would be all that I had said. Hubby shrugged and knew better than to argue when I was in this mood.

He responded, "We'll take a drive into the mountains on the weekend and see what we can find. I think the Kilmar Mountain Store up in Harrington has a bulletin board with ads of land for sale. Let's start there. And I'll treat you to Maria's amazing *Italiana* food, if you're good."

I nodded in agreement. What a treat to take a ride into those beautiful mountains and end the day with a meal at the quaint Kilmar restaurant. In the years since we'd moved up here, Maria and I had become great friends. The Italian cooking she and Roberto, her husband, served up was simply to die for!

Saturday came around soon enough, and the kids were off with their friends early, so we set out after lunch on our treasure land hunt. We knew the mountains north of us a bit, but our familiarity with the area remained limited. We drove for a few hours, looking for signs and real estate advertisements.

About to call it a day, we spotted a dirt road that drew our attention. I looked down at the paper Roberto had given us. "Hubby, do you think this might be the road with land for sale?"

"If it is, Angelina, you'd better get yourself a good 4x4, because this looks more like a bush trail than a road."

We decided to check it out for fun, laughing our heads off as we bumped around on what was obviously used as a trail.

"Imagine if our land is up here and our families come and visit? They'll have a field day with this one!"

Our families had different ideas about how they wanted to live, and being stuck in the mountains on a dirt road didn't appeal to any of them. We drove for about twenty minutes on the winding road, admiring the views. The road passed right beside a lake, where ducks and a beaver went about their business, completely ignoring our intrusion.

Suddenly, my spidey senses, as I call them, came alive. I grabbed Hubby's arm.

"Hubby, slow down. There's something here."

He hit the brakes, and at that moment a white-tailed hawk swooped down and circled to get our attention. I felt more than heard the beautiful creature say, "Follow me."

This was a sign. "Hubby, don't ask questions," I said. "Just follow that hawk."

Hubby had started to recognize my seer moments. A glazed look would come over my face, and my seer eyes would turn jet black. Although present, a great part of me was listening and seeing into another dimension of reality.

He hurriedly shifted gears, and off we went, as the hawk flew ahead. It guided us for miles down a dirt track, and, wonder of wonders, the hawk kept to the road. This alone, improbable and unusual, we saw as another sign. For more than three miles, we bumped along, laughing at the incongruity of everything. We turned a curve and sped ahead. I suddenly noticed the hawk had vanished.

I yelled, "Hubby, stop! We lost the hawk somewhere. Please back up!"

The words were barely out of my mouth before Hubby realized the same thing and had the car in reverse. Twenty metres back, a road curved to our left that we hadn't noticed. Turning onto the road, we spotted our hawk, circling ahead. Just a few feet in, I noticed a sign nailed to a tree.

As we got closer, I laughed hysterically, not believing my eyes. I pointed ahead to the sign, and we looked at each other in amazement. It read, "Land for sale," with a number to call.

The hawk made one more swoop and flew off. We drove ahead a bit, and there in front of us was the land.

The next day we called the landowner, and within a few weeks we owned those acres in the mountains. The land had a plateau facing south towards a summit we could build on. A few months later, Hubby discovered several springs that could provide our water source, and, of course, we looked down onto a small deserted lake. Little did we know at the time that another nearby plateau would be the future site of the institute.

Out of all of our experiences, this one perplexed Hubby the most. It opened him up to the concept that life consisted of more than logic. I remind him of this whenever my ideas seem strange to his way of thinking. This side of me just gets stronger and stronger as things move forward, and it's a good thing Hubby is so resilient and open to the "mysteries of life."

Finally, years later, my inner voice told me about the importance of these mountains in the coming events.

> *Your mountains are a central location of Mother Earth's consciousness. She is a being like you, and She also has her centres of power. You must use these to support what you and others, Angelina, have come to accomplish in this life. Only with the help of Her powerful energy forces will you succeed in this endeavour.*

I now know why instinct guided Hubby and me to build the institute in this place. It lay in the calm of a vortex of energy so great as to be indistinguishable from its surroundings.

More words from the past come forth, whispered within me, preparing me for what would come.

> *The struggle of a great evolutionary shift has arrived. Life, man, and all of Mother Nature's creatures suffered for eons and eons, reaching to something beyond man's ability to understand, often defined as heaven. Today, the world's overpopulated state bears witness to all of the souls who chose to live during this amazing time. On a global scale, everyone is being offered heaven on Earth. Angelina, you have come to help the world understand exactly what that means, how it looks, and what people need to "remember" to embrace this. The mystical*

domain once accessible only to a few of the holy is now being presented to the collective.

The scent of evergreen branches brings me back to the present, as the memory of those words recedes into my past. It is way too early for these deep, serious thoughts.

I enter my office, and the phone rings. It must be important, because the first students won't arrive from the city for hours. Caller ID reveals my long-time friend Tia.

"Good morning, Tia. You're awake early. What's up?"

Full of excitement, she says, "I have great news! My granddaughter Katharina had her check-up yesterday at the children's hospital. And guess what? Katharina's tumour is gone! She's been given a clean bill of health, to the bewilderment of the doctors. Congrats, Angelina! I knew you would come through and help my sweet little one."

Tia's voice breaks from emotion, and I breathe in a great surge of energy to remain grounded. A swell of gratitude overcomes me. I look up and nod to the Powers That Be, in thanks for their support and for this miracle. These moments, these rare gifts of life, make everything worth it—all of the sacrifices I make to hold these powerful forces. It demands so much at times that I want to give up. This news is like manna from heaven. It gives me courage for the times of struggle when doubt surges.

"I'm so happy for you, Tia—and for Katharina, of course. How are the parents reacting?"

Katharina's health issues are intricately wound up with her parents' behaviour, expectations, and demands. Tia tells me they have made a lot of changes for the good of the whole family.

Hanging up, I turn my gaze to the panoramic windows. Visitors comment that it seems as if we live outdoors. The beauty of nature hurts my eyes, with acres of mountain bush dusted in snow, above the deserted lake just now freezing over.

I pull out Katharina's file and update her records. I maintain these for all of my clients, as would any professional. I am a soul practitioner, the oldest field of medicine known to man. Some people ask me what, exactly, do I do? Yet not many speak the language to understand my answer. My world is filled with magic, synchronicities, miracles, and wonderful places few can ever imagine. This world of soul, of high energy, transformation, and initiation, has always been diverse and mystical. My answer is to simply shrug and give an evasive comment about natural medicine and healing. Most people suspect I'm not telling them everything. Yet they don't push any further, fearing to know the truth.

The quietness soothes me, for I am alone at this early hour. While perusing Katharina's file, I glance at the clock. I still have time before class to re-read the events of that miraculous day. I clearly remember the fateful morning when Tia came to me, desperate that I help her young granddaughter Katharina. Their nightmare dilemma had begun weeks earlier, when Tia noticed something protruding from the right side of Katharina's head. She mentioned it to the parents, but they simply put it off to rough playing.

As the week progressed, the protrusion grew bigger, until the parents finally recognized its abnormality. They brought Katharina to a special children's hospital, where doctors ran scans and did blood tests. Yet to the consternation of the team of doctors, nothing made any sense. Baffled by her symptoms, they admitted her case was unusual and not textbook. The medical team finally decided that a fast-growing cancerous tumour had penetrated into Katharina's brain and spread to the soft tissues. They wanted to start her immediately on aggressive chemotherapy to shut down her overactive immune system, which they surmised might be the problem. Within a few weeks, the tumour had already more than doubled.

On hearing this news, both parents, as well as Tia, were horrified. True advocates of a natural lifestyle, they knew allopathic methods had more harmful side effects than healing benefits. The latest discoveries about the ineffectiveness of certain cancer treatments had them questioning their options. Tia knew they'd be receptive to a session with me, so, on her suggestion, they showed up on my clinic doorstep.

That Wednesday morning, Little Katharina made a vivid first impression on me. Shy at first, this tiny blonde sprite came into the clinic with her head bowed, peeking up at me from under dishevelled shoulder-length locks. I smiled gently and extended my energy in warmth to welcome her. She opened up as a flower does to the sun, and a beautiful, powerful light emanated from her. She grew still for a moment before looking me straight in the eyes with her big browns. Her first words to me melted my heart: "Well, hi, Angelina! I just LOVE your sweater!"

I responded, "Thank you," in wonderment. I fell instantly in love with this child. In that moment, I resolved that this beautiful soul would not die, if I had any say in the matter. As she took off her coat, chatting away with her mother, I noted the huge pointed cone shape protruding from her head. Judging by her actions, it didn't seem to bother her in the least. Extremely intelligent and mature in her speech, she had so much energy. I could see why the doctors felt perplexed by her case. I found this more and more interesting, as the minutes ticked by.

The mother, more reserved, soon opened up, and it became obvious where the child got her intellect and awareness. Katharina also greatly resembled her grandmother Tia in that respect and had her brains, to boot!

As I began asking questions, I felt a need to go in and check out Katharina's subtle energy field, to determine what to do about this tumour. Helping this child would be sourced from the dimension of soul, where miracles originate. With permission, I lay my hands on the tumour. The energy hit a solid wall of resistance. I persisted, for deep down I knew this child had to live.

Katharina kept chatting away, much to my happiness. Gradually, the energy flowed in and around the tumour and softened its tissues.

Next, I intuited to unblock the child's left foot, where the energy seemed stagnant. I mentioned this to the mother, who later told me she'd also had problems with her left foot from a young age. This was a crucial clue.

I proceeded to do what I do, as Katharina amused herself with various toys. She kept up a lively conversation, while I studied her and asked questions. Everyone embraced all of this naturally, without question. Next, I turned to the mother.

From years of experience, I know children don't get sick without an outside influence. If the health issue didn't exist at birth, I needed to look for this influence. Karmically linked to a loved one, the child would have bound herself to an adult to fulfil a purpose only seen at the soul level. The foot blockage spoke of Katharina shifting her Chakaura™ structure to try to please someone dear to her. I scanned the mother's energy field. Something caught my attention in the haze emanating from the mother's head. To my surprise, the mother's subtle structural field elongated into a pointy bump in the exact spot of Katharina's physical tumour. I immediately knew the cause of the child's tumour. Katharina had emulated her mom's Chakaura™ structure, a unified field of soul. In the immature child, this had given birth to the tumour.

I'd discovered I could positively affect this structure in adults and produce life-changing benefits for both the parent and the child. I shared my findings with Janet, the mom, that the child had copied her Chakaura™ structure. I felt relieved at Janet's openness to my unusual approach.

The child simply took on her mother's traits, in order to be loved and have her parents' approval. Janet, a disciplined and regimented person, could not be easily impressed. Katharina had tried to mesh with Mom, as Mom attempted to turn her into a "mini me," but, of course, they did this unknowingly, unconsciously.

I recommended that we do a Chakaura™ Balancing on Janet to remove the pattern Katharina had copied, as well as to bring her back into balance. She readily agreed.

As I filled out Janet's dossier, I recognized that she shared similar traits with many seekers who came to me, looking for something to fill a void deep inside. We then proceeded to do the Chakaura™ therapy, setting the course for another future reality.

Before her departure, Janet told me of their desperation to take care of Katharina's health issue with alternative medicine. She had previously made an appointment for the next day with an acupuncturist and also with a reputed healer from out of town who worked with alternative medicine.

When I heard this, warning sirens went off in my head. I immediately saw the danger of having these other people go into Katharina's and Janet's energy fields so soon after the soul work I'd done. I sighed in frustration, unsure how to broach such a delicate, yet crucial subject. I tentatively explained the danger of anyone playing around with her energy field or Katharina's until everything stabilized, which could take a few weeks. To my utter surprise, she understood and agreed. Janet cancelled the acupuncturist's appointment, yet she felt committed to bringing in the alternative healer, due to arrive by bus on Friday. I purposely said nothing, because free will forbade me to interfere.

I told Janet that if Katharina hadn't experienced any changes within three days, they should immediately go back to the special children's hospital, because the doctors had warned this aggressive tumour could kill Katharina. She agreed, and I felt humbled and honoured that Janet and her family had such trust in me.

* * *

Friday arrived, and so did the healer woman from out of town. I'd told Janet I completely supported the dietary changes this healer had previously suggested for Katharina. This family's diet had significant deficiencies in nutrients they needed right now.

The day went by uneventfully, as I put in my regular hours at the clinic. Driving to work, I'd thought of beautiful Katharina. I felt upset that the healer, Carol, might undo all of the good I'd done. On the morning after Katharina's treatment with me, Tia had told me the tumour had begun to subside. Now, three days after their visit, these positive results hung in a fragile balance, easily undone by unknowing behaviour.

The child, when put under my care, had become my concern and my right to protect, as all innocents are. I sent out a command to keep her from harm, as long as the highest good of all be served.

I cut all ties and let everything go. It would be what it would be.

Tia had called later that day and revealed more about the relationship developing between the healer, named Carol, and Janet's family. They exhibited signs of being under an energy-binding spell—bound by cords that function as the highways of our pain and suffering.

I'd explained to Janet some important protocols that all healers should adhere to. Tia told me that when Janet later phoned Carol, the healer, to ask about her practices with energy, Carol became upset, unable to answer these questions. Carol obviously knew nothing about such protocols. Janet then told Carol about their visit with me and their promise to adhere to my precautionary measures. I wondered how the healer would react to that, but time would tell.

I intuited that this gifted healer had undergone no real training to safely channel the amazing energy she could access. I "saw" with my seer eyes that her Chakaura™ structure was cut off at her legs, forcing her to "take on" her clients' "stuff," in exchange for their patronage. Her energy field had split in two at her waist, most likely from an accident. The minute this thought crossed my mind, a visual of her falling and of electrical static flashed in my mind's eye, later to be confirmed by Tia. This incident had cut her off from her power to protect her from herself. The soul does this at times, because our good deeds earn us protection from ourselves. Obviously a good woman who meant well, she remained anchored in old ideas about healing.

That Friday evening after dinner, I unexpectedly felt some sort of energy slam into me. At once I saw it was the healer, Carol. I instinctively put up my shields, and she bashed at me ever stronger.

I sent the command to bring me to her. I bilocated instantly and found myself looking down from the ceiling of a moving bus only half full of passengers. Evening shadows suggested the time. My gaze went to a woman I intuitively knew to be the healer, Carol: tall but petite, with fine features and gold, silky hair. I easily read her mind. Peeved about who had been in the child's energy field, she attempted to know more about me.

Her emotions surged, and her energy came at me again, with all of her strength. Three times being the limit, the laws decreed I could protect myself, and I did.

I shoved her back with an energetic poke, so she could see I wasn't to be played with. This response from my dragon force, the limit of my permissible boundaries, would surely kill if unleashed. She immediately backed off, surprised and quieted. Satisfied that the situation had been neutralized, I gave the command to leave, and I found myself once again at home relaxing. Minutes went by as I settled back to watch my movie. Suddenly, she appeared again, but this time she respectfully came nudging, more in curiosity than anything else. I acknowledged her attempt to apologize. I put up my barriers and went to bed.

Tia later told me of the healer's surprise to see what I'd done to Katharina's energy field, which was everything necessary for Katharina to heal. My respect for the healer went up a notch—obviously, this woman had more ability than first apparent.

Tia also confirmed that Carol had returned home on the bus that very evening, at the time when I had bilocated.

I close Katharina's file. She'd healed naturally during the following months. Tia mentioned that the doctors had wanted to know what had been done, for this case could be described as unprecedented. The medical team determined that the tumour had dissolved, and the skull had regenerated its bone, as the hole in her skull got smaller. I smile my Cheshire grin, knowing that even if I'd explained, it would be way too much for these doctors to believe or accept.

I thank the Powers That Be for their continued support. The child had healed and would do something great in life, for how else could it be?

> *We change this, we change a lot!*

Chapter 3

A Visit from a Spirit Elder: Wonders Never Cease

Reality lies across the veil where dwells the unseen side of life.

—Michèle St.Amour

Susan

I put away Katharina's file. I walk silently toward my office window and sit on its ledge. This event with Katharina triggers the memory of discovering the power of my healing ability. Once again I become immersed in the past and travel to another time. Following the threads of Grandmother Spider, I weave through a space odyssey of bright-coloured filaments of light zipping by. The speed tapers off, and everything becomes slow motion, changing from dark to sudden light. My eyes focus, and I become the Angelina of my past, the present one slipping away as if she's never existed.

    I dreamed once again of my teacher in spirit, our silhouettes sitting somewhere in a desert at sunset. I felt the warmth of the day dissipate and the cold of night seep in, as he explained to me the workings of the universe. This aboriginal Elder initiated me to the fact that, first, my Native roots went much deeper than I knew, and second, I had the gift of communing with and commanding the elements. As I grew into this power, so would my ability to influence the weather and its many moods.

My spirit Elder taught me about the wonders of the gifts we shared. I had no idea who this Native American Elder could be, as he appeared in dreamtime, night after night. We travelled to many sacred places, and he shared countless teachings. These dreams had a certain quality, but unless something unusual catches our attention, we do not question them.

One day I realized how unusual these dreams were and thought maybe I should ask this Elder who he was. In response, the Elder spoke his name. I shrugged it off as simply imagination. The next morning, upon waking, I researched it to appease my logic.

To my amazement, I discovered the reality of his existence and everything he said, though he had passed on to the spirit world many years ago. He had been known for his gift of commanding the elements, for being a powerful healer, and much more. Surprisingly, he looked exactly the same in real life as he appeared in my dreams, based on old photographs I found surfing the Net.

The Powers That Be had sent him to teach me to understand the strange happenings of my first years of awakening, as my dormant abilities began to surface.

He once told me, "Healing forces have the strength of the Creator, which includes the power of thunder and lightning and of all living beings. As a medicine woman, you must bring these forces together, in and around you, so that they convey their healing power to you and to the sick people you will be asked to heal."

A roaring in my ears suddenly pulls me from that memory and into another one, as again I weave and fly through another time vortex. The ability to time-travel is so natural to me nowadays—how did I remain unaware of it those many years before I awakened?

Then everything slows, and as my vision clears, I find myself outdoors, just a few winters ago.

On that blustery winter day, I'd gone out for a stroll on this very mountain. I heard a branch snap, broken by the unusually strong winds. I took a deep breath of fresh air and scanned the area, unable to shrug off the sense of something trying to get my attention. A nagging tingle down my spine would not let me be.

Curious, I went in deeper, to gain a clearer idea of what greeted me so subtly but with such graciousness. Taking a deep Breath of Life, I opened up my senses and reached out. The howling wind suddenly shifted and caressed my face in a gentle greeting. The wind's embrace still gives me chills, though it is a common occurrence now.

I responded to her soft touch with a mental greeting and a slight nod, deemed respectful in interactions with the spirits of things. The trees bowed in unison, returning the salutation. I laughed out loud and sent thanks that life flowed so freely and fully through me now. I decided to send out a greeting of gratitude to an old friend for what we'd shared so many years ago. I reached out to the spirit world, searching for my aboriginal Elder's imprint. It seemed as if lifetimes had passed since I'd seen him.

An unusual change in the wind caught my attention. I shivered, though well dressed for this weather, and my back stiffened. Something entered my energy field, like a wave disrupting my natural flow. Turning, I caught a glimpse of a shadow and smelled the early morning dew, mixed with the scent of dying embers from a campfire. I went deeper into this insight, and the shadow took on shape and depth. I felt the familiar presence of my Elder.

There his spirit stood in all of his glory, smiling and nodding at me. He once again wore jeans and a white T-shirt depicting a Native American logo. His unique hat bore an eagle feather, a sign of his connection to the world of spirit. His medicine man's beaded necklace spoke of the powerful medicines he wielded. He appeared in the guise of himself while in his mid to late fifties, although his athletic build still embodied youthful energy and vitality. His solidity, for a spirit, demonstrated his intense power, even after death. Dark hair peppered with grey at his temples showed blossoming wisdom beyond his years.

I smiled in return, happy to see my old friend. His telepathic skills appeared stronger in spirit than in dreams. He told me how happily he had watched me mature into my skills. I nodded, humbled by his great humility, because I could only hope to achieve his level of mastery.

His silent voice echoed in my mind that our work together would continue, and in the near future he would come to me again. I still needed to remember a lot more about healing, he said, which would come later in life, when I'd remembered and written down everything. I wanted to ask what he meant, but he grinned, tilting his head in farewell. His image suddenly faded and disappeared altogether. That knowing smile was the Elders' way. They knew when to remain silent and allow students to have their learning experiences.

I felt a loss when he left, missing those early days when he'd played such a crucial role in my self-development. His guidance had created the foundation for me to understand and begin to master the strong elemental forces coursing through me. These Muse forces could destroy a person, if the right mentor didn't come along to help the student manoeuvre the slippery precipice.

I stood there in awe, again questioning the reality of this experience. My glance involuntarily dropped to the spot where my Elder had appeared. There lay a gift: a white Canadian wild goose feather resting on footprints in the snow, which had not been there moments earlier. As I bent to accept this gift, a far-away voice echoed in my mind, "*Do not forget your vow to fulfil the quest.*" Then all went silent.

Oh, yes, I thought, *the quest.*

I mentally heard the inner voice I had come to call Teacher:

> *The children slumber and more awaken every day, looking for guidance and direction. It is for those you wait, and those you need to service now. Your life's purpose will allow you to continue on your personal journey to a deeper and freer understanding of Life. The quest awaits you!*

I silently responded, "We will talk of the quest another time. I'm not ready to take that task to heart. So, be gone now and leave me to my musing!"

Angelina as a Young Child

This latest memory recall with my Elder triggers a childhood remembrance of my first conscious experience of my innate healing ability. I hear a hawk call in the distance, as I once again travel to my distant past.

I swirl through the gateway, and, as it clears, I see myself as a young child. Back then, I could see things before they occurred and knew things I should not know. My father also had the gift of seeing things before they happened. The old folks whispered tales of seers and the like, but no one ever spoke of this out loud. It had been forbidden since the unlawful burning of our ancestors during the Inquisition. At first, I told my parents about my experiences, but in time, after I saw the fear in their eyes, I decided to keep everything to myself.

If someone had "the sight," my parents tended to shrug it off. I developed the same detached attitude, as if these unusual happenings didn't exist. They were no longer on my radar.

Sometimes life reminded me of my oddness. The memory of the dove surfaces. I was five and had found a dove in my sandbox. I'd heard it whimpering in pain and crying for help. I gently picked it up, telling the dove it would be okay. It closed its eyes, and I thought it had died. From somewhere deep inside, I knew I could help this creature. Determined that Mom would help me save it, I ran to the house with the dove in my arms, yelling for Mom. She looked at me strangely, as we made it a bed in a cardboard box. I recall her whispering to Dad that I simply would not let the bird be.

I couldn't explain why, but I knew this white dove had to live and that I could save it. It could barely move and was obviously near death. Mom and Dad wanted to take the bird away, angry at my stubbornness. Yet I would have none of it. In that moment, something awakened inside of me, a spark of who I really was.

I held my hands up, then lay them on the bird and said, "Birdie, you shall live. I love you with all my heart, and love shall heal you, for you are a creature of life. Live, be alive, live!"

The sudden energy and white light coming from my hands spoke of things mystical and sacred. It took but a few minutes that seemed to stretch out for hours. As my innocent self wondered whether this magic would work, I felt a sudden movement beneath my hands. What we three witnessed that day defies belief. Obviously now full of life, the bird opened its eyes and began to stir. We brought it outside and watched it wobble and shake off its sleepy state of death. Then off it flew. The look of shock on my parents' faces has stayed with me since then. We never spoke of it again.

Today I know this happened so I wouldn't forget my origins and my capabilities. It served to remind me of another reality, a divine truth about myself gone dormant, because the dove symbolizes the Divine Trinity, the spiritual eye, and the mother Goddess. The Spirit of God descended and lighted upon a dove.

Chapter 4

Chakaura: The Prophecy Begins

Where dreams may come...

—Michèle C. St.Amour

Present Day

My attention snaps back to the present. I need to focus and ground myself. I will soon have to greet the students. My eyes take in the beauty of the institute, a dream waiting to manifest.

Years ago, deep in a meditative state, I realized that the spiritual needs of society had been neglected. The most beautiful golden white light began to surround me, as my body hummed and became energized.

That inner voice of Teacher whispered,

> You will open an institute that you will call the **Chakaura**™ **Institute of S.O.U.L.**

As I silently wondered, *Why?* the voice responded,

> *Chakaura*™ *is a natural combination of the teachings about the chakras and the aura. You must teach how the physical and the spiritual—just like the chakras and the aura—are one and the same: emanations that crystallize from the soul.*

This made so much sense to me—but why Institute of S.O.U.L.?

Then I saw in my mind's eye: "**S.O.U.L.**—**S**ystem **O**f **U**niversal **L**ove."

I recognized the wisdom of this, for everything I taught centred on directing **love energy, the most powerful force in the universe**. And so Chakaura,™ Institute of S.O.U.L., was birthed.

* * *

As the first arrivals for class noisily prepare the institute for Christmas festivities, I hear my name being called and get up from the window ledge. I teach that doing things naturally grounds the soul, which is so crucial for our health. Our society sacrificed vital ancient traditions to modernization. It's no wonder our classes at the institute keep expanding each season, for people love the philosophy of Chakaura.™

The students call me Angelina. I have never felt healthier or more alive. People comment that I look much younger than I am. Little do they know this is simply an attribute of the high energies I embrace. Feeling the weight of my waist-length hair, I note it will be due for a trim soon. This brings to mind a teaching from my aboriginal ancestors.

In modern times of war, Native American braves conscripted into the army were recruited for their renowned tracking abilities. The braves could pick up noises and scents imperceptible to the average man, tapping into a deep intuitiveness well suited to the army's needs. Yet when forced to cut their hair, according to army protocol, the young braves' skills practically vanished, as they lost contact with all of their intuitive sense perceptions. The army soon realized that the hair of the braves acted similarly to amplifying rods, much as our modern-day antennas do.

I make my way to the main area and pause before a beautiful painting of a black jaguar stalking the jungle, given to me by a student. She said my sleek, graceful movements remind her of this wild black cat. Little did she know this cat with gleaming emerald eyes often comes to me in visions or dreams. It is the source of my ability to shape-shift and understand hidden patterns, because it guides me when time-traveling to see the roads within chaos, facilitating my work as a Soul Seer.

As I awakened, I discovered that many of my abilities were reflected in all of these guides, energies, and totems surrounding me.

My Elder taught me that knowledge often presents itself in such a natural way, as with totems, that I had to develop awareness and pay attention to every word and everything I encounter, for that is how the spirits of all things would communicate and guide me. My aboriginal ancestors call these our Elders, the Grandmothers and the Grandfathers, the wise energy existing in all things. There are Grandmother trees and Grandfather rocks, and everything is either one or the other, as defined by its nature, its polarity.

My personal totems are balanced between earth and sky. An Elder once told me this is extremely rare, because few souls blend the two cosmic forces, in fear of being overwhelmed and destroyed by powerful opposites coming together.

A visual of my principal totem, my dragon staff, flashes in my mind's eye, propped up in a corner of my sacred space—a sentinel always watching my back. She brings the element of the kundalini fire to my world, where magic and miracles abound. It has taken me many years to tame this She dragon, now such a part of my expression. Her unbridled white fire slumbered in my womb, waiting to be stirred by destiny. Her sudden fiery and violent awakening almost destroyed me. That was when conscious awareness of my life journey began to resurface, along with its yoke of responsibility.

* * *

"Angelina, where are you?" a student calls out. The voice snaps me out of my reverie.

I enter the main hall. The newly painted entrance has turned out beautifully. The muted beige interior complements the outer walls, finished with natural wood and stone that mesh well with the forest landscape. We built the institute with three floors, and the main entrance features a circular stone drive. We keep the parking area well away from the main building and offer a scenic walk along a wooded trail. Decks sprawl all around, with benches and tables where everyone can enjoy the outdoors. The greenhouse provides us with the luxury of fresh produce year round.

People describe the institute as having a Zen-like atmosphere. The cafeteria is more like a huge country kitchen, where everyone pitches in for meals. My stay in India taught me about *seva*, a communal way of living and dividing tasks—a quality of the feminine energy we teach about.

I join some students in the main sitting area surrounding a beautiful central stone fireplace. "Good morning, everyone. I'm heading up to the classroom in a few minutes. Please be there promptly."

They turn, surprised, because none of them had felt my approach. One in particular knows of my cloaking ability and watches me for clues on how I did this. I grin at her, easily reading her thoughts, as they all scurry ahead of me.

A heavenly scent catches my attention as I climb the wooden staircase to the Great Hall. Visitors often comment on the unique quality and the amazing smells of this place. Most people don't realize energy carries its own specific physical attributes, aroma being only one.

The soothing trickle of the water fountain pervades the main lobby. Our water is spring sourced and flows straight out of the mountain behind us into the institute.

I enter the upstairs gathering room. Everyone is settled, awaiting my arrival. I educate the students on the use of various techniques, from quieting their minds to using energy as an agent of empowerment. These students have trained to perceive what goes on behind the scenes of everyday life. First-year students laughingly describe themselves as being in a Harry Potter–like school. Our concepts and ideas could seem magical, miraculous, and out of this world. Yet a miracle is simply an event our science has not caught up to.

Sitting comfortably, I begin with a centring technique.

"Everyone, please take a deep breath and release all tension from your body. Make sure to position your chairs properly. Ground yourself, and once you feel ready, you may go, and I will call you back when it is time."

One by one, they allow their souls to travel at will, without the restriction of their physical bodies. One, in particular, I must watch, because her etheric body always manages to get stuck at the ceiling, floating around in a daze of confusion and unable to penetrate into the void, where she can experience her soul self. This time she struggles a minute but then disappears, as her mind lets her go.

While the students immerse themselves in this exercise, I glance at a ring of sweetgrass guarding the entrance to this gathering space. I let the memory surface of the summer day when I gathered these very plants.

Last Summer

I remember thinking, *What a beautiful day for a walkabout!* I'd decided to go for a walk to see which medicinal plants might be ready to pick. For years now, I have gathered and dried many plants and made teas, salves, and medicines, a legacy of my attunement with the earth element. I grabbed my sarong skirt and tied it around my waist, as I recalled the teachings Abuela, a Mayan medicine woman, had shared with me. On one of her visits, we strolled through my gardens, and she taught me women always wore skirts in ceremonies, because a skirt put her in her full feminine power. The circle spoke of the cycle of life. As you stood in the centre of your skirt, you found yourself in your "I Am." This centre was your sacredness, your centre of power.

I reached for my straw hat, and off I went. The shining sun had dried the dew on the land. Sounds of many birds singing blended with the odd bullfrog making himself heard. I stopped to send a special greeting to all of these amazing creatures. Silence met my salutation, followed by a cacophony in response to my hello. I laughed at the beauty of nature. I had always intuitively spoken its language. Some called me an Earth Whisperer, because I spoke the language of my aboriginal ancestors. My aboriginal Elder had taught me about my earth-whispering abilities during those dream-filled nights—such a distant memory.

I made my way down the mountain and walked along the deserted road leading to our private lane. Enjoying the sun's heat on my face, I caught a whiff of a familiar scent so dear to my heart, and I sighed in pleasure.

At one spot along the road, I recalled transplanting a patch of sweetgrass years ago. Now ready for its first cutting, I gave thanks again to the Creator for this bounty. Spirit urged me to make sweetgrass oils for ceremonies and special occasions, along with braids as gifts for smudging.

I began by offering tobacco, our aboriginal custom, as a thank-you to the Creator for the gift of these medicines and for the gift of life Mother Earth bestowed on me.

Years ago, Spirit showed me that I was a sweetgrass keeper. Sweetgrass, the hair of Mother Earth, is a woman's medicine, and its sweet, powerful scent calls on the Grandmothers and the Grandfathers, our ancestors, when we need their wisdom and support. I climbed down a few feet into the ditch where the sweetgrass now grew in abundance and became lost in my own little world. I carefully chose the blades of grass, amazed at how it had flourished in that fresh, clean mountain air. Sweetgrass, being temperamental, didn't like to be bound. It managed for a short while in containers but soon demanded to be transplanted into a space that didn't limit its growth. That kind of reminded me of a woman! I laughed at that thought and continued picking each blade with respect and honour.

I joyfully began singing "my song," offering its sweet melody as thanks to Spirit for the bounty in my life. *"Ya-hey ya-hey ya-hey hoe! . . . ya-hey ya-hey ya-hey hoe . . ."*

I had been picking for about half an hour, my basket now half full. Suddenly, I felt a tingling as if someone were watching me. Compelled to stand up, I looked behind me. A young moose stood only six feet away. The moose, relaxed and curious, quietly watched me. I instinctively knew the moose was a "she."

We silently looked into each other's eyes. Time stood still, and a rapid communication happened between us—not with language but just a sense of thoughts and feelings. The moose telepathically asked what I was doing, surprised that I wasn't like other humans she had encountered. Unruffled and simply curious, she bravely took a step closer to me.

I felt as if I could walk up and touch her, but I knew this wild animal should not be taken lightly. She stood more than six feet at her shoulders, and if she became startled, I could get hurt.

Her gaze drew me to glance downward, at the basket of sweetgrass lying between us. She looked as if she might want to have a munch and began nuzzling the sweetgrass I'd picked. Her head came back up and turned slightly to the side. She stepped closer, and I felt her curiosity get the better of her. Her complete ease allayed any fear I might have experienced. I felt such a communion with this beautiful creature, as we communicated in our silent language.

All of a sudden, something abruptly broke our connection. She got nervous and started prancing. Her body language exuded a field of panic. Her eyes took on a frightened look. If she bolted my way, I could be trampled. If I had to run, I could jump the fence on my left, but that might not be safe for long, because her height would allow her to sail over that same fence if she decided to follow me.

As I pondered my dilemma, a truck crested the top of the road on the horizon, and I realized why she was so nervous. She had sensed the vehicle's approach long before my human senses had and was undecided whether to come closer to me or take off.

I knew I had to get her to safety, so I softly shooed her and telepathically told her to go the other way. She hesitated, unsure, but then she came to a decision and took off the way I pointed.

The truck driver drove up beside me and came to a sudden stop. He jumped out of his vehicle in a panic and asked me if I was all right. I calmly told him the moose had come to say good morning and that everything was fine, but thank you for stopping. I assumed the poor man thought I was crazy, but then he recognized me. He stammered an apology for interrupting my picking, bade me farewell, and off he went.

As the sound of his truck faded into the distance, I gazed intently over to the field where my friend had gone. I sensed her presence not far away. I reached out, and we said our good-byes. I finished gathering my sweetgrass, peacefully and gratefully. Who would ever have believed something like this was part of my everyday existence?

When I got home, I looked up what the moose had been sent to teach me. Synchronicity and life's languages always guide me. I knew this encounter had not been coincidental and pointed to a sign I needed to heed. It turned out the moose was connected to the feminine energies, as well as to the cycle of life and death. I laughed, because hadn't I just been thinking about this before picking sweetgrass?

The sacred gift of the appearance of the moose would be considered auspicious. Since I teach about the sacred and ending a cycle in my life, I felt fortunate to have the support of moose energy on my journey. The fact that a moose had also crossed my path the previous week should have alerted me to pay more attention to its message. Spirit must have decided that the message had to be "in my face" this time! I laughed at the humour of life. The Powers That Be knew me so well.

The moose, a powerful omen, had teachings I had to learn. I then heard the now familiar inner voice of Teacher say,

> *So you got my message through the moose? I thought you'd enjoy that one!*
>
> *Angelina, you have to make more of an effort to listen to your intuitive nature. Just last week, as you know, a moose crossed your path with a very important message, and you ignored it. This is not acceptable anymore. I had to create this new encounter with the moose to force you to move out of time and think in a nonlinear way. Man's troubles are due to the fact that he attempts to understand the mysteries of life from his linear way of thinking. Do not fall back into thinking that time is real. You have grown beyond that.*
>
> *Never forget that you have learned to think with the mind of Soul, but you must exercise this ability all the time and not just when you fancy to. All of the answers people seek but can never discover through a linear way of thinking exist in this place I speak to you from.*

This place exists at my core: my SoulCore. Sages and mystics referred to it when they journeyed to find their redemption. This space in my heart is exactly where I found mine.

I once thought of *soul* and *spirit* only as ideas, loose concepts without relevance or form. All of our ideas ground themselves in time: the past, the present, or the future. We have voluntarily adopted this severe handicap as our lens of perception, but it comes with a learning curve we have to master, if we want to know our inner selves.

"All answers lie within ," said Teacher, "beyond the illusion of time."

As I listened to Teacher's last words, a student's coughing interrupts my thoughts. Twenty minutes have gone by, and I tell the class, "You may bring yourselves back now from your meditation."

Chapter 5

Angelina's Story Begins to Unravel

"Nothing ever goes away until it has taught us what we need to know."

—Pema Chödrön

Present Day

As I sit before this senior group of students, silence encircles us, while they practice yet another mindfulness technique. I can't stress enough the importance of maintaining the health of the nervous system by doing daily exercises to dissolve accumulated stress in the body. It is one of the secrets to developing the ability to know, and interact with, Higher Worlds.

The institute, feeding a deep twenty-first-century spiritual hunger, is fast becoming known as a place that offers deep, lasting, transformative teachings. Yet this particular path, the art of the Royal Way—once meant only for those of a specific royal bloodline—is certainly not for people who want a quick fix or those with weak resolve.

I look around, wondering how many imperceptible spectres of light are listening to my thoughts. They are always there, supporting my destiny.

I sense these others—invisible but real to me—in an odd, nonlinear way. They always surround me or communicate from an unseen source. I rarely glimpse their luminous countenances. They reveal themselves only in times of despair, when I need something tangible to hold onto my faith that I am on the right path.

Seeing my reflection in the window, I'm reminded that my dark looks and fine features, highlighted by dark eyes, result from the coming together of many nations, associated with our aboriginal, English, and French ancestry. Yet my children give away our Scottish bloodlines with their glorious red locks and stoic, fiery nature.

Our whole family is striking, and the contrast among our looks often draws attention to us. My darkness was complemented by the blond hair and light skin of my deceased husband, Daniel. At the thought of Daniel, a wave of sadness runs through me. Years ago, Daniel sacrificed his life in exchange for mine, so that I could fulfil my destiny.

Daniel left us when the kids were in their teens, during the time when I began to come into my powers and my seer's gifts. Tears fill my eyes, and my heart swells with love for Daniel. But now I have Hubby, and in many ways both men are so alike that the void the children and I lived with for a few years after Daniel's passing is filled with love once again.

Hubby very much resembles Daniel, though Hubby keeps his hair longer than Daniel did, and he also has an awareness about energy that Daniel never had. Daniel spent his days building an empire, away at some meeting or on an errand for work. Yet he always made sure that we were financially comfortable. His foresight proved to be a godsend, because, after he left us, the first years were emotionally and spiritually draining. Luckily, we had financial security.

I glance outside and pick up Hubby's athletic stride, so like Daniel's, as he walks to the barn just north of the centre. I smile with affection for this amazing man, who is now as much a part of my life as Daniel once was.

Hubby never wed or had children of his own, unconsciously waiting for the fateful day when destiny would demand he "step in." Daniel is still with us in his own way, and we have Hubby to thank for that. As was planned before our births, Hubby incarnated in case he would be needed. Hubby made room for Daniel's soul within himself the day Daniel suddenly died, so Daniel could fulfil his soul contract. Hubby has us ever thankful for his own sacrifice. I often wonder whether Hubby's ideas in fact come from Daniel's soul, which lives on in Hubby.

I sink into the past, to a time before I met Hubby. Daniel and I—both young ourselves—were the parents of two children in their early teens. The scene comes alive before me. Daniel had come home early from work, saying he wasn't feeling well. I hear voices from a distance, and as the images get clearer on my mind screen, so, then, do these.

"Angelina, where are you?" Daniel yelled, walking into the living room.

I quietly sat on my favourite loveseat in the bay window, reading a novel. "I'm here, sweetie." I noticed his grey complexion. "Daniel, you don't look so good, dear."

He nodded in agreement, saying he hadn't felt well all day and decided to come home early. The kids weren't home from school yet, so I told him to lie on the couch while I fetched him some water. The water running in the kitchen stopped me from hearing his cry of alarm. Then a crashing sound got my attention, and I ran to the living room. By then, I found Daniel lying on the floor, clutching his chest. Obviously, he had suffered a cardiac arrest or a stroke.

A look of fear and pain contorted his features, and my instinctive response was to place my hand on his heart. My full force went into my demand that it stop and be gone. This reactive, instinctive act created a domino effect I couldn't have foreseen. I went in with my full, uncontrolled power, and the damage this did ended up being worse than the actual stroke.

Daniel, as surprised as I was by my actions and words, also noticed in that moment a jolt of energy moving up my arm to dislodge my shoulder, then shooting down to my chest. Immediately, Daniel felt relieved of his pain, but he saw that I had taken it on. I doubled over in shock.

In that moment, Daniel looked into my eyes, and we both knew my death would be the outcome of this. He couldn't have known why, but from somewhere deep inside, he saw it as an unwavering truth. I fell onto my back, clutching my chest and knowing I had done something very wrong.

The pain became so great, I began to lose consciousness. I faintly heard Daniel's voice telling me to stay awake and to hold on, as I slowly slipped away. As I went in and out of consciousness, I noticed a bright light beside Daniel that he seemed to be talking to. I shook this off as fanciful thinking and figured it must be part of dying.

Could that be an angel?

I mumbled to the angel, "Have you come to take me to heaven?"

And the angel said, "No, dear. You have just begun your life, and you're much too important to us for death to claim you before your time. Be peaceful, we shall take care of things."

I nodded and slipped away, feeling the pressure in my chest subside.

Daniel, relieved of his pain, reached over to me and instinctively laid his hand on my chest. His touch always had a magical healing effect on me, and this time was no different.

Yet I had done the unforgiveable and used my power in fear of loss, so a debt had to be repaid. Daniel would have survived if I hadn't given in to my fear of losing him. Karmically, a life had to be forfeited to bring the balance back. So that was how we lost Daniel, but only years later did I discover how Hubby played such a crucial role in all of this.

Daniel's death would be the catalyst to my returning, ever so slowly, to consciousness, to my purpose for living. As the years unfolded, I came to know this life as but one chapter in my book of lives. I am part of a soul group, keepers of the knowledge and the practice of the Pathways of Heaven.

Chapter 6

Journeying into the Akashic

*"The more we understand ourselves, the
more we will understand others!"*

—Michèle C. St.Amour

Present Day

The students now begin to stir, as they complete their latest exercise and ready themselves for the morning's teachings. Minutes have passed during my musing. Looking up at the cathedral ceiling, I smile as another memory surfaces, of Hubby and me spending many hours framing and closing the institute's main building. I find it odd the way I keep recalling the past. This isn't like me at all, because teaching and maintaining the high energies I'm responsible for require me to be of "no mind," in the present moment.

A few students notice my faraway gaze. Marty asks what made me smile so nostalgically. The others turn in our direction.

I tell them, "I remember installing those very rafters with Hubby." I point above, and they all look up.

"We finished just in time to lay the roof before snow settled in that winter. Would you like to hear about that day?" I ask.

They all nod, enjoying the rare times I share personal experiences. I decide it would be a great exercise for them to practice holding numerous timelines in mind at once and to have a first-hand encounter from a teacher's point of view.

"Well, come stand in a circle."

Everyone gathers around, as I search my memories for where to start. I hem and haw, making exaggerated faces, as I consider options. My mannerisms have them all laughing, creating the space I need to bring them journeying. As my memories move back through time, I decide to begin with the day's end.

You see, I don't hold a memory as most people do. Memories weigh us down. The archives I access for my memories are my personal Akashic library. Why waste precious energy storing all of this when it already exists in an external hard drive?

To recall the past, I bring it forth from the Akashic grid. I will use this technique so the students can feel and see this memory recall, first-hand. I open a portal with a specific set of commands and gestures. Suddenly, we find ourselves standing in the centre of a shimmering sacred space, as a veil of energy surrounds us.

Everyone feels the energy rising as an electric tingle. The students sigh in wonder. As the force gleams and everyone adapts to the higher frequencies, a holographic scene of a past memory surrounds us and slowly becomes visible, much like watching a 4-D movie in an amphitheatre. The scene sparkles and remains blurred, and I hurriedly tell the students to ground themselves and bring their energy up. They immediately do so, resulting in the holograph becoming crystal clear and lifelike.

We become immersed in the holograph; each person is the observer, as well as the main character. A splitting into two or more levels of awareness occurs, as one must become the person in the memory, while another part of oneself observes it. This requires holding two states of awareness at once or, in other words, two minds—not easily done.

People have a difficult enough time simply mastering one mind, let alone two or more.

Our senses tune in to the sounds, the sensations, the tastes, and smells of this voyage back in time. The scene depicts a clear, crisp 4-D picture of Hubby a few years ago, relaxing after a day outdoors. The night-time darkness reflects into the house from the many windows facing east and south.

I speak slowly and softly. "I remember hearing the howling wind in the background, melding with Christmas carols heralding the coming holidays."

With my words, we hear a familiar Christmas song and feel the battering wind against the windows. *"It's a holly jolly Christmas, and in case you didn't hear."*

The students laugh nervously.

I continue, "The early evening light and the warmth from the blazing fire on that Sunday created a cosy atmosphere in the chalet. Seated in my comfy chair by the fire, I recall my joints aching, then relaxing as I rested."

A few students squeal in surprise, as everyone feels my aching joints and then the relief of resting. Throwing my head back, I laugh with the sheer joy of sharing my memory so literally.

"As you can see . . ." I direct their attention to a section of the holograph. "Hubby indulged his passion for sustainable living, inspired by dozens of new magazines a friend gave him."

Everyone notices the pile of used monthlies lying on the floor beside Hubby. The top picture portrays a family tilling their garden, and the heading reads, "Old Forgotten Ways Made New."

Hubby sat opposite me in an area we'd dubbed our "winter spot" by the porcelain wood stove. The dogs lay sprawled at our feet. We heard the crackling fire and we felt its warmth.

"Hubby really loves homesteading, doesn't he?" a student comments.

I respond, "Yes, he does indeed."

Hubby and I are so well suited, but, of course, we have come together in so many different roles over many lifetimes, we have lost count of them all.

"Living up here in the mountains, we've met many others like us who want to return to a more natural way of living. The unhealthy aspects of living unsustainably dishearten us. Many move up here from industrialized farming areas polluted by over-chemicalization and dangerous processing techniques."

"My parents are industrial farmers, and they really don't see what they're creating," says another student.

"Yes, I know, and it's really sad, Sheila," I answer. "We're not even aware of how we're destroying and pilfering from the very hand that feeds us, Mother Nature."

People from around the world come to this region. In the beginning I found this curious. As time passed, the sacredness of this area revealed itself to me, and I gained a deeper understanding of why so many were drawn here.

We stand in the holographic image of the warm chalet, enjoying this moment of peacefulness they rarely got to witness in my life with Hubby. Being private people, he and I seldom invite others to our home.

Some students remark on the chalet's elegant furnishings and beautiful antiques. My likes often reflect memories I harbour of past lives, which played an influential role in who I am and what I do today.

"Hubby and I spent the morning into the early afternoon strapping rafters onto the institute's roof in blizzard conditions, readying it for the tin. Some people describe us as eccentric, but there is nothing more gratifying and exhilarating than working as a team with the energy of the storm blazing around you."

I tell the students to brace themselves, as I wave my hands with silent words to transport us back in time. A whirlwind of energy surrounds us, like a vortex of blowing snow. The holographic image shifts and shimmers. A loud noise fills our ears and then quiets to a soft hum, as the energy clears to a mirror image.

We find ourselves outdoors earlier that day. I remember the fervour of nature filling my every cell with energy. My voice, full of passion and exhilaration, directs the holographic images to reveal the memory I'm sharing. The joy Hubby and I felt living so close to Mother Nature was apparent on our faces. This life was not for the weak at heart. Nature can really test you, until you understand Her true nature.

Everyone can see Hubby and me standing precariously on the roof, as we reinforced the rafters. Our next step would be to lay the tin, so the weather couldn't damage the inside of the framed building. The institute's new curriculum would not begin until next fall, so we had plenty of time over the winter to complete this project we held so close to our hearts. I'd rented a place in town temporarily for my practice, so no deadline took away from our pleasure in that moment.

"I recall that during our work, Hubby had to go get more nails. I stood on the rafters and breathed in the energy of the storm. Ice pellets mixed with snowflakes slapped my face with a light but not uncomfortable stinging sensation. What a feeling!"

With these words, the students feel a sensation of ice pellets hitting their faces, and they shriek in delight. All the while they observe Hubby climbing down from the roof and heading off to fetch his nails. Hubby, a robust, healthy woodsman, had the steady, solid gait of a man well grounded and self-assured. His manly demeanour housed a soft and sensitive nature, in contrast to his protector energy, which played such an important role in my life. A very good-looking and knowledgeable man, he drew the attention of men and women alike. With his inviting, friendly expression, he possessed a rare, endearing honesty and a no-nonsense manner.

Joan, another student, pipes up, "I love it when you bring us journeying, Angelina! I can actually see and feel what you're sharing!"

Hearing my name makes me smile, because we encourage using first names for the intimacy this engenders. Many think this name suits me, for they say I am an angel who came into their lives at a time when they wanted to give up. Yet being an angel is not always my way. During the reality of transformation, my own inner struggle with change sometimes has me in a devilish mood. The true nature of transformation is a continual shift from one to the other. Certain students also need prodding to trigger a shift of awareness, so at times I demonstrate guidance that is far from angelic. I'm so glad the students have persevered in the challenges of this path. The everyday people we dub Muggles, taken from the popular book series, would call this time travel impossible, but I teach that miracles are simply things not yet understood.

The scene in the holographic imagery shows me dressed for the weather in a heavy one-piece turquoise suit. A black angora scarf covered my head, because hats no longer suited my energetic needs.

I resume my tale: "As I stood in the storm, enjoying the moment, I caught the subtle scent of homemade donuts. It crossed my mind that someone I knew was making donuts and thinking of me. I scanned this insight more deeply and caught a glimpse of one of you..."

I purposely don't look at anyone in particular before continuing, "... who shall remain nameless, but you know who you are."

I grin but keep this mind thought separate from the holographic memory, so that I don't expose the student until receiving her permission to share. The room fills with the smell of fresh-baked donuts. Lunch is not far away, and a few stomachs grumble. We laugh at that!

When I notice the student's surprised nod of consent at my questioning gaze, I speak to her directly. "You were in a tiny, airy kitchen with a woman I guessed was your mother. Both of you were laughing as you sprinkled freshly baked donuts with icing sugar. What a delicious smell and what childhood memories this brought back, of a time when my Mamère and I made Christmas donuts."

Now everyone knows who I'm talking about, as they see her clearly in the holograph images. They turn to Jo. She smiles in acknowledgment.

A gust of wind brings our attention back to the place where I stood on the rafters. I again see myself braving the elements, as I observed with my third eye vision the kitchen scene of my student and her mother baking donuts.

Another whiff of fresh-baked donuts assails us, and again we sigh in pleasure. I turn to the students, "I remember thinking Jo's mind thought had reached out to me as she wondered whether I would like donuts, and this created the connection."

It's often that easy: a simple thought can have far-reaching consequences, binding us. There is no such thing as idle thinking. Karmic repercussions from our thoughts, whether intentional or not, always play out in the realities and adventures of our everyday lives.

I notice the students are beginning to have difficulty sustaining the energy to continue this exercise in group time travel.

"Okay, everyone, pay attention. I will begin to close the session, so I want you all to bring yourselves back."

I gently close the holograph, allowing the students time to adjust and return. Glazed eyes suddenly become clear, as they bring their awareness back to the present moment. I keenly observe each one, because a few of them still tend to let their ground slip away and return to journeying. Finally, I'm satisfied with their presence.

"Okay, students, story time is over. We will meet here after the Christmas lunch for our end-of-year presentations. Make sure to cut all bindings with this as you leave. I don't want any of you ungrounded in a past realm. And record your impressions before you leave. I will expect those as part of your regular synthesis."

I sever the connection, and the portal disappears. Everyone's awareness is back in the classroom. They silently make their way to the cafeteria, recognizing by my tone of voice that I wish to be alone.

Chapter 7

Some Things Are Best Kept to Oneself

"Silence is a virtue often forgotten."

Present Day

The last student leaves the room, and the hall rings with silence. The students don't realize I didn't share the full story with them. Some things are best kept close to ourselves. Vague sounds from the cafeteria, of chatting and sharing lunch, waft up through the floor. I allow my mind the luxury of again recalling the events of that day, years ago. Back in the holograph, I'm standing on the rafters once again.

While I waited for Hubby to fetch more nails, I glanced at the mountain behind the framed hollow building. The sounds of nature lulled my senses. I felt the gaze of one of the forest's wild, furry inhabitants. As I scanned with my subtle senses, I had mental flashes of our downy neighbours hunkered down for the storm in their warm nests, yet one had peeked up, sensing my presence. I nodded a greeting to the small critter, and it nodded in return. It scurried back to its warm burrow and settled in for the rest of the day, wondering at the funny habits of humans.

As Hubby headed back my way, I glimpsed a shadow in the corner of my eye and felt a shiver from something ancient but dangerous. I turned my head in the direction the dark form had taken, but now all was quiet and seemingly peaceful. Yet deep down, I knew to pay heed, for lurking shadows could only mean trouble, waiting to strike when my guard was down. A light carrier always had to be vigilant, knowing she was constantly being stalked and watched by the entities many called evil, which waited for a moment of inattention or weakness before striking.

Hubby suddenly yelled out, "Found some long nails in the basement! Are you ready?"

My attention returned to the rafter I stood on. Hubby always had a naturally grounding influence on me. We finished what we'd set out to do that afternoon, and, laughing, with hair soaked from the falling snow, we hurried back to the house to warm up and settle down for the night. It was close to sundown and our stomachs rumbled in unison, as we smelled the fresh bread I'd baked that morning. We looked at each other and laughed at the synchronicity of our reactions.

The dogs came running and barked their happy greeting. They sent us mind thoughts that it was time to eat. I shook my head silently, answering that it was still a bit early. I sat beside the woodstove to relax. At this, they cocked their heads, grunting in displeasure because I didn't buy their story that they were starving. I laughed, sharing this latest with Hubby.

Used to the dogs sending us mind pictures, he chuckled good-naturedly. Our eldest male, Buddy, was utterly obsessed with our food. We often cracked up over his heartfelt attempts to get a taste of our meals. Oddly, anyone who took the time to look deeply into his eyes would see the old man inside who sent thoughts of wisdom my way. Hubby wondered how real this aspect of Buddy was and whether it might only be our active imaginations. I knew better, though, because others had commented on Buddy's unusual human-looking eyes. I knew deep down that a very old soul resided in Buddy.

A few times I'd caught Buddy taking on the boomerang energy from a karmic act for one of us, which wasn't his responsibility. I often told him, "Now, Buddy, you're not supposed to 'take on' our stuff. I know you love us and want to protect us, but this is not the way in our household!"

One time he cut his foot severely, when I knew my own foot should have taken the blunt force of what had inadvertently been my own doing. I scolded him afterward and explained that this type of behaviour was unacceptable. The animals often protected us and saved us from our own stupidity and ignorance. Yet it wasn't their job to do this, if it brought them harm and they suffered in vain, because most humans never realized their own mistakes this way.

For years now, old souls have come to stay with us in the guise of animals. These animals began arriving just prior to my destined time of awakening, and their numbers increased as the years went by, which meant we needed to exercise precaution. The odd discerning person might comment on their unusual character but then shrug off these ideas, because no framework of belief existed to explain this phenomenon. Best to simply attribute it to fantasy and notions!

In the holograph, I got out of my chair and walked to the kitchen to prepare dinner. Every year we grew more of our own food. We felt gratified to be self-sustainable, in our simple, wonderful life.

After dinner, we settled before the fire. Hubby and I then dozed off, relaxed and comforted by a day well spent. The dogs lay at the foot of the woodstove, soaking up its warmth. The students had witnessed this scene in the holograph experience. My book lay open, precariously perched on my lap, as I dozed.

The memory recall of this scene separates, and I travel through the tunnel of time, with the coloured thread lighting my way. The dizzying effects always make me feel disoriented. Then everything slows down, as the holograph of this memory weakens, and I come back to the here and now.

Present Day

I sit quietly in the hall at the institute, dazed and struggling to get my bearings. Bilocating with such depth of spirit demands more discipline and more time to recover than simply viewing scenes "out of time." My stomach growls, in need of food, and jolts those last pieces floating around right back into my body. I realize I'd better get some lunch before the afternoon celebrations begin.

The "end-of-year presentations" are full of laughter. We have a fun-filled gift exchange, but the day soon ends. To cheers and wishes for "Happy holidays!" the last of the students and the staff take their leave. As I close the institute, I give thanks for all of the support life and the Creator have brought me. I walk to the main door, as silence echoes throughout the empty spaces.

A shiver runs down my spine—a sure sign to pay heed. I stop and turn toward an oddly familiar sound. I strain to make out words in the distance.

Some form of energy is attempting to gain my attention from another dimension. In the shadows of the staircase, a movement catches my eye. I hear a clear voice.

It's the young girl who passed away years ago, not far from here. Hubby discovered a few barrels of her clothing neatly tucked away in the side of the mountain, hidden there by her assailant. Her spirit had been roaming, confused by the circumstances of her death. A petite young dark-haired girl, barely out of puberty, she often makes an appearance when I'm alone at the institute. A few of the more astute students have spotted her presence on occasion. I told them these Earth-bound spirits were simply holographic remnants of tragic souls confused by their sudden passing. In time, the remnants would wear out.

I nod a greeting, wishing her peace and telling her I have to be on my way. Her face saddens with my words, and although I know it's useless I decide to take a few minutes to see if I can help her. She'd met all of my previous attempts with resistance and confusion. Not all Earth-bound spirits feel ready to move on, and it takes a wise seer to know when to lend a helping hand.

I take a tentative step her way, asking her whether it's time for her to return to her soul host. Can she see the light and her family waiting in heaven? She doesn't answer right away, her expression unreadable.

I wait, knowing time is irrelevant in the spirit world. This mirage is simply a small piece of this girl's greater self, left behind to heal. The spirits and visitations people speak of are holographic remnants of what once was. They retain a very limited consciousness. This is a form of purgatory, releasing heavy negative energies that have no place in heaven.

She moves closer and becomes quite solid. She never had the ability to be so present before, and this alone catches my attention. She speaks in a childlike voice, saying her name is Mirah and they sent her to warn me.

"Angelina, be wise, for what is to come stems from the evil lurking around all holy places. "

I'm surprised at her words, but I note she has referred to this spot as the holy place. I ask her what form the evil takes, and she shakes her head in sadness. She has warned me of danger in the past, but now it seems more urgent. I ask her again, "What evil and who has sent you to warn me?"

Time passes, and it seems she won't answer me. I'm about to give up and bid her farewell when suddenly she stands facing me less than two feet away. Her eyes implore me to be careful. "The evil wants you gone, the same evil that once wanted me gone."

Slowly, her image begins to fade.

I ask her once again, anxiously, "Mirah, what form does this evil take?"

She answers in a far-away voice, "From those you once trusted, beware of their guilt, for they covet what is yours."

With these last words she disappears. Funny how just today I'd thought of this same type of encounter with the shadow, while Hubby and I were installing the rafters. I now know it is created of pure mischief, which became a real problem during those first years when the institute came to life.

Shaking off the dread, I remind myself not to give this more attention than warranted, because that opens the door between good and evil, making me vulnerable. I will write all of this down. If I don't catalogue my memories of these events, I often forget them.

I let myself out through the main door. The echoes of the door closing and the lock falling into place interrupt my sad thoughts about Mirah's life ending so violently.

The enjoyable walk home takes barely a quarter of an hour. It's still light out, and the sun has just settled its rays to sleep on this portion of the world. I ponder this danger Mirah warned me about, curious about the source of the evil. This isn't the first time I've faced "evil," and I doubt it will be the last. Much evil simply consists of "mind states," shadows swaying and influencing those weak of heart or spirit. Negative, judgmental, envious people are susceptible to these energies, which stick to them like glue because like draws like. Heavy, sinful thoughts overwhelm people of fearful constitution into committing evil deeds. Spirits and the unseen have no power, except for what they can make someone believe and create.

I look upward and give thanks to Mirah for her protection and, with a side glance, put my "People" on alert. These "People" were sent to protect me and mine by the Powers That Be against those that would see us fail.

I arrive home, where Hubby has made a simple meal. After breaking bread, we relax by the fire. It began to snow in the early afternoon, and I make sure by the Powers That Be that everyone at the institute has gotten home safely, especially with it being the holiday season. Then I doze off in my chair, as is my habit.

The crackling fire startles me from my slumber. I look outside to see a blizzard and figure we'll be snowed in until morning. Because we built the chalet high up on a mountain, no vehicle will be coming up or going down until then.

We constructed both the house and the institute according to self-sustainable ideas. The glass-walled sides provide awe-inspiring views of the valley and the neighbouring mountains.

Oh, well, I'll worry about getting to the office in the morning.

I have a new client coming in to the clinic, but thankfully I booked her appointment at mid morning. Hubby and I will have plenty of time to get down off the mountain in the morning.

I nudge Hubby awake, and we stumble up to bed. The dogs follow, and as a pack we cuddle and slumber off to sweet dreams.

***

The next morning we wake up to a beautiful sun. I arrive early at the clinic, so I have time to plan the sessions for the fast-approaching New Year. The first year after opening, the demand grew for my unusual services and programs and had me in a whirlwind of expansion.

A knock brings me back. My client has arrived. I answer the door and beckon her into my office.

The woman sits anxiously before me, expecting me to *heal her as I have her friend*. She has no clue I can so easily read her silent thoughts. What exactly does this client, Judy, think I can do for her? I see her troubles, but I doubt she wants to hear what I really have to say about her situation. The truth of her plight is hidden beneath her desperate silent plea that I be her saviour.

Judy is in for a huge disappointment, because I'm no saviour. In fact, we all have the power within us to save ourselves. That's what I help people discover and develop. I often tend to play a Skakus role, which suits me fine.[1] Yet the Powers That Be have a funny sense of humour at times. Every once in a while, they bring me a client who pushes all of my buttons and stretches my patience. Today is one of those days.

Judy, one of millions around the world, is so deeply lost in her fears that if I were to "heal her," as she asked, the shock of such an instant release would most probably kill her or at least sink her deeper into misery. People don't understand how much stress healing can put on one's nervous system. As Judy describes her constant state of irritability, anger, and general unhappiness, I observe her deep bitterness and melancholy. She is drowning in them. She is buried alive beneath all of her "stuff."

Judy is a typical spiritually starved and ungrounded victim of our times. She is sinking so deeply into her worries, she may not emerge unscathed. The stress of her constant questioning depletes her entire

---

1   Skakus is a master with a wry sense of humour who trains and mentors Jesus in *The Nine Faces of Christ: Quest of the True Initiate*, by Eugene Whitworth (Moradabad, India: Great Western University and Arcana International, 1972; Seattle, WA: Great Western University and Eichmann Publishing, 1980, first U.S. edition; first Devers Publications edition, 1993; rev. ed., 2011).

person, and I wonder whether I can catch a glimpse of Judy herself. If not, then I cannot help her. I need something of her essence to grab hold of, because the natural laws of healing forbid me from intervening without a soul's consent. The karmic debt following a transgression of this law is not something I choose to experience again. It was enough that Daniel lost his life from my last epic mistake in this type of situation.

Then, out of nowhere, I silently recite, *Fool me once, shame on you. Fool me twice, death to me.* I grin at the twist I added to the old proverb. More and more so-called well-meaning people violate this natural law.

Judy describes her worries for the umpteenth time. Though I've let my thoughts roam, part of me keeps listening to her grievances. Judy doesn't realize that complaining and "letting go of steam" are simply saboteur tactics to keep people busy and thus avoid dealing with their "stuff." Talking away the pressure of her life, losing herself in the troubles of others, and blaming her friends and partners for her lot in life bury the issues ever deeper. Judy goes on and on.

In frustration, I ask silently: *Why do you bring them to me when they are in this state?* She is probably beyond my help, and she doesn't want to hear the truth.

Judy finally has nothing more to say, because I refused to fuel her complaining. Exhausted, she sits quietly and looks at me expectantly.

Oh, what to do, what to do? I wonder, as I give her a comforting smile.

I stare down at my notes, buying precious time to tap into the *"usually wonderful insight I have that is not guiding me today."*

Then, suddenly, my head snaps up. In that moment I see something in Judy's eyes, and it is all I need. I swiftly send out a thank-you to "my People" and mentally outline my ideas for her.

My smile puts her at ease, as she waits for my feedback. It dawns on me that she will greatly benefit from a Chakaura™ Balancing, and her main problem lies in the state of her present misalignment. She is so energetically bound, no amount of talking will have any effect. Once we get her restructured, we can then address the remaining ideas she has about life that drive her mad with worry. The Chakaura™ Balancing therapy will most likely get rid of more than half of her worries and fears, which simply consist of bindings from past experiences she no longer needs and cannot rid herself of. So in this alone, she will be freed.

Once again, my moment of self-doubt has all been for naught.

Judy is unusual in one respect: she has not yet been a victim of our medical system, resorting to medication to ease her symptoms. Though well-intended, pharmaceutical drugs usually do nothing but numb the symptoms and make things worse. Judy has also not turned to any addictions to suppress her issues, so this is a plus.

She is not that far gone, so I feel hopeful. Yet she does habitually run a circuit of healing modalities. Judy, like many spiritually starved people, gobbles up just about anything spiritual and esoteric she can find.

I know, deep down, that "if the experience existed, then someone out there needed it." I silently send love out to the souls of these spiritual wolves praying on the ignorance of people, for *Karma is a much bigger bitch than I could ever be!* It's heartening that society finally accepts alternative healing. In the past, my kind were hunted and burned.

With the words "Now, Judy," I calmly but strongly grab her attention and stop her racing mind. I explain the situation, while holding her awareness with an energetic force she cannot refuse, because it's founded in the energy of love. I share what I see as her dilemma, and I suggest how she can broach her issues. She accepts my ideas gratefully.

We will begin with a Chakaura Structural Balancing.™ Then, if this suits her, she can enrol in our self-development program, which will provide knowledge and techniques to empower her, as well maintain her Chakaura™ alignment. She agrees and stands up with a smile.

My next appointment is due to arrive. Another day has gone by, and I add yet another series of experiences to my records. When I began to awaken, I searched for teachers to help me bring up buried memories of my past life training, but so few people had the depth of knowledge I needed.

Then my story began to unravel, and I began to understand why.

I close the door behind my last patient. Soon I will need to write about all of this. Spring will be a good time, because spring brings the energy of birthing, of new beginnings.

"Yes," the voice of Teacher whispers, *"in the spring."*

Chapter 8

The Beginning of the End

*Concealed within us is all the wisdom there is or ever was.
It is in the unveiling of this knowledge that we awaken.
The secret to "remembering" is in the
journey to self-realization.*

—Michèle C. St.Amour

Present Day

I wake up to a beautiful spring day. Weather experts described the fierce, long winter as the coldest on record for many years. The sun hasn't yet peeked over the neighbouring mountaintops, but the skies are visibly clear. The air has a fresh crispness that one feels only in the mountains. Classes are out. We have just finished the institute's winter programs, with yet another year of students graduating and looking forward to their summer break.

Today I will start to compile "the book." It's already late May, and we've turned over the garden beds, so they're ready for seeding. Hubby and my daughter, who now lives with us, got up and left early, to go to work down in the flatlands. I set up a makeshift office on the deck, surrounded by nature and its energy.

Sipping a cup of tea, I lean back, then take a deep breath and look at my blank computer screen.

"Where will this begin?" I ask out loud.

I sit quietly, with faith that "the voice" of Teacher will come and get me started.

"I know you're there and you can hear me. I'm ready when you are." Silence greets my words, and I shrug away any doubts about timing and readiness. As the seconds tick by, the forest sounds lull me, and my mind wanders. I enter a state of quietness.

A long-ago memory comes alive, surfaces in a glimmer, and plays out before me as a holograph, reminding me that this destined day has been long foretold.

It happened in my mid twenties, when Teacher's voice was a mystery to me. One day, I heard a whisper in my inner ear, "You are going to write a book."

I felt a bit taken aback, but the more I thought about it, the more the idea of writing a book felt right. Yet I didn't trust this strong inner prompting so easily. I had always been an avid reader and excelled in English, but to actually write a book?

I couldn't imagine where to begin. Young and full of hope and dreams, however, I felt that nothing was beyond me. The sky was the limit. I constantly challenged myself and looked for exciting new adventures. It never took me long to get bored with a new activity, compounded by the energy of youth. Off I would go, in pursuit of another experience to spark my interest. I never sat still for long, with my active, fiery temperament.

Yet something about this book idea sprung from a deep longing in my soul. When insights like this hit you, you cannot deny their power, no matter how unrealistic they seem. Bound to this was sadness that had been with me as far back as I could remember.

Little did I know, in those early days, that despite being physically mature, spiritually I was but a child—a child who nevertheless had the gift of foresight. I could see what would happen in the future. This gift tended to surface through my dreams when I let my guard down. Yet just as often it came forth in a moment of daydreaming.

My ignorance of this unique ability unconsciously influenced my decisions during my life. I didn't know this legacy had come from my family of seers. Our kin rarely talked about it and then only in constrained, hushed moments when someone mentioned a premonition he or she felt compelled to share. After the murmured disclosure of the odd occurrence with a trusted family member, it would be laughed off as a coincidence or something else, for no one dared speak of it publicly. Society had long marked these types of insights as "evil" or "works of the devil," so in our family it became taboo to speak of them openly. For this reason, I never paid much attention to my own premonitions.

Yet when the book idea occurred, I decided without question I would write it.

I laugh to recall my zealous fervour and unwavering discipline, important factors in most projects I took on as a youth. I didn't realize I had merely seen into a possible future, so I took it for granted that I would write a book immediately.

My next dilemma became, "What will I write about?"

I racked my brain for days, but no ideas came. The more I thought about it, the more I determined that I had nothing to say that spoke deeply from my *SoulCore*.

"Now, isn't that an interesting word I just used?" I'd asked out loud. The word had surfaced out of the blue, and it sounded good and right in some weird way. As weeks went by, no matter how much I searched for a plot, an idea, or a story, disappointment set in, and I continued to stare at a blank sheet of paper.

I just don't get it! I thought. *Why would I have this idea and not be able to follow through?*

I shared my predicament with my best friend, Sofia. She always had a grounding influence on me, and this forced me to develop patience with her quiet ways. She was short and not very athletic in build or temperament, so we balanced out each other well. We'd met during childhood and, to this day, remained the best of friends.

"You know, Sofia, I actually don't have much to say to the world. But why would my urge to write be so strong?"

Never one to hurry, she thought about this for a moment. Then she said calmly, "So it must wait. This idea has to be put aside until life brings you a subject to ignite passion and spark enough to share."

I finally gave up and shrugged aside the book notion. I went off looking for a new adventure, completely forgetting the idea of a book until many years later. I now know that when I do finish this book, it will begin a whole new era. It will signal the maze of my destiny to be revealed.

The buzzing of a hummingbird brings me back to the task at hand, as I once again stare at my blank computer screen. I have to laugh, because now I have the opposite quandary from the one I had in the past. After organizing more than a decade's worth of manuscripts, I realize one book will never be able to hold all I want to write about. "Where will I start? What teachings and wonderful journeys will I share?" I ask myself out loud.

With a sigh of resignation, I know deep down Spirit will guide me.

Teacher has prepared me for months, energetically, emotionally, and mentally, to maintain a link with her, as she mentors me in writing of knowledge once veiled or forgotten. Butterflies surface in my stomach. *It's hard to believe this day is finally here!*

I roll my eyes and look around, wondering, *Where is She?*

I know She is always with me. Teacher once told me that in the past, She was forced to be quiet, due to my inability to calm my mind or bring my energy high enough for Her to come through. Back then, Teacher had been vague and distant, like a barely noticeable memory. During those first years when I began to awaken and ask questions about life, Teacher surfaced as faint silent thoughts. The more I practiced meditation to calm my racing mind and learned how to bring my energy up higher, the more easily I heard Her words of wisdom in moments of silence. At other times, however, Teacher remained in the shadows of my consciousness, and I simply referred to Her as "the voice."

Some people would describe this as wisdom communicating through me, but it was more than that. I had suppressed Teacher at a young age.

She was the part of me that had gone to sleep when I had asked to forget the All I was born remembering.

She began to surface ever so slowly and gently in harmony with the awakening of my Muse.

My physical, emotional, and spiritual bodies required many years of transformation to adapt to the higher frequencies I needed to embrace in full consciousness the wisdom of this Goddess of lore, Teacher. Years passed before I recognized who and what She was, though I'm still not fully convinced I know Her as I should.

I notice that the incense has burned out, and half an hour has gone by, as I wait for Teacher to appear.

Yet I discern Teacher is still not ready. I sink back into my thoughts and let whatever wants to surface come. Images of past events flash by. My body had been horribly twisted from a slew of unhealthy practices—bad eating habits and mismanaged energy. I often succumbed to bouts of down moods. I wasn't ready to embrace the full energies of the Dragon, which some call the Goddess or the Muse. My body needed time to repair the severe damage from my life choices.

Only as my Dragon began to rouse did the tree of life offer up all of its secrets.

Today, the first stage of my process is almost complete, so I need to close this chapter by sharing this story, as Teacher commanded. Today is the beginning of the end of ignorance about my soul journey.

I once again listen for Teacher. Since this is our first run, I'm not yet familiar with what She expects of me.

I'm about to give up when suddenly She appears. She greets me with a great surge of liquid fire running through my body. I feel an energetic presence that is undeniably sacred, mysterious, and not of this world.

"*Are you properly grounded, Angelina? Have you created the sacred space, as I instructed you?*"

"All is in place, Teacher, as you willed it."

Teacher then runs me through a series of ancient techniques, adapted to our times, to be sure I'm ready for the task at hand. I feel the buzzing and numbing effect of high energy surround my sacred space.

She continues, *"You will begin by telling your story as the memories surface, to set the stage. This will occur in the same way that has happened since you first sat down this morning."*

I laugh, as it dawns on me why Teacher didn't present herself sooner. During the prelude to her appearance, I was actively being taught to recognize how the information I'd write about would surface.

"I will add my comments as I see fit," says Teacher. *"You will type or record all you receive as you 'see' and 'hear' it."*

I start to type, as the memories of the past appear before me. And so it begins.

Chapter 9

The Forgotten Self

*The journey of life unveils layers of
ignorance hiding us from our truth.*

— Michèle C. St.Amour

Angelina's Story Unfolds

As the words flow, a holograph plays out in my mind's eye. My fingers can barely type fast enough. My foggy memories as a child called Angelina dance by, filled with mystical dreams and the wondrous feats I performed. I relive these formative years as a young child, who believed that deep inside me lived the magical creature I'd read about in fairy tales and seen in Disney movies. The images swirl and weave through many time frames, until they settle on one particular event.

Angelina's Early Years

Around the age of five, I knew deep down that I could fly. Now I watch as my five-year-old self jumped off a six-foot fence without a thought of failure, demanding to fly. Of course, this insight represented a metaphor for spirit flight, and I fell flat on my face. I ran crying to Mom with two scraped knees. Adults reinforced my imprudence when they laughingly said, "Child, how could you think such a foolish thing as being able to fly?" Yet deep inside, I knew something they did not. I had a vague memory of being capable of so much more than they could ever imagine. During my entire life, this deep sense that I needed to remember something haunted me and gave me no peace.

Today I describe this idea of flying as *"la pensée magique."* Flight of the spirit had been so common to me, before I asked the Powers That Be to let me forget my true self.

Angelina as a Teen

My mind's eye fast-forwards the scenes playing out, to stop in my teenage years. In that series of memories, I still instinctively believed in magic and held onto a notion that something else existed beyond what people described as reality. Teacher interjects,

> *It is a common thread binding all humans. These beliefs live in all of you, though you never really talk openly about them for fear of being ridiculed. They fade as you get older. They will often make one last attempt to take hold and be birthed, until the day you become completely disillusioned with life and bury them deeply under logic and belief systems. It is a flavour of the society you were born into and one reason you asked to forget your beginnings.*

While viewing a scene of myself and my young friends dabbling in occult practices, I wonder if they ever think about those magical moments anymore. The games we played and the world of make-believe we delved into zip past. How many of us have sat around a Ouija board and tried in vain to communicate with another world, another reality beyond this one, that we instinctively know exists?

In the memory surfacing, I'd spent a rainy afternoon with friends, trying to get spirits to talk to us through this Ouija board. We set it up in the dark basement, with only one candle for light. The empty house seemed eerie. Although our parents had never said not to dabble in the occult, it just felt taboo when we brought out the board. Enveloped in a mystical, esoteric energy, the Ouija board seemed secret and forbidden.

"Hey, Julie, are you making it move?" I remember asking, when something seemed to be happening. Of course, the board never did anything, and knowing what I know today, I'm glad we weren't successful. Or maybe we were, and we never recognized it? Repercussions from dabbling in things not fully understood are far-reaching and at times extremely subtle.

In the world of spirit, everything is connected in a place beyond time and space. Some call it the great web and others the divine matrix. It is the fabric that glues all things together. Children remember this place. This web, once triggered by the right energy, can turn illusion into reality with the flick of a finger, much as sorcerers and witches did in times gone by. I constantly tested the boundaries of my reality when I was young. Just when I almost believed the delusion of the collective that magic did not exist, it would show itself to me. A miracle would happen, which rekindled my belief in something beyond.

I stop typing, lost in thought, as I realize the school is a place to experience the magical web of life.

Teacher nudges me to get back to writing.

The scenes paused during my "break," and as I resume, I watch an immature Angelina find magic in books and movies. At a very young age, I read whatever I could get my hands on from the world of make-believe: UFOs, magic, time-travel romances, anything that allowed my imagination to soar. Books I'd collected over the years littered my room.

I spent hours in other worlds, escaping from this one, which seemed unreal, cruel, and irrational. I also involved myself in athletic pursuits, from dance and music to competitive running and team sports. They helped me ground the powerful energies of my ever-present creative primal force, my slumbering Muse.

From the time I could walk, my family told stories about how I dreamed, talked, and walked in my sleep. They often joked about my escapades, their way of relieving an uncomfortable notion that I wasn't like other kids. I constantly questioned the reality presented to me by adults and peers alike, but after being ridiculed once too often, I became conditioned to keep silent. Teacher once again intercedes.

So many things about you were normal, but alongside your normality lurked unexplained happenings and taboo behaviours. You did everything to the limit of your ability and excelled in ways that were uncanny even to you, performing feats that made you stand apart from others, though your unawareness acted as camouflage. We, the planners, had not seen how this would happen, so the Powers That Be sighed in relief to observe that humans did not have the perception to notice the workings of your powers when they arose naturally. We were also very relieved that your own unawareness of your powers acted as a cloak, so not much attention was given to your somewhat odd abilities.

Teacher's words trigger memories of my school years, when I performed way above average in academics, sports, the arts, musically, and the list went on. I'd won numerous awards, when most students would have been glad to simply have one. My drive and willpower had me obsessed with success and personal recognition. Only now do I realize that even though this gift, this power, became my greatest oppressor, it turned into my greatest teacher and supporter.

All of those years when I moved forward in ignorance of my destiny, I knew something more existed, and I would find it one day.

On the surface, I was no different than anyone else at birth, except that "I was born in full consciousness, remembering who I was and why I had come; and then I asked that it be taken away."

Wow! As I utter these words, I sit back in my chair. I stop hearing Teacher, and the shock of my words has my senses reeling. These words, typed so surely and precisely, hit home as they never had in the past. In the typing came full awareness of my origins, and the floodgates of my memories fully opened and bombarded me. So many questions were answered in that one instant, accompanied by a staggering surge of energy that almost knocked me off my chair.

Now I understand why Teacher would not begin until I was fully fit, physically and energetically, for this task. I also better understand Teacher's words, that in the telling of it full disclosure would come to me.

Images flash before my mind's eye, as nonstop memories surface. My head aches from this and the accompanying volatile emotions.

"I, Angelina, was born with complete knowledge of my purpose for reincarnating," I say out loud. I now intimately know at my core that I'm not the Angelina I thought I was.

In a state of shock, I feel like a split personality. Chilled to the bone, I almost wish I hadn't been so eager to open this chest of treasures, as waves of energy rush through me.

I suddenly hear Teacher's calm, soothing voice say, *"In time, this will pass."*

Her words give me comfort. No one had warned me about this, and my surprise prevented my usual habit of blocking anything I wasn't familiar with. The Powers That Be had foreseen I might refuse this last bit of consciousness, so they had agreed not to share with me how it would unravel. If I had blocked this, I probably would have exploded from the forces now surging through me. My hands and legs shake, my head still spins, and my body feels numb and frozen. I feel disconnected from reality. I keep taking deep breaths and do a few mudras to settle my heart area.

I relax into the energy but then become restless, needing to release the unaccustomed electrical bursts. Teacher begins to speak, and I gladly start typing again, welcoming the distraction.

> *This time around, you have brought with you the Divine Mother, the Holy Spirit, and hence you clothe yourself as female, for only as female can you fully express the Dragon Goddess. She carries within her the purpose of life. Without this connection, humanity becomes spiritually starved and sickens.*
>
> *She is the yin and the yang energies come together, the polarities in constant play to create your physical reality. It is in this truth that spirituality becomes science; they are but one and the same—different only in the language expressing their truth.*

The wind suddenly comes up, and I look around, wondering what that's all about. An energy nudge compels me not to be distracted, and I resume typing.

> *In the past, you had this same influence on the world as a male, but today it is time to reintroduce the quality of yin. The feminine aspects of Wo-man will no longer be hidden in symbolism and innuendo simply for the few discerning souls. Now it is time the Divine Mother be recognized and embraced with open arms by all.*

Angelina as a Young Child

The wind comes up once again, and this time a portal of energy settles in the space in front of me. The time when I forgot the truth about myself is now revealed to me. The energy swirls and twists, and I see Angelina at her birth and then a few years into her life, with the full awareness she had back then.

I say to Teacher, "After my birth, the challenge of having to go through the whole maturing process once again was so daunting and so frustrating, I asked to be released from my memories, so I could grow up in ignorance, for I had things to learn from this new era."

With my words, I again experience the reality of Angelina's life. Images and scenes play out before me, clearly explaining the reasons for my decision to become unconscious.

"The Powers That Be originally discussed this before I incarnated in this life, but they hadn't agreed on a consensus." I see meetings with beings of light in an unrecognizable world. A debate was taking place among familiar people I obviously knew then, but who are now a vague memory.

"They thought my time of awakening would be much too dangerous and most likely unsuccessful, if I were allowed to forget during my incarnation as Angelina. They also determined that if I were to forget, I could not lose my powers—these could only be dulled. A person without knowledge of how to manage this type of energy could very well destroy or be destroyed. No soul had ever accomplished or taken on a task this dangerous."

I stop talking. The wind howls, as the portal from whence these memories came gets stronger and bigger. I stand up, as the wind blows my hair back and forth, but I hold my ground with strong energy muscles and willpower. A black hole in space has manifested to bring forth these far-reaching memories. If I'm not careful, I could easily be sucked into it, and all trace of my existence would be gone. Am I being tested once again?

Teacher's voice rises above the energy humming in my ears, which sounds like a jet getting ready for take-off. I hear Teacher and suddenly know I should stop writing and listen for a time.

> *I want you to go deep within yourself and expand your consciousness fully to accept and embrace the Christ Consciousness more than is your habit, so that your mental capacities become diamond-like for the next revelations.*

I straighten my posture, so my spine won't obstruct the pathways of Divine consciousness. The sexual nature of the energy, the Muse coursing through my veins, now completely transforms into pure creative life force. I prepare myself for the bliss that accompanies these experiences. My spiritual centres become fully activated. The awakening of my spinal centres is not a mystical anomaly but a purely natural occurrence under the tutelage and development I have undergone. I travel these main highways to reach my soul.

> *Now bring your concentration to your brow centre, where dwells your spiritual eyes. Turn your attention inward.*

I withdraw from my senses. As my spiritual eyes focus, my mind and my breath reflect calmness. Minutes go by, and I suddenly find myself at the gates of Heaven.

> *This is your first memory. . . . Today we go to the beginning of all things. These first memories are from a time beyond time, where life as we know it had not yet birthed. I, the Teacher, exist in this place and am in "The Beyond." This "Beyond" is perpetually in the Now, and hence I, the Teacher, can observe the function and unravelling of events.*

The Beginning of This Life as Angelina

Opening myself up, I become still. I now understand the need for such a high frequency to travel so far back. I take deep breaths to calm my racing heart. From a distance, a point becomes visible and stirs; a dim light appears. As it approaches, it grows, and, ever so slowly, this individual consciousness arises within me. This turns into an "I AM," which is how I come to know of myself.

I am now part of another world of vaster dimensions. I know from past experiences I have entered Cosmic Consciousness.

Then once again comes Teacher's voice,

> *In the beginning there was NOTHING. From the fathomless stillness of nothingness arose the first Breath of Life. Perfect Bliss expressed itself, to create of itself, in order to know itself. From this nothingness, radiance flashed outward, to then retract back onto itself. This was the first of a never-ending expression of a Creative force so magnificent as to be Omnipotent, Omnipresent, and Omniconscious. Bliss birthed self-awareness in that first moment of expression.*

Teacher recalls this moment of separation, the moment when the Love Energy was birthed: "*It is the most unique and only expression from the Source, which we call Love.*"

I recall being part of that nothingness. Teacher continues,

> *Love is not an emotion but is a powerful energy with unlimited consciousness grounded in your SoulCore. It is the spirit of your soul. It is the Holy Grail, touted for eons: the elixir of life!*

As I sit in silence, I see another energetic pulse, and Creation expresses itself further and further from its primal Source until the world of physical matter comes into existence. I realize this is the "Big Bang," a concept often used to describe the beginning of our universe.

In answer, Teacher says,

> *And so I say to you, this is Creation; this is life in expression.*

> *Your SoulCore nourishes, guides, and lights you. The SoulCore is found at the centre of all living things. It is what every soul secretly seeks to know more deeply and reunite with; that which lies beneath the many shrouds of illusion you call reality. This is your mission: to guide those who are ready to begin awakening and consciously know their SoulCore through your guidance towards self-realization.*

As Teacher's words fade away, I feel the energy retracting back to its Source. My body hums, and my inner senses turn outward once again. After a few minutes, I'm completely back. I do a few grounding techniques to reintegrate all of my energy parts into my physical body. The scene before me shifts back to this era.

"I now observe my birth and see through the eyes of the child Angelina, who I was, in full awareness of my destiny. My parents were chosen for their unique genetic blend of a multitude of cultures."

An image of my parents leaning over the baby Angelina flashes by, then a family tree mapping out generations of my ancestors, mixed with sacred geometry and triangular formulas I don't understand.

"This careful planning began millennia ago, and everything had to be perfectly aligned. I spent my first years trapped in an infant's body, biding my time until I realized this undertaking would be better served if I could simply forget and become like all the rest of the souls around me. And so I forgot."

My vision of Angelina shifts to a few years later, just after she "forgot" her reason for reincarnating. I'm overwhelmed by a wave of compassion for the very young, unconscious Angelina portrayed in the portal. To be so asleep, in ignorance of anything outside my world—it had been so many lives since I'd experienced this blind state of unawareness.

Teacher's voice asks, *"Do you recall why you were so adamant to forget?"*

I answer, "It would allow me to blend in with everyone else, to intimately know the people who surrounded me and be like them. It would help me assist and teach them once I awakened."

I focus on the reality playing out in the portal. I'd recognized the subtle tightening of a noose by a matrix world.

A slithering darkness hides in dark corners, not recognized for its inherently evil ways. Once upon a time man believed in the dangers of the unseen world, but today man has been convinced of its nonexistence. The darkness is now winning because it has nothing to fear, for man can't see what he doesn't believe in or have knowledge of. Part of my reason for being was to reacquaint man with this inner world, liberated of superstitions of ancient times.

And so, my petition to forget began.

The scenes go back in time to the years before I would forget. I observe myself as a very young conscious toddler, praying to the higher-ups and having long discussions with my People. What I wanted to do had never been done before. It was all new for us Planners, so we pondered all probabilities and looked far into the future for every possible outcome to our ideas. From the higher-dimension worlds, we could see far into the future and into the past for guidance in planning. We finally settled on what has now become my reality.

When I say *we*, I mean my Soul and the Powers That Be.

One day when I must have been about four years old, I astral-travelled with my HS (my Higher Soul Self) to a higher dimension to present my case. The memory of that day clearly surfaces, and I now recall that the process of forgetting began the following night.

I stood in a much higher dimension than Earth, surrounded by the most amazing light. Thousands of beings from numerous other realities were present. For one such as I to ask to forget in the middle of an incarnation was inconceivable.

As I stood at the centre of this world of light, I sensed the fascination of many gazing upon my human light form. I had cloaked myself in my Christ; this was a wonder to see.

Silence suddenly reigned, and I spoke.

"I stand before you to present my appeal to return to a state of unawareness, so I may live out the balance of my incarnation in ignorant bliss until it is deemed my time to reawaken. I am aware this has its dangers, but I am willing to take this chance."

My words brought forth many whispers and gasps of shock, but in the end, free will won. Ultimately, I made the decision, as was the custom in the place between Heaven and Earth. Yet it was also the custom to honour all of those involved, so that they might, out of respect, have a say, which would surely reflect on their destiny. One such soul came forward.

"I stand here by you, my sister, and wonder if you have thought this out. If you fail, we have much to lose. You are one of the few who has remained unnoticed by forces that would not have you succeed. The forces man calls evil are everywhere and would have us fail."

I nodded in agreement before answering, "Yes, dear friend, you are so right, but I cannot imagine how I can prevail if I don't do it this way. I understand why I had to remain aware for my physical birth, because the powers of my soul had to be vehicled with awareness so as not to kill my birth mother. Yet now other considerations must be accounted for, which is why I'm here before all of you."

Finally, after eons of exchanges and explanations, the Powers That Be reluctantly agreed to support my decision that Angelina would forget until it was ordained she awaken.

The head of the council succinctly said, "We remind you that no other has ever survived the cruel initiation that this dark night of the soul will ask you to endure, when the time to awaken comes upon you."

I knew deep down it was the only way I could hope to rightfully accomplish this life's purpose. This undertaking was the most crucial I had ever taken on. It was the age of transformation. And so, at the age of four, I went to sleep and forgot.

I didn't foresee that my soul would lie smothered, purposely locked in my heart, where the subconscious is buried. A soul cannot separate from its SoulCore. I later realized that my longing and unhappiness—such an integral part of my existence from the time I went into slumber—stemmed from this unconscious separation.

Teacher once said to me, "I always feel such sadness coming from deep inside you."

You can only feel a loss once you've had something. I'd been torn asunder, and so I would bear this cross as a result of forgetting for a time.

Present Day

I come back to the here and now. Wow! That's a lot to digest. I need a break. This is heavy stuff, even for me.

I close my computer for the day. I have much to think about, and I need to plan some meals, mainly of the non-meat variety. I notice when I eat meat, I become heavy, and my thoughts and dreams have a fearful quality otherwise not present. Maybe a light detox would be good. Off I go to pick up a few groceries. Hubby will be thrilled, because he loves eating simply.

He knew me when I was a junk-food addict, and the other day he commented, "I never thought I'd see you eat so healthfully!"

Little does he know the extent of why I have to do this and my desire to support my journey in any way I can.

Chapter 10

Angelina's Purpose

"When the body goes south and the mind goes north, then the soul is pulled asunder."

— Inayat Khan, Sufi mystic

Present Day

Down below in the flatlands, fierce winds always swept across the fields of cultivated land surrounding the old homestead. Up here in the mountains, windy conditions are rare. I settle outside on the deck, overlooking the lake. It's unusually balmy for this time of year. Straw hat in hand, incense burning once again—but for mood and not bugs—I'm ready for another day with Teacher.

I marvel at the simplicity of life, as a world once hidden in the shadows of my consciousness has arisen. Sharing this world is bringing me to full awareness, as destiny has foretold.

Who am I? I am known in this life as Angelina. Before this incarnation, those you describe as "the ascended masters" or "the Powers That Be" determined it was time the Teacher return to Earth to support a planetary shift.

Teacher makes her presence known with a great surge of energy. This is her cue to take over the conversation.

> *I represent the feminine principle of the Divine. For millennia, I have been an initiator of life, from worlds unknown yet to man, born in many cultures under many names, some remembered and others forever lost.*
>
> *Some of my fondest memories are the lives when I guided and trained initiates on their journey to remembering. Many great names I once knew have now become extolled in your history books.*

Another Life, Long Ago

As Teacher speaks, holographic images of a long-forgotten past play within my spiritual eye.

I feel nostalgic seeing these times I once lived in and revisiting ancient places and people forgotten. Images appear of a strange land of sand and heat, with pyramidal temples of stone. Serene initiates walk about robed in natural-coloured cloth. They move gracefully but with purpose, heading to a central stone edifice.

Teacher explains,

> *In this past, initiates trained for years to prepare for the types of shifts your world is now globally experiencing. They would fast for days and go through cleansing rituals, readying their physical, mental, and spiritual bodies for the challenges they needed to survive, in order to embrace their destined calling of the mystical.*
>
> *The pyramids were in fact temples of initiation, where the students went through their "dark night of the soul" experiences. The pyramid is a natural energy generator. Within its space you can transcend the physical world, for it is a doorway, a sacred geometric portal, to the higher spiritual dimensions.*

Silent tears well up, as I remember the beauty of recalling these dormant memories. It's a homecoming of proportions I didn't expect. I feel a sense of peace. I now understand how the energy of these buried memories fuelled my courage and my will to survive the most difficult challenges.

I see a communal hot bath where many participated in cleansing rituals, readying themselves for ceremonies. I smell the incense, a blend of herbs and spices unique to those areas. It reminds me of my own Three Kings blend of resins but with a mystery ingredient I don't recognize right away. It's similar to a Sufi resin-and-herb blend gifted to me from a dear student. The smoke from the burning medicines actually wafts through the portal of time that has opened, to wrap itself around me.

Teacher explains,

> *Yes, this is possible. These portals are avenues we can travel, and it's why we exercise such caution to make sure anyone viewing is well grounded in his or her timeline.*
>
> *This age has forgotten most of these practices, and the world moves too fast to remember such notions as described in our text on ancient rites. The sacred is mostly forgotten and misunderstood.*

The scene before me shifts to high priests performing gestures I know so well today. They are drawing heaven to earth as they open a gateway to the higher worlds for the initiate trainings.

> *We, the Initiators, grounded the higher energies of the upper worlds into the Earth energies, to support Earth's coming ascension. These initiations—rites of passage once accessible only by mystics and holy men—are now accessible to the world. These are the sacred ceremonies you now observe through the holograph.*

I see a teacher with assistants on each side, as well as lined up behind the students. The colours are so vibrant, and the room shimmers. This formation seems so familiar to me, but, curiously, no memory surfaces. A golden grid of sorts appears in the shimmering all around them. It emulates the pyramidal structure of the building itself.

> *Do not fret—you will remember these techniques when it is time.*
>
> *As people awaken, you will create these energy grid structures to support those guided to you, so that they recognize themselves in their kin, in those brothers and sisters of humanity, and this will speak to them of a truth forgotten, much as you are now remembering.*

As this ancient past plays out before me, I know I will have these memories at my disposal whenever I wish to review them.

Teacher, reading my thoughts, knows this is overwhelming. Her words to me are,

> *With the passing of the numerous Earth lives, this soul we have named Angelina has gained the ability not to lose consciousness on passing from one life to another.*
>
> *Angelina, you graduated to the role of initiator in schools of high alchemy. This helps you understand how one full life lived here on Earth is but one second in the life of a soul.*

I have searched for this world all of my life. My training had revealed bits and pieces, but the full picture then presented to me overwhelmed my senses.

> *I watched your pain, and my forced silence was of your choice. You suffered much in those first years, but, as you see, it was for the highest good of all.*
>
> *Your choice to forget was appropriate, though you clearly carry many scars from it.*
>
> *Some refer to our ways as high alchemy, and names abound for this path—but no matter. This next century will determine the continuation of the species we call man. It is a time of Shiva, of destruction, for only from chaos may new life be born. Yet it is also a time of birth, of new beginnings, and in this we rejoice.*

My mind wanders to past lives when I contracted a "step in" before my reincarnation. However, possible complications demanding a lengthy, disorienting adjustment period led me to opt out of that type of agreement this time around. Teacher adds,

> *As you know, a "step-in" is when souls are exchanged or blend together at a specific time in the life of a person here on Earth, as happened with Daniel and Hubby. The physical body often sustains severe damage during these, and the psychological ramifications can take years to heal.*
>
> *A "step-in" is an event rarely seen, due to the dangers for all concerned and its very limited success rate. Luckily, your soul group had foreseen the possible need of having a backup for Daniel and had contracted Hubby to be available and prepared accordingly.*

Teacher continues, *"Are you remembering any of this?"*

I nod uncertainly, telling her some of it yes and some of it no.

"The sharing of your memories will help them awaken as needed, so you can finally liberate them," Teacher says.

She suddenly calls it a day. It's time for me to mull over all of this, and soon everyone will be home for the night.

Present Day

The next morning, I wake up early from a lucid dream and consciously recall more past-life events. My past has been unravelling nonstop since yesterday.

I glance at the clock. It's 4 a.m., and I should think about getting up. My obsessive book writing takes over my sleep, as much as my waking hours.

Teacher guided me to write the book as a novel, which would free me to disconnect from everything. Anyway, who would believe that all of this could be true?

We often lose precious growth opportunities to let our imaginations soar and be free as a child. When the sages say you must be like a child, it really means to free your mind the way a child's mind is free from ideas that adults program us with, binding us and restricting our creativity.

I drift back in time, feeling the security of Hubby beside me. I've always been *"early to bed and early to rise."* I nudge myself fully awake and gently kick off the sheet. With the summer nights so warm and balmy, sleeping naked is a joy. Yet the morning air still has a nip. Hubby and I often drape ourselves, legs and arms entwined, in our perfect knot. We fit so nicely together, as we *huggle*—our word for "hugging" and "snuggling." His maleness and my femininity complement each other so well. If at some point we become discordant, all hell breaks loose.

I slip out of bed, being careful not to disturb Hubby's sleep. He works long days this time of year, and he needs his rest. I look around for something to wear. I'm discovering an aversion to any clothing that's the least bit confining.

I catch a glimpse of my slim, womanly figure in the cheval mirror, reflecting my state of health. I gaze at my body through the dispassionate eyes of a stranger. I don't often pay attention to my looks, though people consider me attractive.

I'm lucky to still have such a youthful figure at my age. My stomach is flat and my breasts perky. Hubby says he loves touching me, because my skin is so soft. We are a perfect match, because I love to be touched. He says I purr and roll like a cat when he rubs me. He knows exactly how to turn my foul mood into a receptive one.

I turn to pick up my shawl and catch my feline grin in the mirror. *Should I wake him for a rub?* He looks so peaceful, still deeply lost in sleep, that I decide against it. His long tousled blond hair enhances his strong, manly features. He's a handsome devil, and women can't help being attracted to his maleness. I tease him about his baby blues, especially when he's in a cuddly mood.

He's an unusually caring man and, surprisingly, very nurturing. He takes such good care of me when the Dragon within makes Herself known with Her energy surges, creating havoc in my system at times for days on end. I spent quite a few years broken and barely survived Her awakening in the time before Daniel left us. None of us had a clue then what was happening, and conventional doctors even less. I shake off the sombre mood, grab some clothes, and jump into the shower.

After dressing, I go to get my laptop. Today Teacher urges me to notice the teachings and memories surfacing the minute I open my eyes in the morning. Her relentless prodding has begun to get on my every nerve. When she notices my ill temper, she tells me each memory has a place in the book, and I am not to argue this point.

I sigh at Teacher's no-nonsense manner, wondering who this reminds me of? Then I realize that my own students would also describe *me* this way at times!

With the weather overcast and quite cool today, writing on the deck is not an option. The best place will be in my comfy chair by the wood stove. The house is quiet. I make my way to the kitchen and put on the percolator coffee.

The first one to rise has the task of making coffee. Waking up to the sound and smell of this old-fashioned brewing method is a ritual in this house.

I pour a cup and sit down to review my notes—manuscripts of my thoughts and experiences, written by a much younger me . . .

> It is said a shaman is born from death. Every spiritual healer must go through this rite of passage to transition from one consciousness of reality to another.
>
> I've searched to understand the physical, mental, and spiritual changes that resulted from my lengthy convalescence. I need to know the purpose behind my experiences. Why has my life been such an ordeal, filled with inordinate drama and countless initiate trials?

I hear Hubby stirring and, not long afterward, everyone else moving around. The once-quiet house comes alive with activity and animals looking for their breakfast. The morning activity doesn't bother me in the least, and I just keep reading. My family simply goes about business as usual, after years of living with my eccentric ways.

"*Mom is busy, so do your thing and go,*" they would say and bid me farewell, rushing out the door. They know I'm distracted and lost in my imaginary world.

This morning, while reviewing my manuscripts, I noticed my daughter clearing some intense energies. She had been giving in to her temper lately. Her moods could be taxing in normal times, but this morning she ran around frantically, upset that she would be late.

After fifteen minutes of listening to her, I said calmly, "You need to ground yourself before going any further, or you will have an accident. You're all over the place, and this never brings anything positive!"

She stopped and looked at me in frustration, about to blow her red-headed top. I raised my left eyebrow as if to say, "Really?" and she turned in a huff. She knew I was right. She took a deep relaxing breath and did as I'd asked. Not five minutes later, she'd become her calm, collected self, thanking me with a sheepish smile for my concern and advice.

I shake my head and return to my manuscripts. She was the last to leave, and I am finally alone once again. Her actions bring to mind a recent event.

Chapter 11

The Lecture—Grounding

As above, so below; as below, so above

—Hermetes principle

My daughter's "little episode" reminds me of a lecture I gave a few months ago on the importance of certain techniques, grounding being the most crucial for health. Synchronicity has pointed to something I spoke of that day. I bring forth the words in my mind and weave the threads of time until I'm in a postcognitive time warp, focusing on this date in my past. Then everything slows and becomes still. The scene before me comes into focus.

    I stood at a podium at the local university, presenting a talk to hundreds of students on the science of transformation, an art of high alchemy, and about healing from an energy perspective. As the attentive audience listened, I could see my words had an impact.

I wore a well-cut black suit with a soft lilac cotton lace blouse under the tailored jacket. My delicate black pumps matched my outfit, and I'd secured my hair back with a tie, though a few wisps framed my face.

I made these presentations wearing professional attire, bringing respectability and a no-nonsense attitude to the subject. Still, I heard a mix of grunts from the sceptics and ah's from the receptive ones, and "Oh, my God" rang out every once in a while. I grinned at this, for in a crowd so vast, many would refute my facts, while others' lives would be forever changed. And why wouldn't some people resist? If they accepted what I said, they would no longer have any excuse to be miserable or use the role of victim or martyr for their own ends. Some embraced empowering knowledge, and others denied themselves this responsibility. To each his own in the end. My role is simply to offer alternatives to what they know already exists.

After introducing myself with a brief account of what I did, I spoke for more than a half hour about various topics.

"When going through an emotional or mental crisis, you need to be grounded. Each thought and every emotion you experience has a toxic by-product that you must eliminate in the same breath as its creation, to maintain health, neutrality, and centeredness. These toxic by-products of your thought processes hold you in certain behaviour patterns. That's why it is crucial to learn the workings of the mind using the techniques we teach at the institute. These techniques should be practiced unceasingly, to be effective, and not only in a crisis situation."

The room remained quiet, as the students absorbed my words. Then hands went up. I often permitted questions, to encourage interaction with the students. I nodded to a young woman.

"You mean our psychological and spiritual processes have toxic debris attached to them?" she asked.

"Yes," I answered. "I have witnessed, over and over again, the truth of the Hermetic axiom and its law of correspondence: *'As above, so below; as below, so above.'* This principle embodies the truth that a correspondence always exists between all planes or dimensions of reality. I relate this to the biological and energetic function of every life form, but in this instance let's use man as our example. The physical body exists in a world or dimension of matter and takes life force sustenance from the earth. It always has a by-product from its activity, and it's the same with emotion and thought. The breath is inhaled, the positive is used for life, and the negative is exhaled as non-serving. Its by-product of carbon dioxide then feeds the earth. You take in food for nutrition; your body consumes what benefits its life force and then releases the toxic waste, which in turn becomes fodder for the earth. In this, we clearly see the law of correspondence playing out. Do you all agree?"

All heads nodded, curious where I was going with this.

"Well, we also have our emotional, mental, and spiritual processes, which are not on this plane or dimension of matter but which exist in higher ones. The basis of our energy healing teachings at the Chakaura™ Institute is the principle that all psychological and spiritual processes also have negative by-products, much as our biological functions do. We must eliminate unnecessary substances for spiritual health and vitality to be present. If not, they create emotional, mental, or spiritual blockages that our society calls 'stress'—another psychological process with proven biological ramifications that are often deadly."

I clearly had everyone's attention. "At Chakaura,™ we define a blockage as something that doesn't move and that constricts the flow of energy or vital life force. This follows the law of vibration: Nothing rests; everything moves; everything vibrates.

"Modern science, as well as each new scientific discovery, endorses the fact that everything is in motion and vibrates, and nothing is at rest. Matter is simply an energy particle vibrating at a very low frequency, creating the illusion of solidity. This alone proves that all of man's experiences have by-products, for the frequency of vibration defines every aspect of man.

"Next we must look at the principle of polarity, and I quote,

> *Everything is Dual; everything has poles; everything has its pair of opposites; like and unlike are the same; opposites are identical in nature, but different in degree; extremes meet; all truths are but half-truths; all paradoxes may be reconciled.*
>
> —The Kybalion

"In this lies the principle of the life cycle and health. Each positive process has a negative corresponding element—the yin and yang of life. In man, the negative is simply the by-product of experience and hence must be released for the cycle of experience to be complete. We eat food, we digest it and get fuelled by its positive life-giving substances, and then we release the negative by-product, in a specific time period associated with the vibrational frequency of its dimension of manifestation, which is that of heavy, dense matter. On that release of the by-product, the cycle is complete and becomes a past event. If, for any reason, the body withholds any part of the toxic waste, it creates blockages and ill health, because it takes energy from the body, instead of giving energy to the body. So, anything taking energy from the body is unhealthy and stressful and can eventually be life threatening, a negative charge. And anything giving energy to the body is healthy and life giving, hence a positive charge. Combating the negative stress of a toxin we didn't properly eliminate may exhaust this positive charge.

"All thoughts and emotions have toxic by-products that, if not released, will take from the person and create ill health. The release time frame for this is slightly shorter than the time frame for a breath to be complete, because our psychological processes vibrate above the dimension of air."

Hands went up once again. I nodded to an excited young gentleman wearing wide-rimmed glasses.

"So," he said, "you're stating that our psychological processes follow the same principles as our biological processes, but the cycle takes place much faster, due to the higher vibrational frequency at which these psychological processes occur?"

"Yes, we have discovered this and have it proved over and over again in our programs at the clinic and at the institute. Our life-changing protocols, grounded in the science of transformation, are founded on these principles of life."

Another hand went up, and I nodded for an older man to ask his question.

"Would this mean, then, that a person's trauma and psychological fear, which consist of toxic stress stuck in the person's system created from a past experience, can be released simply by eliminating the blockage that is the negative by-product of this experience?"

"Yes, that is correct," I answered.

A hush went over the crowd, as the ramifications of this statement became clear. I waited to let this sink in before continuing.

"Of course, each thought and emotion of that experience must be addressed with a very specific technique we teach, so it's not always cut and dried, but it's a starting point. If you take this a step further, you realize the memories of past traumatic experiences remain alive in the mind, directly attached to the toxic waste stressing the body. In this way, a lot of our memories point out our 'unfinished business.'"

I mentioned that man must become conscious of and must develop grounding in a specific way as the first basic technique to let go of his psychological toxins.

I continued, "I have yet to meet anyone who truly understands grounding and how to properly develop and manage this *energy muscle*, as I call it. Some spiritual schools refer to it, but even they lack knowledge about the intricate details of this energetic mechanism. Grounding is crucial for our physical and psychological health, as well as for self-realization. Without it, not much would exist beyond our physical experience.

"Society has archaic ideas about grounding, such as the practice of telling people to imagine their legs to be tree roots or that they are a tree. This is illogical, if you think about it, because a tree has no consciousness related closely to man's, and it never moves; it stays stuck in one place. It's imperative to realize that whatever you conjure up, all of its properties will come to you—not just a select few. This is what many forget when they begin playing creator with visualizations."

From the back of the room, a deep low voice rose above all of the others. I peered through the shadows, trying to discern who this might be, his tone oddly familiar to me. Everyone in the room turned, curious to see who had caught my attention. The person was obviously male, but I couldn't identify him until he stepped out of the shadows. Smiling, he sauntered down the aisle. I grinned in return, recognizing the swagger. No one dared interrupt, impressed by the commanding presence of this charismatic man.

"So, Ms. Angelina."

I nodded, restraining a smile and trying to remain serious.

"You say stress is killing our society with toxic-based diseases, a fairly new phenomenon. It's mainly because society is no longer grounded, so its 'physical and psychological garbage can' has overflowed, creating a slew of sicknesses, such as obesity, cancer, depression, immune system deficiencies, and so on. We are an extremely toxic species, evidenced in the fact that we have become so self-destructive, even destroying what keeps us healthy. Our unsustainable lifestyles are killing our resources—resources we need to be healthy if we want to stay alive as a species. We are slowly killing ourselves with our own toxic waste—not just physically but also psychologically and spiritually."

He paused, waiting for me to make a comment. I simply nodded in agreement. His grin took the edge off his words, but they still made the impact he wanted. He continued in a voice that brooked no resistance.

"This means we are walking time bombs, as we carry the toxins of our past, putting greater pressure on our nervous systems. We are blowing up into overweight balloons from them, becoming zombie techs desperately trying to avoid and block our toxic ills with mind activities and slowly poisoning ourselves with our toxic lifestyles, until one day a great wave will come and take most of us away."

I took up his monologue, finishing it with, "In fact, these things you define first lead to depression of all systems, which is simply a body screaming for life. Hopefully, people will wake up before the wave comes and takes them away!"

Everyone then realized I knew this person very well, and we were having a word-sparring game. "I'd like you all to meet my loving husband, Hubby, who is a naturalist and a tree hugger extraordinaire, with little patience for anyone who disrespects his back yard, which is nothing short of Mother Earth!"

This took the edge off our doomsday repartee, for the reality of what we had discussed encompassed a truth few had the stomach to face. With the world in such serious trouble, we wouldn't get out of this mess without suffering grave consequences.

I closed the session and watched many students approach Hubby. His natural intelligence and self-confidence drew an equal number of males seeking a father figure and females attracted to his raw sexuality. Luckily for his sake, he had eyes for me alone. He looked up as these thoughts crossed my mind, and he winked, reading me perfectly. I telepathically sent back, *Wait till I get you home,* and his answer was, *I can't wait!* I burst out laughing.

I bring myself back to the present and smile in memory of how Hubby kept his promise and had been anxiously waiting for me when I returned home. Years have gone by since our first meeting, but the spiritual aspect of our relationship gets better and better as we get older. His adorable playfulness quickly turned to soulful lovemaking. That night, we fell asleep wrapped in each other's arms.

I lean back in my chair, contemplating my writing. It's already mid day, as I immerse myself in memories. I think of Hubby and the time he surprised me by coming to that lecture. We suit each other so well.

Knowing it's such a busy time of year for him, I can't get upset if he's always gone. At least this time he's working close to home, and we have our evenings together. Often, he travels to remote places to survey and can be away for months on end, with very little communication between us.

My Cheshire cat grin warms my insides, as I remember more recent connections between us. I put aside my writing and decide to prepare a romantic dinner for two, because tonight we'll be alone.

Chapter 12

New Beginnings

"Enlightenment—that magnificent escape from anguish and ignorance—never happens by accident. It results from the brave and sometimes lonely battle of one person against his own weaknesses."

—Bhikkhu Nyanasobhano, Landscapes of Wonder

Present Day

I slowly awaken to feel Hubby's warmth beside me. Remembering our late-night rendezvous, I run my hands across his muscular chest, loving his strength as his maleness warms my hands. He moans in pleasure. He got home late last night, and by the time we actually went to sleep, it was even later.

Watching him resting peacefully, I don't have the heart to wake him. I scoot over to my side of the bed, so as not to disturb him further. He sighs and goes back into a deep sleep. The memory of his feathery caresses soon has me purring like a cat. Now, watching him sleep, I wonder if I should reciprocate?

Making love with Hubby is a spiritually harmonious experience, something I've searched for all of my life. We share something that all couples instinctively want but don't know how to achieve.

Hubby and I have a spiritual union, based on the joy of love and gratification, both physically and spiritually. We have mastered redirecting strong sexual energies upward within ourselves. It is the true role of two opposites coming together in union. This redirecting of the powerful creative forces stimulates, strengthens, and renews our bodies.

Eyes now closed, I recall his slow, sensual stroking of last night. I arch my back in pleasure, as I run my hand across my body.

I can see and feel Hubby's caress, as he took the time to waken my She Dragon and charm Her. His gentle, yet firm hands moved over me, head to toe, knowing exactly where to touch. His ability to "feel" and hear my needs in my silence made him the perfect partner. He never dove in but waited and nurtured the fire.

Hubby knew I had to feel completely safe and protected by him before I would surrender myself. He was the carrier and I, the receptacle. He managed, protected, and guided us until we were no longer separate, rising above physical reality as our energies danced and wound ever upward until melding.

By now, I'm lost to the memories of last night, but part of me wonders how this happened so easily? I glance over at Hubby. To my surprise, he's lying on his side, facing me, head propped up with his hand, languidly watching me with a "cat's got the mouse" grin. His stillness speaks of just how concentrated he is, as his mind merges with mine and sends thoughts to warm me.

His hypnotic power often finds its way into my conscious awareness. He can do this so easily, and it irks me to no end. His keen mind and his knowledge and mastery of energy are so natural, he can capture my attention with a simple look or touch. My ability to pick up mental thoughts and his to send them initially surprised us. We realized we had something special and were meant to come together as one.

Now my confusion disappears, for the bugger has participated in this from the get-go. He smiles his crooked smile, as his sleekness slips over me. He prods the She snake to rise from her den at the base of my spine. He pulses his energy up in union with his rhythmic strokes, as he wraps his male energy around Her, embracing my She dragon in a caress. Unified, he begins to raise us up and transform the raw sexual desire into the heights of pure love. We rise and together we explode into the cup that receives our blessing.

We both sigh inwardly and exhale outwardly, as the fire energizes every cell throughout all of our fields. It has never been just about physical release but about coming together in a union of love energy. This is the true nature of desire, with its inherent goal of nourishing us with pure spiritual life force.

Hubby's breath becomes still, as he slowly moves to lie by my side, holding me to him. That moment when we become two from one united energy often shocks our systems, so we learned to be gentle and take our time before separating. Hubby runs his hands down my body, as the last waves of energy flow through us. Fully awake now, I encourage him to lie back and let his body rest. He needs to be strong and fit for his long days at work this time of the year. In the time it takes me to get dressed, he is softly snoring and back in his own dream world.

As I make my way to the washroom, I can feel the energies Hubby awakened, feeding all of my cells. It reminds me why I wanted to get up and get to it so early this morning. I listen for Teacher and wonder whether she had anything to do with this morning recreational pick-me-upper. I hear a soft chuckle from afar. Grinning, I shake my head at Teacher's nosiness. The energies I channelled in those last "sit downs" had affected me a lot more than I realized.

I lean against the washroom counter and gaze at my reflection. Weeks have gone by since the morning I wrote about the dormant memories of my past. Since then, I've been clearing toxins on a physical, emotional, and spiritual level. It never dawned on me that I had been initiated by Teacher that day. As with all initiations, the surges of energy She ran through me jump-started a deep process of letting go, triggering "a clearing" in the way of a healing crisis. A whole slew of deep-buried issues surfaced with the higher force of my Muse.

I hadn't seen this coming. Hubby had been worried, even though he's well aware of the clearing processes my writing often engenders.

I enter the shower stall and turn on the water. Its warm, sensual softness soothes my overly sensitive skin. I'm quite tanned from spending many hours outdoors. The noise of the spray lulls me into reverie, and I recall first meeting Hubby so many years ago.

First Encounters with Hubby

Hubby literally bumped into me in the aisle of a department store one fall day, when the kids and I were buying supplies. The electric jolt that ran through me as our bodies touched immediately caught my attention, for my senses had gone dead numb in the years since Daniel's death. I hadn't had a reaction like this to a man for a long time. That alone got my curiosity, so, as he apologized for being so clumsy, I surreptitiously looked him over from head to toe, liking what I saw.

He'd knocked my packages to the ground, and as he leaned forward to gather them back up, I had a chance to catch my breath. I noticed his strength and hardness, well displayed in snug jeans that were not too tight but not loose, either. His broad shoulders spoke of an outdoorsman, unlike the false builds often created in gyms. Again, a flash of Daniel appeared in my mind's eye, and I thought, *Not only does he look like Daniel, but this guy even smells the way Daniel did, with a clean, musky, woodsy scent.*

I found his resemblance to Daniel quite odd but simply put it off to imagining. I caught myself fantasizing about him, as I noted the hard lines in his snug clothes. He glanced up just then with that wolfish grin I now know so intimately, to catch me staring. I could have sworn he could read my mind. Little did I know that, in fact, he had done just that. I held his stare, meeting him head on and not the least bit intimidated by his raw male sensuality. My eyes sparkled, and my own feline grin responded to his wolf. He reacted strangely, pulling back in surprise, and in turn I read his mind. Never had he met a woman who could handle his raw maleness without being intimidated or resorting to a childlike state of insecurity.

At that moment, the kids came rushing up to us, both talking at once, after I'd sent them on a scouting mission for a list of items. We often split up, all of us out to get the items we most preferred. They were so handsome and smart. The loss of their father had taken its toll, but their youthful resilience was apparent. Within weeks following Daniel's death, they settled into a routine that helped me also adjust to the loss of the first love of my life.

Now they both stopped talking in unison, because they, too, noticed this man's deep resemblance to their father. He had obviously bumped into their mother and was now recovering her parcels. They looked at me, perplexed, picking up the tension in the air. I shrugged, not knowing what to tell them. He handed me my packages, and I said thank you. Then I scurried off with the kids before they could ask too many embarrassing questions.

Our second encounter would be the beginning of a deep, lasting relationship.

I'd stopped at a friend's for tea to tell her about the peculiar happenings of that day. She always had the ability to anchor my wayward notions. As I pulled into her driveway, I saw a strange blue car parked there.

I knocked on her door, and it suddenly opened. Before me stood that god-awfully handsome man the kids and I had bumped into recently. A shiver ran down my back, and a surge of energy moved up my spine. He seemed as shocked to see me as I was him. I felt stunned at this unexpected encounter and turned beet red in embarrassment. He regained his composure much faster than I did. Natasha came up behind him.

"Hi, Angelina, I see you have met my cousin Hubby. Come in and get acquainted. He is just back from his travels. He often works abroad and has only just stopped by for some of his things."

I looked around, noting bags and boxes of personal items.

"Well, well, who have we here?" he said quietly. "Haven't we 'bumped' into each other before?"

His smile and raw sexuality made my knees tremble, and the energy surging up my spine hit the roof.

Who was this man who made me go weak inside and seemed to know my deepest secrets? His hawk-eyed gaze didn't miss much, as he cocked an eyebrow at my dishevelled hair and coat. I suddenly felt uncomfortable, as the heat inside me rose again. I hadn't glanced in a mirror since leaving home and realized I must look a mess after a full day of running errands.

Why was I so affected by this man? I became upset with myself—and with him, too, for being so damn handsome in a rough, tough guy way. Rugged men were so rare today, and he was obviously a real man, no mistaking that.

His head turned to one side, as he looked me up and down once again. I flushed a deeper shade of red, and this time I felt as if I would lose the little control I had.

How did this Hubby guy suddenly make me feel so exposed and vulnerable?

As I gazed deeply into his eyes, why did I see the reflection of Daniel looking at me?

I felt dizzy and lightheaded, and the energy once again surged up my spine but with orgasmic force. I shuddered and groaned in response to the powerful rise of this creative muse. I lost consciousness, just as the thought "Why is this happening again?" entered my mind. I sank lower, and my last sensation was of his warm, comforting arms catching me. Then I completely blacked out.

The shower water turns cool, bringing me back to the present. I dry myself, slip on some comfortable clothes, and tiptoe down the stairs, not wanting to wake anyone at this early hour.

I've avoided writing all summer, only dabbling in it here and there.

The summer has been busy, but that's no excuse. I'm worried about my evasion tactics. With fall fast approaching, I will once again be teaching at the institute, with little time for writing. I turn to the stove and wait for the coffee to perk.

My avoidance was understandable during those few weeks when I didn't feel well, but something else nags at me. Along with my clearing, I'd become distracted and anxious about neglecting all of the tasks necessary to maintain our lifestyle. When we shut down the institute for the summer holidays, I get a break from running two homes, because the institute is also our home away from home. Yet summer demands that I concentrate on our private home.

Most people don't understand the time and constant attention required for our lifestyle choice. With the lush forests surrounding us, we must make a continued effort to maintain our boundaries, as Mother Nature attempts to regain her territory. Every spring and into the summer, we spend days clearing foliage and creeping blackberries, vines, and sprouting trees from the claimed land, before we even think about the vast gardens. The power of this land is evident in its stubborn urge to return to naturalness. We understand this phenomenon and give thanks for the little space She permits us to domesticate, in our need to be self-sufficient. Hubby and I also took advantage of this break in my writing routine to finish my studio on the upper floor of his workshop.

I turn off the stove and let the grains settle before pouring that first awesome cup. With coffee in hand, I grab my recorder, because I never know when a memory will surface that I need to write about. I'm often not at my computer when Teacher begins to speak or when a memory surfaces, triggered by a smell or an emotion.

I step out onto the deck, facing east, into the morning coolness. Fall will soon make itself known. Of late, the leaves have gotten ready to change and the plants are going to seed. In awe, I turn my gaze to the heavens, to the multitude of stars twinkling in the still dark sky. I'm utterly amazed at its beauty. It's rare to see an early morning sky display so many stars. I spot the Little Dipper, and for the thousandth time, I give thanks to the Creator for all of this bounty.

I sit quietly, enjoying the peacefulness. I hear more memories of past teachings from Teacher. I switch on the recorder as I listen to Her inner voice, then speak out loud, knowing that Hubby, still asleep, won't hear my soft words.

> *The passing of time is continuous in the physical world, and light is your timekeeper. Each cycle of night and day marks the aging and cycles of each soul on Earth. Heartbeats are numbered, as is each breath and each life.*

Teacher's words sink in on another level of awareness, bringing forth hidden truths. I realize the soul never ages and never dies, for it is immortal. The haunting cry of ravens as they gather, telling of tales yet to come, brings my attention back. The raven is a seer's ally, and it bodes well that I pay attention when it speaks.

Within minutes, the sun peeks over the horizon in a burnished copper glow, as the equinox of the morning—that moment of stillness between night and day, in which neither exists—gives way to sunlight hours. In that moment of stillness, I feel my connectedness to the Divine. The fog rises and dances away from the heat of the coming day.

I spot my flower gardens and make a mental note to harvest more Echinacea roots this coming week for my winter tinctures. My years of wild-crafting and making earth medicines have resulted in a glorious setting of medicinal gardens that require regular nurturing. I filled the drying shed with an abundance of herbs, but it can surely accommodate a few more.

I walk towards my new studio above Hubby's gabled garage. My hooded caftan and woolly socks keep me warm in the damp, chilly air. With each measured step I take, the light crunch of sandy stone reminds me how quiet the mornings are here. In the dim early dawn light, this area still remains in shadows.

The last nocturnal creatures scurry back to their burrows, to hunker down for the daylight hours. An owl hoots, and its mate responds in kind. The bats are still flying about, feeding off the last flying insects of the season.

I step inside the garage/workshop, inhaling the smell of a new building. I switch on the solar-powered lights and eagerly take the stairs two at a time. My new haven away from reality gives the family a respite from my need to be active before the sun rises.

My habit of writing first thing in the morning suits everyone just fine, including me! The best time of day, in my opinion, is around 4 to 5 am, just hours before sunrise. Those hours, before night becomes day, are so silent and calm. Most people are still lost to their dreams, so the airwaves are slow and silent, unlike any other time of the day.

As I open the door to my sanctuary, I think, *This is truly like stepping into a mystical world, a sacred space of my creation.*

The unique scent triggers memories of times past. I have filled this sacred space with all of my mementos, things that have brought so much richness to my lives. Yes, my *lives*, for here I can be free and display things from my past lives without needing to explain to the unaware, always so full of questions. I've scattered little bits and pieces of my history on shelves and tabletops: driftwood, feathers, and various symbolic statues. The décor reflects my spiritual ancestry, hinting at the source of my past and present knowledge. Discerning eyes can easily map out my history when viewing my collection, but few will ever be invited to enter this room.

I light one of the many candles lying about. The warmth of the coming day will soon dispel the coolness. The shadowed walls reflect the candle's luminosity, creating the perfect blend of ghostly light. My mahogany desk nestled in the windowed gable overlooks the northeast face of the mountain. It contrasts beautifully with the creamy walls.

This gable easily provides the light I need to write. I sit down and switch on my laptop, leaning back into one of my few concessions to modern furniture: a cozy leather chair.

As the computer boots up, I gaze out the window. The sun has begun to cast its light on the mountain ridge. I sigh, amazed that Hubby and I are stewards of this land—this place the locals call "God's country." Little do they know there is more truth to this than anyone could imagine. This thought reminds me why we settled here and the reality of what I sometimes call "the curse" of seeing the future. As Dad has often said, "The visions come out of the blue, with little explanation, and just as suddenly they are gone, leaving you bewildered and in a state of confusion for weeks."

Prophecy is an odd thing. At times, prophetic visions are clear and unquestionable, yet other times the visions are out of chronological sequence, difficult to grasp and decipher. A true prophetic encounter requires many lifetimes for a soul to develop awareness, before being able to master and define a vision. When my ability exploded, few true seers—and hence few teachers—remained in the world whom I could ask for help. Now Teacher answers almost every question—*when it suits Her*, I think with a wry grin.

Not long after I received the prophecy of the Wise Ones and the time of purification, I began to have intuitions, dreams, and visions defining the prophecy's true meaning and my role in it. The prophetic words "Go to the mountains" still echo in my mind when I stand on top of their peak, gazing for miles through a natural valley leading down to the flatlands. In "this place," new ideas and a new awareness will be birthed. Only during these last years have I truly begun to unravel these mysteries.

Chapter 13

The Quest

"Start by doing what's necessary; then do what's possible; and suddenly you are doing the impossible."

— Francis of Assisi

Present Day

As I glance around, the goose wing shield catches my eye. It reminds me of a time when I lived down below.

I know soon things will change and never be the same. In the candlelit darkness of my mountain studio, I bring to mind past days of stupor and forgetfulness, when only a fragment of my true self existed. A shimmering portal opens before me, against the backdrop of dawn's inky darkness. And so, I travel back to the past once again . . .

The holograph of my memories appears. I enter a once-familiar landscape. A time-traveler of my own life, I need to see something I've subconsciously buried. I tweak the threads of time, guided by an inner urge.

Everything is dark. I breathe in deeply, turning my concentration inward and naturally guiding my energy upward. The pulsing of purple begins as my body goes numb. The droning energy foretells my complete disconnection from this reality. Everything transforms into the pitch of night, with a slowly approaching dot of white light on the horizon. Suddenly thrust into the centre of this great eye, I travel through a space odyssey at the speed of light. Billions of white light filaments pass, as I'm propelled along the great web of Grandmother Spider.

Everything begins to slow, as a scene from my past comes alive. I see Daniel, at a time shortly before he died, when we lived in the old Victorian house in the flatlands. I sink into this reality but remind myself to stay grounded in the present and not attempt to make any changes. To change the past could have far-reaching repercussions.

Daniel and I raised our children here. During the fall, migrating geese often rested in the vast fields surrounding our property. I frequently heard their calls while I worked in my studio nestled at the back of our property, surrounded by cornfields. Hearing the cries of the geese, I felt kinship and oneness with these amazing creatures. Hundreds of them came in droves each year to rest here. The distant snow geese resembled white specks sprinkling the bare fields, like the first snowflakes of winter.

On that particular day, the voice of Spirit, but whom I know today to be Teacher, whispered that soon I would have to take a walk, for the goose spirit had gifted me with some feathers. I shrugged off this intuition, not yet comfortable with these inner promptings. I attributed them to a flight of fancy, but they kept nagging at me and urging me to pay attention.

Finally, a few weeks later, I decided it was time to walk the fields and look for treasures.

The next morning, I waited for the sun to warm the air before going feather hunting. The children had gone to school, and Daniel had also left for work. I felt much better today and more hopeful, after years of not being well.

All of a sudden, I heard a series of gunshots coming from the back fields. I rushed to the window to witness several hunters, with decoys, shooting at the geese as they nestled unawares. With those first shots, hundreds rose into the air, rudely awakened and frightened into disarrayed flight, as they searched for their mates. I felt horrified at what I witnessed. The fear of those beautiful creatures seeped into my body, right down to the bone. In shock, I didn't know what to do.

Our previous neighbours had never allowed hunters on this land. I didn't know our new neighbours yet. Appalled, I soon discovered that these hunters had permission to hunt. In time, I spoke to our neighbours, raising my concerns. They agreed put a stop to all hunting, but only after the fact.

A half hour passed, as volley after volley of shots rang out. The scattered birds dropped from the sky, as the hunting dogs ran out to fetch the kill. I turned away, crying and praying it would soon be over.

"Please, Spirit, make these men stop, for they know not what they are creating."

This kind of unacceptable kill disrespected man and creature alike. When had we become so disconnected from the hand that fed us? When had we lost the knowledge of a true huntsman and the protocols of life exchange?

As I watched the hunters return with their kill of the day, I decided to have some words with them about the sacredness of these birds. If I could help them do the right thing and prompt them to at least give thanks for Mother Earth's bounty, the spirits of these geese would rest in peace. I heard the wailing of the birds' mates and sensed the disruption of each bird's soul, after being shot emotionlessly, in ignorance of its spirit sacrifice.

I walked along the path that led to the returning hunters. As I calmly approached them, they must have wondered what I was all about. I stopped a few steps ahead of them, barring their way. We stood for a few moments, simply staring at one another, before my gaze went to their kill.

They shuffled around uncomfortably, sensing they had inadvertently done something wrong. I was obviously of Native blood, and almost everyone has an idea about our custom of offering respect and thanks with each taking of life. I sensed that my thoughts had unconsciously penetrated their minds.

They stood motionless, pinned to their spots by an energy so great, no one could ignore the moment. I held them steadfastly, as I spoke a language of silence they clearly heard. I let my thoughts sink deeply into their souls until satisfied that each of these men knew he had done something wrong and unforgivable. I had no clue how intimidating I could be back then, for I was unaware of my powers.

Only recently had I realized I had the ability to transfer thoughts and emotions to others, so they could be made aware of something they chose not to see or feel. Yet I had never thought this unusual, because Daniel could do the same. His stare could freeze any man in his tracks, so I never questioned what some described as my piercing gaze. By now, these men were squirming in discomfort, and it was time for me to speak my truth.

In a strong but calm voice, I explained, "My ancestors' customs are to always offer thanks and prayer to animals, Mother Earth, the Grandfathers and the Grandmothers that give us life, before and after a kill. It is especially important in the case of these geese, because they mate for life, and those left behind will remain alone and barren and mate-less until death claims them."

By then, we could hear the remaining geese lamenting and crying. It sank in deeply with these men, listening to my words and those of the geese spirit. They knew I spoke the truth. They avoided my gaze, not knowing what to do next. I took pity on them.

"I strongly suggest you apologize to the spirits of these birds for not first offering thanks for their sacrifice and asking forgiveness of the ancestors and of those left behind. It is not only about the kill; it is also about not wasting and about making use of all that each creature has sacrificed for you to be able to live. In the Native tradition, all parts of an animal or a bird are used and blessed. Only what is strictly necessary is ever taken."

I stared at the numerous birds they had killed. This was sport and not a matter of survival, which is the only acceptable reason for a hunt.

In the end, this went well, and they expressed their interest in Native beliefs about animals in general. They asked if they could bring the wings to me, so that I might put them to good use and honour them properly. I agreed, though I doubted anything would come of it.

The following day, my girlfriend Victoria and I walked the fields. Spirit gifted us with many feathers, some even from the snow geese. In appreciation, we gave offerings of tobacco and gave thanks, promising to honour and hold dear these precious gifts from Spirit. We then prayed at the spots where we saw blood from the dead birds, so that their souls could rest in peace.

A few more days passed and still no sign of the wings from the hunters. Victoria commented that they probably hadn't given it another thought, and it was now in Spirit's hands. I agreed.

One evening, after dark, Daniel went outside and came back to tell me about two bags in the garage, full of goose wings. Stunned, I ran out. It had been quite some time since the hunting incident. Amazed at what I saw, I was guided to bring the wings in to dry. On opening the bags, I noticed some were fresh kills, so it seemed the hunters had brought all of the wings from their week of hunting. I silently thanked the hunters for listening and respecting my beliefs, as well as honouring the birds. I looked heavenward, giving thanks. There might still be hope for mankind.

I spent the next few hours opening the wings and stretching them to dry. My blood sang with old songs of my ancestors, and I could sense the Grandmothers and the Grandfathers surrounding me as I hummed the beat of old, long-forgotten chants. Once done, I stood awed at the energy and sight of all of those wings.

A few weeks passed. Victoria told me I had been given a great honour to be the caretaker of the wings and that I needed to give thanks for it. I agreed, though I didn't know why I had drawn those wings to me. There were eight sets of snow geese wings. Everything had meaning, and I would soon unravel this mystery. The peculiar thing about snow geese was that from afar, they seemed to be pure white, but in fact the wings were striped with dark tips—such a beautiful expression of the yin-and-yang interplay of life, represented in the spirit of this bird.

After a month or so, as the winter solstice approached, the inner voice encouraged me to take down all of the dried wings and bring them into my sacred space. Then Spirit guided me to gift the wings to warriors of light from various places. These wings would aid in protecting and anchoring the light of consciousness. The first wing would go to a dear healer friend of mine, Margie, who lived in the States.

I started to work on Margie's wing on the eve of the solstice. As Spirit guided me, wondrous things took place. Items I would need appeared out of nowhere, as the voice of Spirit told me how to adorn the wing. The high energy soothed my still scarred soul. This was a blessing. The inner guidance got stronger and stronger as the months of my healing journey went by. I felt a powerful urge to connect more to my Native roots. Finally, after hours of being immersed in my creative Muse, I held up the adorned wing, very happy with the outcome.

As I gazed upon its beauty, I heard that inner voice whisper to me,

> *You have been gifted with eight sets of adult wings. You are to gift eight warriors with these.*

Next, I needed to create a shield to anchor the healing core energy.

> *You will paint a shield on hide, and it will be created from all natural things.*

Spirit guided me to separate the wings and create their pairs. One set would go to a medicine man I knew and the South American tribe he communicated with. This place would be important for our future, because there dwelled the heart of the world.

The voice said,

> *He is to give them the right wing, and he is to hold the left one of the set.*

This was the second set of wings I'd been told what to do with. I had faith that when it was time, Spirit would instruct me.

Next, I was told to write down the following in a letter to be presented along with the wings. The words were as new to me as they would be to those chosen, so, as I wrote, I spoke the words aloud.

> *Brothers & Sisters,*
>
> *I am Moonwalker of the Spirit.*

I have been blessed with a sacred quest from the spirit world.

It has been told to me by the whispers of the wind that you are to receive this sacred gift, symbolic of the great spirit of the Canadian goose.

The Canadian goose is a symbol of unity for those travelling the path of Light, because it protects and guides. It will help you ground and bring protection and guidance to those in need. You have been chosen in honour of your dedication, courage, and wisdom.

This wing you are being gifted with, which carries the Great Spirit of the Canadian goose, will serve to link you and others. These wings will start a healing resonance within the great universal grid of Grandmother Spider.

This gift will help create and strengthen a telepathic and energetic connection between the holders of all sacred symbols for the future.

These wings reflect a call to the Spiritual Quest! So be it!

This is heard in their call if we listen carefully, for a time in the future, in its season of spring, the Grandmothers and the Grandfathers, our ancestors, will bring great surprises to all of us, and the Spirit of the Goose will call out to us of this time on their return. We are to pay attention and listen for them.

It is an honour to gift you as a warrior to receive this offering from Spirit.

Osh Ta Lo

As the seriousness of the quest came crashing down on me, the task I'd been asked to shoulder seemed overwhelming. I realized what an honour I had been granted but, at the same time, how significant this sacred quest was. The responsibility started to weigh heavily on me.

The song of low-flying geese snaps me back to this reality. I laugh at the irony of life and the amazing synchronistic events that occur daily now. Here I was lost in the beginnings of this quest and brought back to the present by the very same creature that had bequeathed it to me.

I remember the vision of the Wise Ones leading people north through chaos to a safe place, and I know this goose quest is intricately linked to that prophetic vision.

This was the beginning of a great quest and a journey that I and many others would never forget.

Chapter 14

Cycles of Life—Endings, Birth, Beginnings

"This Holy Instant would I give to You. Be You in charge, for I would follow You, certain that Your direction gives me peace."

—A Course in Miracles

Present Day

I focus on the goose shield, as the aromas of herbs and oils bombard my senses. Those prophetic words of the past—*"Go to the mountains!"*—echo through my mind once again, as the memory of the quest fades away. Only minutes have gone by, yet my memory about the geese seemed to last hours.

    I slowly walk around the room, looking at what I've accumulated. I never really understood the connection between "our mountain, our dream" and "go to the mountains." Everything manifested over the years in bits and pieces until the puzzle became legible. It's often like this. Little morsels of information come through in synchronistic dreams, visions, and intuitions, some taking years to unravel. I've had to develop the patience of a saint and the wisdom of knowing that all is revealed in its time and its place. Sometimes I become frustrated by constantly being bombarded with clues and guidance I don't understand. Yet this never diminishes my awe at the mystery of life on Earth.

I so love the exotic smells in this oasis where I come for inspiration. I burn incense and medicines to help with concentration and relaxation. This morning's aroma brings to mind my time in India. I recall the amazing resilience of a people living in poverty but with such a heartfelt love of life. The caste system is still very much in place, though, and the Indian culture often cloisters women and requires them to follow ancient customs, despite society heading into a new era. The old dominant yang energy is at war with the yin, feminine energy—there, as everywhere in the world. As the time of ascension approaches, many things must shift and transform to adapt to the energy of a new era.

I was drawn to India to seek answers and learn more about my unusual intuitive perceptions and experiences. India, suffused with spiritual energy and the legacy of immortalized sages, held a story and a past for me. I needed to unravel this story. Modern society simply could not help me. I had exhausted any aboriginal teachings, seeing that much had been lost with Christianity's influence on this beautiful ancient culture.

With the sun now up, Hubby silently goes about his errands, knowing I'm not to be disturbed. As he walks by, I lean out the window and whistle a sexy tune, noticing how beautiful this man is. He turns to me with a wolfish grin and asks if I want something before he goes? I smile at his teasing. He didn't get to sleep until midway through the night, and now he is openly hinting at . . . ?

I shake my head at him, smiling. "You'll have to climb up, because the door is locked."

Heading my way, he answers, "Since when has a door stopped me?"

I squeal and tell him he'd better stop right away or else.

"Or else what?" he purrs.

I take a second to think of what I can threaten him with, something that he holds dear.

"I won't make you supper tonight!" There, that was good one.

His answer is to turn up the energy with a look. I yell at him to stop, and in pity he backs off, laughing under his breath. To this day I can't figure out how he can get through my defenses with just a look, and he's not giving away his secret yet. Since I taught him energy has no walls or boundaries, he's found a clever way to explore this.

Hubby realizes by my tone that I'm in the middle of something, so it doesn't take much convincing for him to go on his way. My family learned long ago to respect my need for time alone, and they don't interrupt me during my seclusion. They often have no idea what I do when I sequester myself away from the world, but they don't ask many questions.

I think about Hubby, and I'm reminded how nice it is to be loved and appreciated by your partner. So many relationships have gone awry during these last few decades. Did people give up too easily? Was it much harder to work through problems than walk away? We can't avoid our life experiences, because karma decrees we are simply doomed to repeat them until we master them. Then again, the laws of relationship have changed, so it isn't easy to be part of a couple either.

I light a few more candles to dispel the shadows before finally settling down to write. I wonder where to begin. I am out of the zone and looking for guidance.

Teacher gently comments on my procrastinating thoughts:

> *Well, finally. Good morning, stranger. It seems you've decided to heed my call to get back to it! And it's about time. I have made every excuse to the Powers That Be why we have not yet completed this project, and I have run out of reasons. You've become an expert at blocking me out. You've spent the last hour jumping between all kinds of memories, while conveniently ignoring my presence.*

How will I pick up where I left off? I haven't been able to finish this thing. Again I wonder why, because I do enjoy writing with Teacher.

"Is it laziness on my part?" I ask myself out loud.

I decide that no, this isn't it, for I'm not generally a lazy person.

I hang the DO NOT DISTURB sign on the outside of the door. There's nothing worse than being jerked back into one's body when traveling in spirit. To refresh my memory, Teacher guides me to pull out some old manuscripts, dated years ago. I become lost to my younger, less mature voice.

A light breeze rustles the leaves in the trees. Time disappears, as I bring my energy up for this Akashic jaunt. Teacher instructs me once again to open a portal to time. My mind's eye opens, and so I travel. The images fast-forward, as I look for scenes that haven't yet revealed themselves to me. I skip most of my teen years, which I surmise I'll deal with on another occasion. I know I encountered some crucial teachings in those years. Next, the scenes depict my first years with Daniel and begin to slow. Why did I have to go back to this time? What did Teacher wish me to see?

Much like a movie, the scenes of my past begin to play. I become a younger Angelina, recounting this time in my life.

Life with Daniel: The Early Years

I am in my late twenties, as my two wonderful children approach their teens. Daniel and I have been together for just over a decade, raising our children in a beautiful century-old home down in the flatlands, an area full of history. It's a magical place of peace and serenity—a perfect setting in a remote countryside surrounded by farmland. We have easy access to the major cities and enjoy the conveniences of a metropolis, having the best of both worlds. We live a life that blends our country's French and English heritage.

Then the holograph fast-tracks back to when Daniel and I met in high school: I, an innocent, impressionable teenager, and he a mature, emotionally hurt young adult. Despite our age, we were mature beyond our years. Life deemed that we grow up before our time. That destined meeting, the beginning of a passionate relationship, had us on a rollercoaster ride, fighting fate in our ignorance of what was meant to be. I then find myself once again melding with this younger Angelina, as I wrote:

Daniel comes from a traditional home with parents who love deeply and passionately and have an active social life. The importance of family always comes first. His parents married young, with hopes and dreams of material freedom. The children were raised to be independent, and Daniel grew up before his time, already an adult in his teen years.

Daniel's youthful mom and his handsome father lived life to the fullest, and I often wondered how they could be so full of vitality. Their resilience spoke of health and a strength of character not easily matched. They were good, heartfelt people and openly affectionate.

My siblings and I had much of the same, except Mom became extremely ill when we were young. She kept busy working and creating a normal life for us, while dealing with her illness. We never doubted our parents' love, though, for they went out of their way to try to make up for the disruption Mom's illness created in our lives. Even so, we grew up very fast. At a young age, I became a surrogate mother for my brother and sister. Through weeks of Mom's treatments, I often kept house, made meals, and took care of my siblings when life became too much for my parents. This forced us to adapt to living with sickness, responsibility, and uncertainty on a daily basis.

Death stalked us, day by day, and we became numb to its reality. We, as a family, learned to block out the emotional upheaval and, for survival's sake, became adept at creating the illusion of normalcy. Yet blocking these emotions also kept us from openly expressing our love for one another. I never noticed this until I saw how affectionate Daniel's family was.

Mom struggled with her sickness for many years. Now, the memories begin to surface of a time I rarely visit. The scenes fast-forward to that fateful summer when everything changed.

While in my late teens, I discovered I was with child. Mom wanted me legitimately married, because in those times, society still frowned on a woman having a baby out of wedlock.

The day I announced Daniel's and my intention to tie the knot, she surprised me by her words: "We're going to have to find a hall and call the caterers. Three months, Angelina, is not a long time to prepare a wedding. I will call Father John immediately and see which dates the church is available."

She stunned me with her matter-of-fact acceptance of everything.

However, Dad reacted to my announcement by bellowing, "How is that young snip Daniel going to care for a wife and a child?"

I realized why Daniel hadn't wanted to be there when I announced the news, for he had intuited Dad's reaction, contrary to my fear of Mom's.

We embarked on a whirlwind of activities. Being from a fairly wealthy background, Mom wanted only the best for me, her firstborn. I spent my days at a summer job and early evenings at appointments to choose flowers and invitations and organize the meals and the seating, until finally the time arrived to meet the priest for the church ceremony.

Scenes of this time flash before my eyes. Only weeks before the wedding, Daniel, Mom, and I had sat in the church, discussing the wedding ceremony with Father John.

"Father John," I asked, "we were wondering about decorating the church for the wedding ceremony. Is this permitted, and, if so, what is the procedure?"

Father John, a cordial fellow, red-nosed from his love of the occasional drink, paused and then softly spoke. "Well, Angelina, I'm not too sure how to say this."

He hemmed and hawed, obviously uncomfortable, and we waited patiently for him to continue.

"I hate to speak of this on such a joyous occasion, but in fact we do not allow any decorations on the altar itself. If you are lucky, however, there will be a funeral prior to your wedding, God bless some poor soul's life, and those flowers will decorate your wedding. You are permitted to decorate the entrance, the aisles, and the pews, though, as you wish. Confetti is no longer permitted, since it is so messy and its festiveness does not go with funerals, which are far from joyous occasions. Weddings and funerals are often held back to back at this time of year."

We didn't think any more of his statement, but later we realized how odd some of his comments had been.

The stress of life and Mom's continued struggle with her sickness finally reached a crisis point just before the wedding. She had valiantly pushed her pain away, often limping to and from the many excursions necessary to plan this grand occasion. But lo and behold, it all became too much, and she could put it off no longer. She had some tests done, which confirmed her worse fears: the cancer was back and needed immediate attention.

The day she had to be admitted to the hospital, she took me aside and said, "Angelina, I want you to know my prognosis is not good. I'll be undergoing a series of new treatments never tested on a human. I've been accepted in the first human trials, because it's my only hope to beat this. If I do it now, I may be out for the wedding, but I cannot take the pain anymore."

That previous weekend had taken a toll on her, with the wedding shower and all. I could see the unbearable pain she lived with.

I told her I understood and that all would be well. So, Mom admitted herself into the hospital. Time passed, and we got through the last crazy weeks of planning. When Mom began her treatments, Daniel and I were occupied with work and the remaining wedding preparations.

The holograph fast-forwards through many days, leading up to that last week before the wedding. We had been so busy running around, I hadn't taken time to drive the few hours to the hospital to visit Mom. I woke up that Friday morning, exactly one week before the wedding day, after a night filled with dreams. Mom had clearly visited me in spirit, insistent that I come to her. Though I wasn't conscious then of the hidden depths of my abilities, I just knew without doubt or questioning that she had spoken to me. I immediately acted on it, guided by my gut feeling.

That evening I told Daniel, "I have to go see my mother tomorrow, and nothing will stop me."

He and I arrived at the hospital in mid afternoon of that Saturday. Mom seemed energized and so very glad to see us. Mamère—my grandmother—had been with her, having decided to see her daughter through this latest ordeal.

Mom smiled joyfully. "I'm so happy you came."

Her smile allayed our worries. After a few hours, with Mom laughing and so happy to see us, Daniel and I got ready to leave. We felt certain she would be fine and would make it to the wedding. She had finished her treatments, so nothing would keep her here.

As we began to say our goodbyes, I walked up to Mom, wanting to tell her I loved her. As I stood there, the words I so desperately wanted to say stuck in my throat, and no matter how hard I tried, they would not budge. I stood paralyzed, not knowing why I feared saying those words out loud. A few moments went by, as Mom looked at me with that beautiful smile of hers, and still the words would not come out—a legacy of our upbringing, I later realized. Displays of emotion were simply not our family's way.

Why can't I tell her I love her? I asked myself, struggling to express this deep emotion aloud. Daniel and I left, and I felt guilty, telling myself I would do better next time.

The next morning—Sunday—dawned sunny and beautiful. Daniel and I decided to spend the day on the river, waterskiing with friends. After the last hectic and stressful weeks, we needed to relax and have fun. We felt optimistic about Mom. Her parting words to me had been profound but light: "I'll see you at the wedding."

We spent a relaxing day on the river, without a care in the world. Only a few small things remained to get done for the wedding. Our dresses were ready, and Mom's hung in her bedroom, waiting for her to come home. We felt happy and content that everything would be perfect.

We arrived at my house in the late afternoon. The empty house felt eerie, because normally my siblings and Dad would be preparing supper. As Daniel and I stood at the counter, debating whether to cook a meal or eat out, the phone rang.

I realized it was Daniel's mom when she said, "Angelina, your mom."

"Hi, Rose." I turned to Daniel, covering the mouthpiece, and whispered, " It's your mom!"

Thinking she wanted to know how it had gone the day before, I excitedly said, "Yes, we saw Mom yesterday. It looks like she'll be well enough to be out for the wedding."

As I stopped for breath, Rose's anxious voice interrupted me in mid sentence with, "No, Angelina, your mom."

Her tone and the energy of her words instantly struck me in the gut. On a deep level, I knew tragedy had hit. I folded in two. From her few words, I knew what had happened, and the shock had me speechless and down on my knees. I couldn't speak or breathe. Daniel, knowing something had gone terribly wrong, grabbed me and held me, as I screamed and wailed. He wrapped me in his arms and held me tight, as he picked up the receiver. As suddenly as my feelings had surged, they dissipated, and I became an empty emotionless shell.

"Mom, Angelina is in shock. What did you say to her? What happened?"

As he listened, his grave facial expression registered emotional pain. I slowly came back to myself. Time seemed to have stopped. My entire body felt frozen from the inside out. Something had shut off in me, and I waited quietly for the news, as Daniel nodded and finally said good-bye.

I remember his look of disbelief as he told me Mom had fallen into a coma that morning, and we were expected at the hospital. I nodded, knowing deep down that the beginning of the end had unravelled. An instinct to survive immobilised me. A wall came up, and all disabling reactions disappeared, as I became emotionally detached. A prisoner of my racing thoughts, I drove the long hours to the hospital in silence, as Daniel slept in the passenger seat, having had a few too many drinks.

The family arrived around mid afternoon. We bumped into some visiting aunts and uncles who had shown up just after Mom went into the coma. I hugged my dad and my brother and sister, and we cried such tears as we would never shed again.

Years later, Mamère told me that as we'd entered the elevator to leave on the fateful last day that we'd seen her alive, Mom had turned to her with a whimsical smile and said, "God is with me. I have been granted my last wish that I see my children one final time before I go."

Dad had been to see her with my sister and brother a day earlier. Unbeknownst to any of us, that same week the doctors had told Mom it would be only a matter of days or weeks before she would pass on. They'd kept all of this from us. Her last wish requested Dad and Mamère not to spoil this time of celebration. Mamère told me that she'd held onto the hope that Mom would pull out of this one, as on previous times, but alas, destiny decreed it not be so.

My attention momentarily returns to the present moment. No matter how much I tweaked the threads or looked for the doors into that moment, this remains my last memory. To this day, I have no recollection of how we got home or the next few harrowing days as we waited to see what would happen. I know the traumatic events have not healed and hence will not reveal themselves until I am ready.

I return to my memory recall, reliving the dilemma of the wedding only five days away and whether we should follow through with our plans. It was the main topic of discussion that Sunday. We decided that if Mom passed by noon on Tuesday, it would leave us enough time to lay her to rest before the wedding Friday. We would take this as a sign that she wanted the wedding to go on. We made the decision to have her unplugged from all life support, after the doctors determined that a blood clot to her brain had caused the coma. Survival meant she would be a vegetable until the cancer claimed her. The chemo no longer helped; the cancer was resistant to treatment. We all agreed that this compassionate act must be done.

The holograph goes black, as the memories of the next few days still refuse to surface. My next flash of memory is at midday on Tuesday. I stood outside in the warm sun with one of my maids of honour, who offered her comforting presence. The phone rang at five past noon, and I instinctively knew things were about to change. Dad told me in a sombre tone that Mom had passed exactly at noon, and the family decided the wedding would go on.

Once again, my walls went up, as my heart chakra closed tight in protection, and I became numb to all emotions.

During the next few days, we attempted to deal with the loss of our loved one and jumped into last-minute preparations for the wedding. The funeral home burst at the seams with flowers and mourners. So many people respected and cared for Mom. Her death, so unexpected, shocked everyone. Her relapse had been kept secret. In fact, few ever knew of Mom's sickness, except close family and friends, for she didn't want to burden others with her health issues. This went against her kind heart and caring ways, which she was known for.

Father John opened up other sections of the church to accommodate the growing throng of family members and the beautiful floral contributions that arrived from all over.

As I gazed at her lying in the casket, looking so beautiful, I smiled in memory of the day a few months earlier when we had gone shopping for the exquisite soft rose dress she now wore. She had chosen this gown to be her mother-of-the-bride dress. Her years of sickness had made her unhappy with the physical changes in her body, and she so wanted to look beautiful on the day of my wedding. My mother, a gorgeous woman, had always worked at maintaining her figure. Her wish had been granted when we found her the perfect dress, which made her look so lovely. She seemed at peace, finally.

In a moment of insight, I realized how all of those years of torture, from the difficult side effects of therapy to the fear of dying and leaving a young family, had tormented her. Now her face no longer bore lines of worry.

I recall the day when we both went to try our dresses on. She wasn't walking much, due to the pain in her leg. This had happened only a few days before she would decide to get tested. We arrived at the dressmaker's, and with a smile of genuine happiness she said, "Angelina, I haven't had a dress look so good on me in years!"

Then I took my turn, trying on my dress. I felt nervous about my slight tummy bump, but the style of the wedding gown, combined with my height and slimness, hid the slow-growing bulge of my future daughter. Mom's eyes lit up that day when she saw me in my traditional wedding dress, being properly fitted. She had gotten to see me in my dress, after all. My aunt told me later that Mom had confided her happiness in seeing me that day and hoped to welcome her first grandchild.

The week before the wedding still has huge gaps of missing memory. I later learned this is how the heart and the soul protect us when our grief could destroy us. When we love someone so deeply, losing that person could shatter the strongest of us. This inbuilt survival mechanism shuts down our emotional body until we are ready to heal the grief. I didn't know then, as I do today, that grief is directly linked to energies binding us to others.

The Morning of the Wedding

On that bright, sunny morning, the house became a bustle of comings and goings. Many of our out-of-town relatives decided to stay for the wedding, because, of course, they had come up for the funeral. I woke up in a mood, with very little patience for all of the commotion. Looking back, I see that keeping busy didn't allow us time to dwell on our loss.

The photographer arrived, and we spent the afternoon taking wedding photos. Finally, the time arrived to go to the church. Dressed and standing alone in the salon, after everyone had scattered, I had a rare moment of peace. I stood transfixed, thinking about Mom. No sooner had this thought entered my mind than I felt a shiver of something run down my back, and coldness came over the room. I looked around, feeling a presence close to me. Though I couldn't see anything, I smelled a whiff of her favourite perfume. In that moment I clearly felt her presence. Her last words echoed in my mind, when she promised to see me at the wedding. It dawned on me that she wouldn't miss this for the world. With a sad smile, yet heartened by her presence, I sent her my love.

I snapped out of my reverie when my young brother came running into the house, yelling, "Dad is here! The limousine is pulling up. Are you ready? Hurry up. They're waiting for us. You don't want to be late!"

He rushed back out the door—a testament to the resilience of an eleven-year-old and the moral strength of our family. Dad entered with a sad smile, and we looked deeply into each other's eyes, exchanging thoughts as only we could.

We both took a deep breath, and with a smirk Dad said, "Let the show begin!"

He and I shared a really odd sense of humour—at times wry and sarcastic but lifesaving in times of stress.

I laughed, and off we went. I so appreciated Dad for dissolving the tenseness of the moment. We all piled into the limousines and drove toward the church. The car with Dad and me wound its way through the back streets, then approached a busy intersection. Silence reigned in our car. My siblings rode in the limousine behind us. I wondered how they were faring in all of this, being so young to have lost their mother. I worried for them. I knew that in time, the reality of her death would hit home. I would make a point to be there for them, if I could. As we passed a popular drive-through fast-food place, Dad's voice brought me back.

His words, "Want a fry or something? We should make that groom of yours sweat a bit!" had us laughing until tears of release fell.

This broke the ice—exactly what we needed to snap us out of the mood of mourning that still clung to us from the previous day.

With daylight still lingering, we arrived at the church. The wedding had been booked as an evening ceremony. I stepped out of the car and waited, as members of the wedding party took their positions. The church overflowed with guests, curious about how we would handle this. I felt a bit offended by the openly nosy looks that came our way. Little did I know that my empathy, sensitized by my overly emotional state, had put my guard up.

After much confusion, we all took our places and started walking down the aisle towards Daniel, who stood waiting uncomfortably in his fancy suit. Though not a fan of these affairs, he had agreed to our mothers' desires for a traditional wedding.

Suddenly, midway down the aisle, Dad stumbled. I grabbed his arm more tightly under mine. I knew I had to be the strong one here. I felt his resolve waning and his need for strength. I caught the look of my younger sister and brother, both about to crumble, as they turned towards us. I would have none of it. I smiled, and that smile conveyed such strength that a resolve to see this through came over them. My look spoke a thousand words, and they straightened their backs and threw off their momentary bit of weakness.

We will make Mom proud, echoed in our minds.

I did have one more moment when I felt I might not be able to restrain a surge of emotions. As I listened to Father John's caring words in his eulogy, he respectfully referred to our recent loss. This brought to mind his comment not long ago about flowers decorating our ceremony. I looked around at the abundance of colors and arrangements. Little had we known his words had forewarned us of what would come. Flowers spilled from every surface, courtesy of Mom's funeral the previous day. As I beheld their beauty, my bottom lip trembled, and I felt an unexpected stab of loss in my heart.

The rest of the ceremony went smoothly, and Dad later thanked me for my strength and courage. Without it, he said he didn't think he could have gone through the day with such calmness and resilience. Little did I know then that I had dug in deep for support, to a place within I came to know consciously only years later.

Mom had sacrificed herself so we could fulfill our destiny, as fate decreed.

And so it went. Mom had been laid out on Wednesday and cremated and buried on Thursday. Daniel and I wed on Friday and arrived in Jamaica by Saturday night, for a much-needed honeymoon break from the reality of our lives.

Present Day

I return to the here and now, needing to shake off these old memories. I wipe away the tear rolling down my cheek. My mom's death still hurts after all of this time, and I wonder whether the pain will ever go away. Yet allowing these things to surface enables us to let go. With such traumatic experiences, we should let them rest until they surface on their own. The soul knows the right time to release its pain.

This began a series of dramatic life experiences that drove Daniel and me toward our destiny. Yet as we fulfilled a karmic debt and responded to life as best we could, we remained ignorant of our origins and reason for being.

I see an image of myself years later, looking up and asking, "Why has my life always been so volatile and full of drama? Why have these events happened to me and my family? What lies under the surface, slumbering, waiting—and for what?"

Chapter 15

Angelina's Awakening

"The period of greatest gain in knowledge and experience is the most difficult period in one's life."

—Dalai Lama

Present Day, Looking Back

Now, before I become too distracted by my wandering thoughts, another holograph opens. A whirlwind of energy plays through scenes going back in time. It slows and stops right after Daniel and I wed. I observe these years dispassionately. I kept busy raising a family, running businesses, traveling, feeding my creative endeavours—a slew of activities that today I associate with the Wonder Woman syndrome, a legacy from my own mother.

I feel exhausted just watching this younger me. I've always been overly active and full of energy, but as I got older, I took on so many responsibilities. I made choices that had far-reaching consequences. In time, this caught up with me. A severe physical breakdown had me in its clutches for years. My nervous system let go and landed me in the hospital. My entire awareness of reality forcefully changed from that day on.

In Her Early Thirties, Angelina Revisits Her Personal Hell

Life in the Flatlands became my years of convalescence. One day Daniel had left for work at dawn, and the kids went to school, allowing me the luxury of resting. Lost in thought, as usual, I wrote in my journals to document my thoughts and experiences. Through the corridors of the holograph, the cry of a crow echoed its warning to pay heed. My younger self stood and walked over to the windows of her studio in the flatlands.

Acres upon acres of corn and wheat rocked softly in the afternoon breeze, reminding me that I had become like these plants, learning to bend and sway with the flow of life. To resist my experiences would have been like a tree trying to defy gale force winds, only to break. I had to develop the resilience to bend with life's unpredictable mood swings, while maintaining a strong foundation.

I leave this time period in the Flatlands and drift back to a place I'd avoided: my days of awakening. I observe myself broken, a shadow of my true being. It's so painful to watch. I'd drowned in a storm of emotions and fears for months on end. The medical profession called this major depression, but I came to know it as, first, hell and then rebirth—the death of my ego and the birth of a higher awareness.

I once again relive the turmoil and torment that forced me to understand what hell could be. I burn in an inner purgatory, bedevilled by chaotic emotions and out-of-control thoughts.

I hesitate before completely sinking into this earlier period, fearing I won't survive the telling. Yet deep down, I know I have to revisit this to finally put its demons to rest.

From far away, I hear Teacher say,

> *It's okay, Angelina. We are with you, and we will support and protect you on this inner journey you are destined to relive. Heal, dear, heal.*

Teacher's soothing voice calms my fears as I resist this return to hell. Clearly, I haven't healed and have buried some crucial memories in the recesses of my subconscious. So, I let go and let be. What will be, will be, and so be it.

I find myself in a dark place, surrounded by the burning fires of hell. *This must be purgatory.* I'd almost given up my fight, exhausted from years of deep pain and suffering. Yet still, some spark to survive helped me find the strength to hang on. These memories encapsulated the worst times of my life.

Teacher's voice once again comes through:

> *Angelina, do not lose yourself to this, for you will not come back. Remember, you are simply recalling a memory; it is not real, except for the power you choose to give your fears. Hold on and simply bring forth the pain, so it can, once and for all, be released!*

Teacher's words bring me back. I make sure to ground myself and not get lost in the nightmare. Thanking her, I turn my attention back to this past, firmly resolved not to get misled by it.

Finding myself yet again in that hell, I discover that my pain resulted from a body unable to manage the tremendous energies that surfaced when the dormant part of me awoke. The time to reclaim my powers has arrived.

I can see now that my nervous system smoked, and my body and my mind were ill prepared for the awakening of my Muse.

Now I understand why the Powers That Be warned me that I might not survive this. My entire being rebelled against the burning inferno that stretched my nervous system to its limit, again and again. Days became weeks, then years, as my body had to accept and adjust to higher and higher frequencies of energy. It demanded that I transform and purify every cell and every associated thought and emotion that no longer served my journey.

Images flash before me of the demons I faced in the initiatory journeys. I had to dig deep to hold onto my sanity. I just wanted to be done with it and wondered if it would ever end.

Finally, after three years, I hit rock bottom, depleted.

On that day, I thought about taking my life—not because I wanted to be dead but because I couldn't take any more pain and suffering. My inability to let go had worn me down. I spent days rocking myself, to block out what was driving me insane. As the memory of that day hits me again, I feel a stabbing sensation in my spleen and my plexus.

Suddenly, a light goes on in my head. My reaction reflects the binding scars still attached to these events. They have to be severed, if I want to step away from the wounded healer syndrome and be the best I can be.

I continue to observe this younger Angelina. That day, I fell to my knees in agony, yelling to the heavens for help or death. I'd grown tired of antidepressant pills frying my nervous system and of the doctors' visits, because each time I left them perplexed. I didn't fall within their textbook material. They didn't know what to do with me, except prescribe more medications. I'd had enough of being labelled with a bipolar diagnosis that meant nothing but only boxed me into a list of symptoms and drew malicious presumptions.

I bore this cross until I could no longer keep silent, and then I screamed out for redemption. This broke me free of my prison. The Powers That Be had been waiting for my final gesture to let go of everything.

Let the Healing Begin . . .

My heartfelt plea, as are all pleas for help when in the throes of initiation, was answered, and the journey to wellness finally began. I turned the tide to replenish my soul. I was guided to become a subject in a medical trial, based out of Edmonton, of a micronutrient discovered by two men to treat nervous system issues, bipolar disorder, ADHD, and so on. It later led to a major scientific discovery regarding nervous system depletion. To this day, I give these same empowering micronutrients to people suffering as I once did.

One healing crisis after another ensued, and I slept as I had not in ages. Before this, despite often "resting," I had suffered from fitful, broken sleep.

Healing can be more painful than sickness. I lost my appetite for days on end, as my body purged toxins. When hungry, I had unusual cravings.

I felt tired and had no interest in anything. Life seemed "blah" and unimportant. These ordeals became less severe as I began to remember and manage the tremendous primal force of my Muse.

My body cleansed and healed in cycles. That next three-year transition was a *droit de passage*, "a rite of passage," to higher awareness. I intuited that the initiations related to my aboriginal bloodline, which a very wise seer later confirmed. On the eve of his death, he told me I had gone through a traditional medicine woman's awakening. He said my healing powers came from my mother's people and my seer's ways from my father's.

This rite of initiation had been traditional in Native American cultures for those destined to become healers and teachers.

Time passed, and ever so slowly, my body and spirit healed. I became whole once again.

During my first months of wellness, I experienced happenings I'd once deemed impossible.

Teacher continues my train of thought:

> *People who have had "near-death experiences," from an accident, a grave illness, or a deeply painful incident, will at times have mystical encounters and paranormal experiences, triggering a new awareness of reality and life. A person is forever changed and will never be the same.*

My senses sharpened, and I felt deep empathy with others and an inexplicable degree of sensitivity to their thoughts and emotions. These qualities had always been part of my makeup, but now they'd been fine-tuned. Energy coursed through my body, and I began to read people's thoughts. All of it drained me until I slept for days. Then the confusing dreams and premonitions began. I wasn't crazy, but I couldn't speak freely of my insights, because others would judge me, based on their fear of the unknown.

I discovered a sensitivity to spirits, real beings living in other dimensions of reality. Yet everything was too new and raw. I was like an infant after my rebirth. I had so many unanswered questions; these mysteries played themselves out on a weekly basis. From visions of far-away loved ones to premonitions of coming events, the strange happenings got more intense. I always experienced health problems afterward, feeling weak and sick for days or weeks on end.

A pattern eventually emerged. Yet I'd grounded these new experiences in a more or less stable nervous system, helped by the micronutrients I took. So, despite being overwhelmed mentally by the new world I encountered, I remained physically healthy.

This all happened before Daniel passed on, and it confused and scared him when I spoke of such things. They created a wall between us, because he couldn't understand the experiences I shared with him.

Losing Daniel

Shortly after my full recovery, we lost Daniel. I sigh to recall that painful time. The rest of the memories surface to be healed, forcing me to relive what I have avoided: the day following Daniel's demise.

I woke up in a hospital bed, with my brother, my sister, and my father standing by my side. Their forlorn expressions bode ill, and I sat up abruptly, asking to see Daniel. The familiar looks on their faces told me Daniel had died. We all had that same look when Mom passed on. I screamed in agony that life had taken another loved one from me and in such an unpredictable way. The nurses came running and gave me a sedative. I fell asleep, and when I woke the next morning, my emotions had shut down, enabling me to take care of everything necessary for Daniel's funeral.

Destiny had once again played us a mean deck of cards. The stress of the karmic boomerang of trying to save Daniel's life and the subsequent damage to my sensitive nervous system sent me into a depressive relapse. I retired from life with the kids at my side, as we all licked the wounds of loss.

A few months later, all was back to normal, except the kids and I had gaping holes in our hearts. I adjusted, frozen beyond feeling. Nothing got in and nothing got out. I had the kids, and that was all I needed.

I sink deeply into these thoughts, metamorphosing into this younger Angelina. Nothing else exists but this past. This young Angelina, alive and so real, feels familiar and true. The past lures me into its web, and I lose my grip as I become one with this dream, this illusion of who I once was.

"*Wake up, Angelina! Wake up!! You've gone too deep into the past!*" yells Teacher in a worried, fretful tone.

Present Day

I snap awake with a jump! I feel a retracting sensation in my abdomen, as if someone punched me. I look out my window to get my bearings—it's mid day. I appreciate Teacher's concern, calling me back, because I could have been lost forever in a time warp of my own making, never to return.

Yet reviewing this earlier period forces me to remember how difficult the beginnings can be. The loss of Daniel—his sacrifice—is a deed I will one day pay back in another life, another time. To each sacrifice is a balanced return, and so it is in our soul group. We give of each other, and we take from life to life, and the laws of balance always ask their price.

I had to look back at who I was, to let it go and appreciate who I've become. I'm shaking from journeying into this shadow of my past, but I let go of something that was stuck in me all of these years.

Teacher says,

> *Problems often arise at the change of electrical current during a person's awakening—those "Ah ha!" moments of realization that change you forever. The astral body will suddenly open up and "baptize" a person in a wave of spiritual energy so great that it can do a lot of harm to untrained nervous systems. Not everyone passes these tests, as you can attest by the loss of some very dear friends in your life.*

I distinctly remember one poor soul with no boundaries, no anchors grounding her in this physical life. Poor Rachel—such a gifted person but now driven crazy in a form of schizophrenia by her adventures into a world of mind she was ill prepared to tackle. Though I did what I could to help her, my limited knowledge in those days didn't permit me to lend her support. During those crucial years, I witnessed many struggling with their initiations into higher "being."

Teacher continues my train of thought:

> *You were not conscious of this phenomenon playing out at the time, so stop feeling guilty.*
>
> *This is an ongoing issue, as the time of ascension fast approaches. Few, though, know what is happening, know how to deal with it, or are able to put themselves back together.*

I dawns on me that my nervous system has survived its transformative phase. I've adjusted to transmitting and circulating my soul frequency. These soulful events have revealed my destiny, my purpose.

Chapter 16

Dark Night of the Soul—A Gift

"Every positive change—every jump to a higher level of energy and awareness—involves a rite of passage. Each time to ascend to a higher rung on the ladder of personal evolution, we must go through a period of discomfort, of initiation. I have never found an exception."

—Dan Millman

During the first years after my "dark night of the soul," I spent days in solitude. These mini retreats in the Flatlands saved my life.

I glance over at the mantel, where a special knife lies, gifted to me years ago by an unexpected visitor.

I return to the past, to those long-forgotten days.

Dad had been visiting us for a few days. He often came for dinner and stayed the night, and I appreciated his habit of checking on us since Daniel had passed. That Monday morning, after talking to my son before the school bus came, he headed off for the day. I decided to catch up on chores. Off I went to the garden, humming a joyful tune. Spending long days in the beautiful perennial gardens of the Victorian house enabled me to ground the toxins I'd accumulated from painful experiences. I'd invested my energy in creating things of beauty to soothe my soul's wounds. How wonderful life could be, after so many years of loss, pain, and struggle!

The singing birds and the warmth of the sun soothed my soul, as nature woke up for the day. My growing affinity with the elements and especially with the earth led me to grow herbs for the medicines I use. Soon, the St. John's Wort would be ready to gather.

I decided to sit by the pond in the ornate courtyard of our beautiful Victorian home. This magical place served as a gathering spot for gnomes, fairies, gargoyles, and such. They watched in curiosity as my awakening unfolded. I felt their presence, and years later they appeared in a photograph my daughter took of me. Their gift of manifesting still warms my heart, during a time when I questioned my sanity and my destiny.

It was the summer equinox, and I'd thought about growing more medicinal herbs and making special remedies. It would be nice to create natural products like creams and such. I found it practically impossible to purchase anything natural in most stores.

A light breeze blew on this quiet morning, as I rested on the stone bench by the pond. The trickling water cascaded down our makeshift waterfall into the reeds. The odd "gribbet" sounded in this haven for all kinds of frogs and toads. The night-time symphonies of amphibian mating calls often forced us to close the doors and the windows to get peace. Sometimes the cacophony became so loud, we had to yell to each other to be heard.

I connected to everything around and within me. My energy surged forth. The hum of my Muse filled me with Her healing energy, until my "cup" filled.

I felt the presence of an unearthly being by my side and turned my head. A form appeared from the haze, and the more attention I gave it, the more solid it became. Within minutes, a glorious figure sat beside me.

She smiled. "I have come to give you a gift."

Though obviously not of this world, she appeared so real. Her long golden tresses hung below her knees, and she wore a beautiful gown of silken green moss. Vines held up her mane of flowing hair, and her eyes sparkled like blue diamonds. Her skin shone pearly white, and she smelled of amber, musk, and fresh air. The wind shifted and then carried the scent of lilies, lilacs, and roses. She smiled to see my confused expressions.

Her clothing, created with materials from Mother Earth, grew and transformed on her before my very eyes, as did Mother Nature. Could she be the spirit of Mother Earth? I cast this thought aside, thinking, *What a silly notion.* But she nodded, and I gasped to realize that this being, a deva of Mother Earth herself, had addressed me.

With a comforting smile, she spoke in the recesses of my mind: "I come for two reasons. The first is to tell you that many support you in your life quest. Many of us Otherworld beings follow and protect you, as you struggle to awaken and come into your powers. We will not forsake you. You were born with the gift of the elements, and I am the spirit of the Earth come alive, as a witness of my commitment to your quest. When the time is right, many others will visit you. Before you can partake of the magic of Earth you hold within, you must cultivate your relationship with Her. I will help you. Even if you do not see me, know I am there."

She told me that before I would be permitted to create magical remedies and awaken that power fully, I had to remember how to walk the Earth. I needed to recognize how we abused, used, and consumed Her, so I could help transform these evil, destructive ways. Man did nothing anymore but take from the Earth, without giving back much. Even those who claimed to do good had little knowledge of everything that needed to change.

Man had destroyed the Earth's harmony, and Her health declined rapidly. The Earth deva pointed to the decay on her body, with parts of her putrid and rotting. Tears came to her eyes, as she explained that dying so slowly caused deep pain. Her health directly reflected our health as a species, and we were not separate from Her. Man had objectified Earth, as he objectified all things he desired and wished to control.

She continues, "People will not live long or live happily if they keep dishonouring me and ignoring my natural laws—laws that govern health and prosperity. The consequences of man's egotistical behaviour will come crashing in on all of you. Man's penchant for materialism is out of control, and the growing health issues throughout the globe testify to your ignorance. You sabotage yourselves by killing everything that sustains your health and welfare. Man has forgotten that everything is connected and interdependent. Man is no longer grounded to his reality."

With her ethereal countenance, the Earth deva and I gazed into each other's eyes. I felt such an affinity with her.

As my mind calmed and went quiet, she said, "I come bearing a gift. This gift will protect and help you cut away the decay that would prevent you from fulfilling your destiny.

"Tonight, when the equinox of spring and summer stills, on this day of the full moon a portal will open. Come here, and my gift will be on this bench. Hold it safe and dear to your heart, for it brings you the support you need in coming trials. Hide it away in your sacred bundle, and when the time is right, you will know how to use it."

I nodded, and her image began to fade. I wanted to ask so many questions, but she simply smiled. I knew she would always support me, as long as I remained true to myself and my destiny.

That evening at the appointed time, I stood by the bench, wondering what to expect. In the blink of an eye, an ornate white metal knife appeared on the bench, as if from thin air. If I hadn't witnessed this myself, I wouldn't have believed it. I dared not pick it up right away, for fear this hallucination would disappear. Maybe it was all a figment of my imagination?

As soon as the thought entered my mind, I heard her voice: "Keep it safe, for one day it will serve you well."

"What are you doing, Angelina?"

I heard Dad come up behind me and instinctively hid the knife in my skirt. He was a handsome man and still spry in his aging years. He was quick to smile, and everyone said I got my sense of humour from him. If he ever got upset, it never lasted longer than the time it took to express his displeasure; then in a minute it was over, and he'd moved on to his next thought.

Some people could never understand our ability to turn a blind eye and let things go, the way we did.

"Hi, Dad. I'm just enjoying the evening."

He sat down beside me. "I'm so amazed at what you've accomplished here. I wish your mother had been more like you. We lived in the city because she was a city girl, but I often wanted to move to the country. Your sister takes after your mother, you know."

"Yes, I know, Dad. Though we look a lot alike, my sister and I are very different." We laughed, because it was so true. I was the trail-breaking, live-off-the-land, natural gal type, and she was a citified girl, loving all of the conveniences and security of modern life.

"Angelina, did I ever tell you the story of when you were little and how your mother and I would sit you in the back of the red bug over the motor, in the trunk, and drive you around the block till you fell asleep? You were just a baby then; it was the only way you'd fall asleep for the night."

"Yes, Dad, you told me the story. Then when you brought me in, I'd wake up again, and off you'd go, driving around the block once more, till the humming of the motor put me back to sleep."

"The second time, always the charm, had you sleeping through the night. You were such a pretty baby, and whenever we took you out, people stopped us to say so. You have the dark looks of your Native American blood but the delicate frame of your French heritage."

He paused, and I knew he was once again thinking of Mom. On that note, he said his goodbyes and was off.

* * *

I bring myself back to the present. It's time to call it a day. We always eat very late at this time of year, because Hubby never gets home until well after dark. I glance over at the knife again, thanking it for all of the times its magic protected me. Another time, another story.

I cook the evening meal. Tired and dishevelled, I decide I can spare a few hours to relax before everyone gets home for dinner. I leave the food on the stove, ready to be reheated, and doze off. The last thought that crosses my mind is, *I'm so tired*.

I wake up the next morning in bed, wondering where the night went. I vaguely remember Hubby and my daughter coming home and that I ate dinner with them. But now my dozy head still can't get rid of dreams of fairies and gnomes and those "fairy-tale" worlds. Hubby, already up and gone, has left me a note saying good-bye and that he loves me.

He's a biologist, specializing in the conservation and protection of nature. He's often asked to assess a site for future development and its impact on the flora and fauna or to evaluate the destruction caused by a spill or a natural disaster. This usually involves devising a recovery plan, which takes months and doesn't permit many visits back home. These are the hardest times for the kids and me, because he's such a positive supporting influence in our lives.

I grin, recalling our special connection. No matter where he is, we have that. Whether we're side by side or miles apart, we connect to each other in a special way.

I walk downstairs. The sun is already high. A quick coffee, and off I go to write. I do my usual preparatory techniques, but something isn't quite right. The energy coursing through me is unusually powerful today.

My energy surges up again. If I don't redirect some of the pressure, I can't settle down to write.

Enough—right now I can't afford to be distracted by this energy. Something is up. I can feel it and smell it.

Chapter 17

Seeking Answers

"We are not Gods or enlightened masters, but we are people who have great gifts to give. We are Messengers sent to alter the course of mankind.
Nonetheless, we remain human beings."

—Godfrey King

The Next Morning...

I try to settle down to write. The energy keeps coursing through me in waves. Now I definitely know something is coming. I realize that today I feel whole again and of one mind. It has taken me many years to adjust to the fullness of Angelina's energy. I better understand the need to revisit the past. What wisdom we have when we souls plan our incarnations. What courage we manifest once we step into these physical bodies!

I stand up and find myself gliding to the centre of the room. Invisible hands guide me, as the energy in my womb explodes upward. My mind disappears, and my heart centre fills with a love so great, it expands until it can take no more. Bliss fills me, and my head falls back, as my arms open up to an unimaginable beam of love energy. This light bursts into millions of light rays of Christ Buddha energy, out into the world, dispelling the shadows of my loft and filling every corner with radiance.

Heavenly music fills my being. I stand on tiptoe, arms outspread and head thrown upwards, floating in a sea of blissful sensations. I look towards a point far ahead, my mind's eye blinded by the light of pure consciousness.

Ethereal beings flash by, and winged beings of light appear. Crowds of beings watch me zip by, and I finally slow down as I approach the One Source. Alone now, I kneel. No words are exchanged, for they are not needed, nor do they exist here. I am bathed in love, and it all becomes clear to me: This is home. This is what I've searched for since incarnating as Angelina. My time of forgetfulness has ended.

Words I once heard in a movie surface: "God dwells in me as me." I dissolve into my bliss. I feel my heart, my soul Source, and my salvation. I make my way into the Divine Light of consciousness, embracing it and diffusing everything else. Home, home, home...

From afar, I hear Teacher's panicky voice:

> *Angelina, you must come back now. Do not get lost to your bliss. It will swallow you whole and is not meant to be more than transitory. Come back, my dear, come back!*

Teacher's words jerk me back into my body, as my heart centre closes. Chest pain folds me in two, as I lie on the floor. The room becomes steeped in shadows. I hadn't conditioned my heart muscle to experience this communion with the Divine. *How did I know of this?* I ask myself. I have a vague memory of bathing in this as a young child before my slumber. Humbled, I know I am far from accepting my Greater Self's full power. Will I ever become whole again, as I was at birth? I can only have faith. That and courage will sustain me.

Many teachers guided me along this path of life. They taught me about the ego and my strange newfound abilities, as I began reclaiming my healing powers.

Traveling back to the years of my illness shook me up. Teacher's words stay with me:

> *When you're caught in your hell, you haven't a clue about the real reasons why you are suffering. You just want a solution and an end to the pain. You enter a place of deep inner contemplation, looking for answers that will alleviate the hurt.*

The crumbling of my outer world triggered my metamorphosis. A seal within me had broken. My time of slumber had ended. Yet I couldn't use my will alone to transform myself. I needed the right tools.

The first step demanded that I "train my brain" to focus. Those initiatory years forced me to develop mind muscles that had gone dormant. The new Angelina had no control over her thought processes. She suffered from a common affliction called "racing mind."

Those earliest years taught her through the avenue of pain and suffering. After three years of blocking out her pain for hours on end, she had become adept at stilling her mind. It was the greatest gift she could have given herself.

I stop to ponder that dark time. I referred to Angelina of that time as "she" and not "I." Why is the Angelina of my past not the "I" I associate myself with anymore? Why do I feel so disconnected from the Angelina of my past?

Teacher says,

> *I have been waiting for you to ask this question. We decided that this knowledge had to be withheld until you matured.*

Teacher definitely has a way of getting my attention. I'm "all ears" now, wondering about still-buried secrets.

> *You experienced a "step-in. This is a contract between two souls to share a body for a certain determined time, then switch. We often see this type of agreement between young souls and more mature ones who no longer wish to relive the birthing and maturing stages of life.*
>
> *The Powers That Be could not chance a full step-in with the magnitude of energy of your Greater Self. The average nervous*

system could never take such an expansion. It is simply not humanly possible. We decided to experiment with blending separate forms of existences: a partial step-in with a dormancy stage of your Greater Self. Many Masters were called to hold the space for this process to be successful. This is why your audience is so illustrious. This type of experiment could never have worked in the past.

It all makes sense now. My memories of this past Angelina seem so disconnected and disassociated from the person I have become. She was but a shell of me.

Years passed, as I unravelled along with my inner world, and this new Angelina came into being. Ever so slowly, the Greater Self awakened in me. Then my journey really began to get interesting.

Present Day

The sound of the loons brings my attention back. I'm sitting at my desk on a high mountaintop, still caught in the residue of my bliss. How long will this stay with me? It can last from hours to days into weeks.

"What goes up must come down," Teacher pipes up.

I grin, knowing this is her way of grounding me. "Yes, it does, dear, and thanks for pulling me back. I was dangerously close to getting lost."

"You're welcome, Angelina. That's my job!" and she laughs.

Teacher guides me to pull out another old manuscript. The first manuscript that catches my eye chronicles my introduction to Cheyenne by Morning Glory, a North American shamanic healer.

Daniel had left us by then, I had not yet met Hubby, and life was more or less back to normal. With no financial concerns, I had the luxury of continuing my healing journey. I still didn't feel my best, and I had more questions than ever.

And so I read . . .

Daniel is gone now. It is just I and the children.

I have developed a perceptual and empathic affinity with the elements. My experiences probe beyond the collective norm. The number of people who could help me dwindles, as these events become stranger and more otherworldly. The bizarre occurrences keep gaining momentum and power. Overwhelmed, I repeatedly have to adjust my perception of reality and remain grounded.

Desperate to understand all of this, I scour books and the Web for answers. Numerous people have come forward to speak of their "awakening" and their ability to help others. Yet after making a few attempts to connect with some of them, I always come away disappointed. They are seekers no different than I. This dilemma plagues our new millennium.

Help was out there, and I had to find it. Someone, somewhere, could guide me through my despair and ignorance. I spent days searching for that mentor, a person or a group. Teacher remained only a voice that surfaced once in a while. In my desperate search for mentorship, I recognized that the world was as spiritually starved as I was. We had thrown off the cloak that organized religion had bundled us in. The ideas and the superstitions of the past no longer served us. Now the abyss of change beckoned mankind.

I came across Morning Glory's website by sheer accident, searching for answers to strange, inexplicable phenomena during the later years of my awakening. I decided to open up communication. Morning Glory headed an organization of unusual shamanic practices that seemed oddly familiar to me.

Morning Glory, in her mid fifties and obviously not Native American, nevertheless donned the dress and spoke the part. She called herself a shamanic practitioner, and I wondered whether she was just another "wannabe" playing "Native Indian," as my father would say, in a quest to belong to a tribe of sorts.

Teacher comments,

All tribes had their own ways and superstitions enrobing their practices and rituals, but in the end they all originated and sourced their knowledge and power from the One.

I nod in agreement, as Teacher continues to share her wisdom.

The Celtic and aboriginal traditions are but a few that have not been completely wiped out by organized religion. Man's ignorance of the workings of his inner world makes him vulnerable to being controlled and manipulated through his fear.

Teacher's words profoundly affect me, as I remember my own vulnerability during my awakening. Teacher continues,

Organized religion came into existence because of a deep need to guide man and introduce governship and another way of worship. In the past, your practices were raw and wild, with human and animal sacrifice founding your beliefs. Organized religion was the next step in humanizing your life experiences, while introducing pagan rituals in a more organized and less violent way.

These words pull forth memories of when I studied healing at a local university. I discovered that ancient pagan customs formed the basis of most rituals in organized religions. I felt stunned to learn this, because the Catholic Church's Inquisition was all about eliminating pagan rituals and practices. It seemed ironic that the Church so feared what its elite members themselves worshipped.

Teacher's words surface above my thoughts:

Systems must change and adapt to the needs of the people. More and more people have discovered they are souls, spiritual beings living a physical experience. There is a worldwide desperation manifesting that reflects a deep desire to anchor into a belief system that's better adapted to a freer, less invasive form of worship—to help people deal with their inner changes, as well as feed their deep spiritual needs.

I go back to reading the manuscript—the part where I decided to follow my gut and communicate with Morning Glory, the shamanic practitioner.

I once again sink into this past.

> Hi, Morning Glory,
> Being instinctively guided to your website, I wonder if you can help me understand many mysterious and paranormal happenings occurring in my life.

After a few email exchanges, she suggested I contact a former student of hers, Cheyenne, who often tutored people in my situation. Cheyenne, a healing practitioner living in the Adirondack Mountains, had expertise in energy healing, mentorship, and training.

Morning Glory explained,

> I'm presently preoccupied with a pet project of mine and have no place for a new student at this time, but I'm sure Cheyenne can offer you the guidance you need.

Her words about energy healing piqued my interest. For the last few months, a series of paranormal events had left me anxiously searching for answers. For days on end, I'd experienced a sensation of being infused with tingling throughout my body, and I wondered whether it had a connection to energy healing.

"Where is it coming from, and how is it turned on or shut off? Why is this happening and how come, deep down, I know this energy intimately but have no conscious knowledge of it?"

I learned that energy healing, an ancient technique, worked by taking in a subtle energy force that surrounds us, through a simple ritual of "Initiation."

Putting my manuscript down, I laugh at the irony. The world of subtle energy is so much more than what most people would have us believe. It is far from harmless, and I soon learned that it wasn't simply about directing healing energy. Certain healing practices can be very dangerous. A particular incident comes to mind.

Years ago, at the beginning of my clinical practice, a young woman named Josephine showed up at my door, begging for help. She had been on an emotional roller-coaster ride for days—in fact, ever since she had undergone an energy healing session with a local healer.

I sat her down and asked, "So, what happened at that session that has you in such a mess?"

"I don't know," Josephine told me, "but halfway through, I wanted to get out of there!"

As I continued to question her, it became apparent that the healer had triggered this response. I listened carefully, looking for clues and insight. Then I saw a glimmer of something suspicious. I asked her, "Did this person talk about doing something to your chakras?" By then, I was very familiar with chakras as organs of consciousness.

"How did you know that? Yes, she said my chakras were closed and needed to be open and balanced."

I swore under my breath at the stupidity of some people, then I felt a pinch and a nudge.

"Angelina, you know better than to think that!" Teacher whispered in my ear. I grimaced, not liking that she was right, again! I asked for forgiveness for my moment of thoughtlessness. But God Almighty, did I get frustrated at some of the things people did.

I looked at Josephine, knowing what had happened. I went about correcting the problem, while respecting the laws governing chakra consciousness. When will people learn that you do not play around with chakras? "Open your chakras," indeed. Within minutes, Josephine felt better and was on her way, thankful for my intervention.

I decide to dig through my visual photo library and command it to come forth. My mind's eye sees pages from my book of life, turning at the speed of light. They slow and come to a stop, and I read:

> Energy healing brings an understanding of mind and body, that "the mind affects the body and the body affects the mind."

Yet it goes far beyond the universe of the mind. We all conduct the symphony of universal energies and must adhere to specific laws.

Teacher's voice pipes up.

> *That is why you have come, my dear—to help those who are prepared and mature spiritually to move forward in a way that is empowering, liberating, and limitless.*

I know the soul is the source of everything.

Synchronicity—a creating force commanded by thinking—this mysterious force, grounded in my soul, links all events together in my life and always with a specific reason. For me to ignore these latest promptings about Morning Glory and Cheyenne would be just plain stupid.

Teacher asks, *"Has synchronicity not been your guiding force from your birth, my dear?"*

Chapter 18

Meeting Cheyenne

"We can suffer anything if there is a purpose and a reason."

—Michèle C. St.Amour

Memories of a Past Mentor

I'd spent a few days hesitantly pondering Morning Glory's suggestion to contact Cheyenne. On the third day, I emailed an introduction of myself. I briefly explained my situation and Morning Glory's referral. I sent it off and waited anxiously for a reply.

Just as I was about to give up hope, I received an email. Cheyenne indeed claimed to be an energy healer and offered many other alternative modalities as well. Cheyenne's specialty seemed to be guiding people undergoing some type of "spiritual process."

The email read:

> Morning Glory mentions you were having some strong experiences. The modalities I work with support healing, followed up with spiritual counselling. For all healing and energy work, I will do this at what we call "a distance."

Though confused, I decided to wait and see. After my further questions, Cheyenne explained, "These modalities for healing are not limited by time and space, hence are just as easily acquired and done at a distance as in person."

I realized that energy healing must follow the same principles as my work in psychometry (the ability to clairvoyantly read pictures, people, or places from the energy attached to an item).

I could feel things that were imperceptible to the average person. This clairvoyant ability surfaced in those first days of my recovery, quite by accident. A friend of mine asked for advice about a person she wanted to date and handed me his picture. The instant I looked at the photo, I went into a detached trance, as feelings and mental images assailed me. All of the information I shared with her later proved to be true.

Cheyenne explained:

> Often, during energy sessions, I have intuitive impressions, and, if meaningful, I will share them with you. The same will go for you.

Cheyenne said early on, "I only work with people willing to 'do the work' and make whatever effort is needed to accomplish the targeted goal."

Cheyenne stated, "Yours is a common experience, and most clients with life-changing illnesses, as you have suffered, are undergoing some type of 'spiritual process.'"

Cheyenne went on to ask me, "What do you need? What do you want? What is 'wrong,' if anything? What are you seeking? From the little you have said, it sounds like you may be experiencing a spiritual awakening. And if this is correct, what is (are) the problem(s)? What do you think is happening?"

I pondered this, and a few weeks passed as we assessed my needs. I described the various new sensitivities that accompanied the healing of my sickness.

Once we decided on my most pressing needs, Cheyenne planned to match those with the modalities I would learn. Finally, here was someone who might be able to guide me and answer the gazillion questions running through my mind!

Cheyenne clearly stated,

> To make the most out of a spiritual awakening requires will, discipline, and patience; these are essential components of success. These things cannot be rushed or put on a timeline. It takes the time it takes, and, in all fact, it can span lifetimes.

I grin, for this is precisely what I inform my students to this day. Yet this timeline frustrated me to no end in my eagerness to move forward.

I asked Cheyenne, "So, how many years, specifically, before I am stable and will acquire a strong, healthy foundation?"

The answer, "many years," seemed like forever to me. I couldn't imagine many more years of what I had lived through. I didn't know how different these would be—and little did I realize they would go by so fast.

Still, not being afraid of a little work, I leaped at this chance to heal and harness powers I had chosen to forget.

We began with Cheyenne asking me to "describe and detail the sensitivities you wish to understand and master."

During the next few weeks, I explained some of the experiences I'd had.

> Good morning, Cheyenne.
>
> The events I'm sharing are out of time sequence. In the end, it's most important that you understand the issues I'm dealing with presently.

RE: I discover dowsing.

I discovered that I have sensitivity to water, and I'm able to dowse for underground water sources or veins simply by feeling. Early one mid-summer morning, the phone rang, and I wondered who was calling at such an early hour. I could already feel the humidity of what promised to be a beautiful, balmy, sunny day.

Jeannie, my next-door neighbour, said in a panicked voice, "Hi, Angelina. I hope I'm not disturbing you. I have a favour to ask."

Without much thought, I answered, "Sure, Jeannie, fire away. What do you need?"

Jeannie, a full-figured woman, had a kind face and a strong voice. No stranger to hard work, she could keep up with any man in the barn. She was always ready to offer a hand. Though not as petite as I, she had fine features that made her pretty and appealing.

She explained that their well had suddenly gone dry, and it was imperative that they dig another. "We were told to get a dowser to source a water vein, but the dowser we were referred to can't come till tomorrow."

I racked my brains to remember what a dowser was. Oh, yeah—a dowser was someone with a gift for finding water with a stick or a rod. A memory flashed on my mind's screen of a picture of a man holding some kind of stick and walking around. Beyond that, I wasn't educated in this specific technique.

"Without enough water," Jeannie said, "the cows will sicken and quit producing, so it's crucial that we replenish the water supply immediately." Jeannie and her husband ran a dairy farm.

In the meantime, I offered them water from our pool and said they could fill a tanker with it. "I can refill the pool overnight. We have an amazing well that never runs dry."

They decided to do this until they resolved their problem.

I then asked Jeannie, "Can I do anything else to help? You and Fred have always been there for me when I needed support."

My gratitude surged for all of the times they'd helped me after Daniel was gone.

Jeannie hesitated, then blurted out, "Could you come this morning and look for a vein of water with me? I'm not sure how it's done, but I figure we can give it a try, especially with your sensitivities lately."

Jeannie had been a witness and a confidante to some of the amazing things that had happened since my recovery, so, of course, she *would* think I could help. I still felt surprised, though, at her question. I needed to think about this and told her I'd call her back in a few minutes.

Jeannie knew I'd been dabbling in unconventional things, but I wasn't sure whether I wanted to open this "keg of worms." What if I could do it? Then what? Yet even worse, what if I couldn't? I think that worried me more.

I got Jeannie back on the phone and asked, "What exactly do you think I can do to help?"

Jeannie sensed my trepidation. "I thought we could do the stick thing that I've seen other dowsers do to find water." In the next breath, she pleaded, "Please do this for me, Angelina? You're the only person I know who may be able to help us. I know you can do this, even if you aren't sure of it!"

Finally, I said yes. I finished my chores, and off I went.

When I arrived at their house, Jeannie was already in the front yard, walking around holding a Y-shaped stick in front of her. The dew-covered grass sparkled in the mid-morning sun. I got out of the car to a cacophony of noises only ever heard on a farm. Fred, her husband, was in the barn, watering the cows as best he could with buckets carried over from the house, which had a well of its own. He'd dug up some milking cans in an ancient shed that he'd used back in the day. He'd never thrown the cans away, in case the automatic milking system ever gave out. The employees ran to and fro, trying to keep up, as the milking cows bellowed for water.

Jeannie came running to me. "Hi, Angelina! I'm so glad you came. I've been trying to figure this thing out, with no luck, so maybe the two of us can do better."

She wore her regular farm jeans and a T-shirt. Her hair was wild, as usual, and her smile genuine. I couldn't help but smile in return. She often appeared childlike, with an underlying innocence that only young souls exude.

As she turned away, gesturing for me to follow, I scowled to myself, wondering what I'd gotten myself into. After a few minutes of deliberation, we decided she would scour the front yard, and I, the back. She had two Y-shaped wood sticks ready.

Jeannie instructed me to use the stick as best I could, while showing me how she had once seen it done on TV. She said that the stick would be drawn to water if an underwater source existed. She handed me one stick, and I thanked her, as we both eyed it in confusion.

I shrugged. "I'll do the best I can, and one of us will figure this out."

She nodded, and off she went. We'd decided that I would check the open area behind the storage shed.

I made my way toward that area, stalling because I didn't have a clue where to begin. It had gone quiet by this time, as all of the animals were now satisfied.

Angelina, what were you thinking? I asked myself. *This is just plain crazy, even by your standards.* I rolled my eyes, as I stood alone behind the shed, feeling silly. I searched my memory for ideas on how to do this. My inner saboteur rose up, and I reproached myself for even thinking I might be able to help. I wanted to give up and run.

As my uncertainties took hold, I walked toward the front yard to tell Jeannie it wouldn't work. Then I noticed how serious she seemed, resolutely attempting to find water and expecting the same from me. She had her eyes closed and concentrated on walking slowly, while holding the stick in front of her. She was so earnest in her intention that I felt ashamed for not even really trying. I quietly sneaked back to my spot behind the shed, before she noticed me. I decided to give it my best and at least try. So, where to begin?

I searched my memory for what I knew or had read about dowsing. A flash of pages appeared before my mind's eye, as the photographic memory I'd inherited from my mother answered my question. It had been a curse to her, because her generation was steeped in superstition about these things. We spoke of it only in whispers, but in this new era I could be frank about my abilities without fear of retribution. I mentally rifled through the pages of time, until I came to the spot I needed. I held the mental picture and asked that it be magnified. I then read to myself in a low voice:

> Dowsing is said to date back into ancient history and was a type of divination using a rod, a stick, a staff, or a wand. Dowsing was once used to find metals in the

fifteenth century. It was denounced as the "workings of the devil" in the mid 1500s, where apparently the term "water witching" originated. It went underground when it was proclaimed that dowsers were practitioners of evil.

I laughed at this, yet understood why my mother never spoke of this mind-seeing gift she and I shared. Deep down, she believed it was evil, and that she had "cheated her way through life," due to a gift she saw as the devil's work. A respected and intelligent woman, she had risen through the ranks of her schooling three years ahead of her age group. By the time she was seventeen, she had graduated from college and was teaching. My father told me this gift had weighed heavily on her, for she felt as if she had been a fraud her entire life. Maybe that was why she got sick so young and passed on when we were but teenagers. Even today, some people still maintain this ignorant belief in "works of the devil."

Our own neighbours across the field, for instance, who were friends for years now crucify me. They discovered that I had an interest in unconventional alternative healing sources, and the prejudice flourishing even now led to their ridiculous attitude.

I bring my attention back to the divination document.

> The practice today is referred to as water divination. Some dowsers use rods made of copper formed in an L shape or rods made of wood. It is common to feel a downward pull on the stick with jerks or writhing in one's hands. These movements are signs indicating a water source beneath one's feet.

I saw these words in my mind's eye like snapshots, created from things I'd read in the past. If I had seen something on television, it would have come forth as such. I flipped over more pages, detailing the history of dowsing, until I came to one with the heading "Make and Use a Dowsing Rod." I scanned the instructions.

> Start walking slowly and mentally ask your dowsing rod to indicate when you pass over water. Be aware of the

rod's movements. Keep a record of your various findings for reference, and don't give up.

"Easy to say," I muttered. Logic told me to hold the two Y ends of the stick, one in each hand, and point the single end out ahead of me. Later, I discovered that I'd been holding the stick all wrong.

I then deduced a need to quiet my mind, and the word *meditation* popped into my head. I asked out loud, "How do I meditate? It's not part of my repertoire."

No sooner were the words out of my mouth that I flashed on an exercise I'd read about in a New Age book.

It's not a meditation, but close enough, I told myself.

The exercise was supposed to allow a person to contact his or her spirit guides. I closed my eyes and reviewed the exercise. Once I felt centred and calm, I began to walk, holding the stick out before me. I did this for a while, feeling sillier and sillier as time ticked away and nothing happened.

The stick hadn't moved—nothing had happened.

I stopped and walked over to a stump behind the shed to figure out what to do next. I sat down and leaned against the cool metal shed, feeling the hot sun beat down. Insects buzzed and the milk machine hummed in the background. It was eerily quiet, and I wondered what the heck I'd been thinking when I told Jeannie I would give this a try. Deep down, I was afraid of the truth. If I could do this, then what would it mean? I'd dealt with so much these past months—I couldn't take another shift of awareness so soon. I was about to give up, but that inner voice urged me on, and I decided to give it one last try.

I stood up and took a deep breath, then went back to the spot I hadn't checked yet. I closed my eyes and focused all of my attention inward, as I walked slowly. In silence, I asked to be shown where water might be.

After a few minutes I entered an altered state of consciousness. My body hummed and zinged. I was there but not—as if I'd become split into two. My body felt numb, and I became disconnected from everything, including what I had attempted to accomplish. At some point, I had to "let go," even though I had no idea what that meant. Then it happened.

All of a sudden, as I walked, my body shook uncontrollably, and I wondered if I were having a seizure. Then, just as abruptly, the shaking stopped. I retraced my steps. I walked along the same course in the grass behind the tool shed, and the same feeling occurred. It dawned on me that there was a pattern and that water might be running below my feet. I just knew this was it!

I tested it again and again, with the same results, so I decided to call Jeannie over. She ran to me, full of excitement. I told her what had happened and showed her over and over again to prove to myself, as much as to her, that I wasn't crazy or making this up.

"I knew you could do this, Angelina!" she said.

Together, after an hour of mapping out potential water veins, based on my shaking fits, we decided that I probably felt water, and only the dowser could confirm it the next day. I remember feeling silly halfway through a shaking fit and asking her whether she wanted a milkshake while I was at it? We both laughed. I always use humour, much as Dad did, to break a tense moment—though not everyone appreciates it.

We decided to keep this to ourselves until we had more concrete proof. We made sure to mark my spots so that only she and I recognized them. Then we had a cup of tea, and I said my good-byes, promising to be over bright and early when the dowser arrived the next day.

I got home just in time to cook the evening meal. The kids came home from school, and the house filled with laughter and activity. They asked me about my day, and with a secret smile I replied that it had been a good day and very enlightening. They looked at me strangely, and I shrugged, muttering, "You know me and my strange ways."

Both kids smiled and let it go, asking me what movie I wanted to watch that night. I had decided not to speak of my experiences until I knew Jeannie and I were on the right track. The kids didn't know how to deal with the strange things that had happened since my recovery. It was best that I didn't share more than they could handle.

The next morning, after the kids had left, I made my way to Jeannie's house to observe the dowser at work. In his mid forties, tall, with cropped blond hair and blue eyes, he acted very matter-of-fact about what he did. He asked all kinds of questions that at the time didn't make sense, but today I completely understand the relevance. He walked around the front yard and then intuitively, without any urging from either of us, made his way to the section behind the shed where I'd found the suspected water sources. We had not left any visible clues about our discoveries the previous day, and to our amazement, he said, "This seems to be the best place to dowse."

Jeannie and I looked at each other, trying to hide our excitement.

He looked around and made a few test runs, holding up his dowsing rods. He used a set of rods made of copper, being two pieces of bent wire, and he marked many of the spots we'd marked secretly during our dowsing experience. My shaking fits obviously had something to do with underwater water sources.

I asked the dowser, "Is it possible to locate water without any tools simply by a person feeling?"

He responded that he'd never heard of such a thing, though he supposed it might be possible. That was all I needed to hear. Jeannie and I again exchanged excited glances. The dowser left, after suggesting that the spots I had intuited were possible sites to dig a well. The best well would furnish a minimum of fifteen gallons of water per minute, and a dairy farm of this size could need more. When Jeannie's husband, Fred, came in from the barn, we told him everything that had occurred, and, though sceptical, he agreed to look at our findings.

Once he saw the area dowsed by us and the dowser, he had misgivings and asked whether I could find another, more easily accessed spot. Fred, a jolly fellow and game to try anything, wasn't superstitious. He was an educated man and had seen and heard things in his life that simply could not be explained, so when we shared my experiences of the previous day, he didn't bat an eye and simply nodded.

"Angelina," he said, " I believe you can do this, but the area that you and the dowser mapped out simply will not do. Can't you look at other spots where it would be more convenient to dig?"

I responded, "I suppose I could!" Yet I made it clear that I couldn't guarantee what they would find. They both agreed not to hold me responsible if things didn't pan out as hoped. I decided to do this the next day, because time was a factor.

Early the next morning, I stood on the back deck, waiting for the tanker to finish emptying our pool before I went to Jeannie and Fred's to dowse. I looked over toward their farm, where grain fields separated our properties. It was another warm, balmy day, with the quietness of early morning. The rhythmic hum of the truck pumping water lulled me into an altered state of consciousness, where the subtle and the real world became one and the same.

I heard noises on my left. I looked over and upward and saw three white-tailed hawks circling an area above a tree line that separated our land from Jeannie's. Truly a wonderful gift! It was auspicious to see not only one but three hawks in one viewing. I had been researching the customs and beliefs of my Native American ancestry, and I made a note to check what the hawks wanted to tell me. I grabbed a few fresh cuttings from my apple tree in the Y shape I needed and rushed off to the neighbours' place to dowse.

It turned out that I had found viable sources, and they did dig for water, but although they found it, the well produced only enough for the house, not for the barn. Happy with my success, Jeannie and Fred asked me a few weeks later to come back and try again. I agreed.

We decided that I would attempt an area on the far side of where they had dug.

I found myself walking along the fence line separating our properties. My findings showed a lot of promise, and the sources seemed extremely strong and viable in this area. This spot was by far the best yet and almost too good to be true, by the readings I got. By then, I'd taught myself how to find the depth of the water and the gallons per minute using a pendulum. After an hour of marking, checking, and rechecking, we took a break.

As we sat on the rocks lining the wall between our two properties, I looked over at my house and could clearly see the swimming pool and my manicured gardens. It suddenly dawned on me that I had mapped the exact spot where the hawks had circled a few weeks earlier, while the tanker emptied water from our pool. Astonished, I realized that the hawks had intended me to look in this place. I shared this with Jeannie, and she was equally amazed. Hawks, I realized, are one of my animal totems, and this would not be the last time a hawk guided me to my destiny.

The morning when they planned to dig, they invited me to come and watch. The well-digging truck had just arrived. While I walked across the field with Jeannie at my side, talking up a storm, out of the blue their drilling truck suddenly stopped running. At that same moment, I began to feel nauseated, and the closer I got to the drilling site, the sicker I felt. I shrugged it off to having taken my micronutrient supplements on an empty stomach and approached to sit a few meters from the truck.

The drillers cursed and swore, not understanding why the drilling truck had suddenly stopped and wouldn't start. They kept checking everything, with no luck. It was a mystery to them, for nothing appeared broken and all systems read normally. Scratching their heads, they decided to recheck again in case they'd missed something.

By this time, I had intuited that my nausea somehow tied in with the sudden short circuit of this truck. My nausea had not abated and seemed to be worsening. A memory surfaced, of this happening with our car, and I wondered whether my nausea could be related?

I yelled to them, "Maybe it's an electrical short circuit?"

I waited around with Jeannie for about half an hour, as they opened the hood and checked all possibilities. We decided to go to the house for a cup of tea, because I felt sicker and sicker. By this time, Jeannie also began to feel lightheaded and nauseated. Sensitive herself, she easily picked up feelings from others.

We made our way back toward the house, and about halfway there, my nausea began to abate. In sync with this, the driller truck sputtered and suddenly started, to the consternation of those attempting to fix it. Jeannie and I looked at each other and simply knew that the truck's not starting and my sickness were somehow connected to my new abilities. We didn't know how or why, but somehow I was responsible for this.

It took them all day to dig, and I watched from a distance, not wanting to chance a repetition of the morning's equipment failure. I knew the water was deep but also from a very good source. By end of day, they had hit a vein and had started to cap the well. Long story short, they dug in the exact spot where the hawks had circled, and they found more water than they knew what to do with.

So, Cheyenne, that was the beginning of a career in water dowsing. I've since discovered that I become a human antenna and can see where the water is located before I even go to an area. It helps, with some places being acres in size.

I've developed a technique to find interconnected underwater sources, because these offer the most gallons per minute as a water supply. Now, using a pendulum, I can foresee the depth of the ground where the veins are located. I never miss, which often freaks people out. I simply ask the question, and the pendulum gives me the answer through a process of elimination.

Once the well has been drilled, I always ask about the depth, and the same question for gallons per minute, so that I can substantiate my findings. To date, I have been contracted to dowse dozens of water sources, with each and every one of them resonating with my findings. Some of the locals call me a witch; my neighbour across the way has now forbidden her family from having anything to do with the kids or me. Imagine, in this day and age!

For a few weeks after this discovery, I found it difficult to be on or around any large bodies of water. The event had opened up yet another Pandora's box of treasures, in which seemingly innocent experiences could result in severe consequences, if I weren't careful. Considering that I spent weekends boating, how could I explain to the kids my new-found aversion to a pastime we loved? I decided to grin and bear it, in the hope that my system would again adjust, as it had in the past when a new ability surfaced. This led me to develop techniques of integration to make myself less vulnerable and less sensitive when near water. In the end, it all worked out for the best.

I also told Cheyenne, "I get weak and tired for days and sometimes weeks after something like this surfaces. It drains me, and my body needs to adjust and replenish."

Sharing my experiences with a sympathetic ear felt therapeutic, and I finally decided to spill my guts and see what Cheyenne was made of. Either Cheyenne would say I was crazy and would want nothing more to do with me or would be genuine and help me. I had nothing to lose and everything to gain. The next day I would put it all in writing and find out.

Chapter 19

To Explain the Inexplicable

Mysteries are only such 'til truth is revealed.

—Michèle C. St.Amour

Still Recalling the Past

I pull out another manuscript, which begins...

> I've avoided writing about the more extreme versions of my experiences. They seem so otherworldly, and I'm afraid to appear crazy. How do I get this across to a stranger, who knows nothing about my normally grounded personality? I resolve to finish what I started.
>
> I follow up my report on dowsing with a more confusing phenomenon. I hope Cheyenne can shed some light on it.
>
> Good morning Cheyenne,

Here is another issue I want clarification about.

RE: Getting Plugged In

> Most days I get infused with energy, which I call "getting plugged in." This started soon after I began taking those micronutrient supplements. After three weeks, my body and nervous system began to heal at an unprecedented rate, demanding that I wean myself off the high doses of medication the doctors had prescribed over the years. It was a miracle to feel normal again! Within three months, I was clean of all meds, and these "plug-in" sessions began.
>
> I realize that an overtaxed nervous system caused my severe depression. Sometimes I didn't have enough fuel to make the wheels go around. At other times, the opposite occurred: a build-up of energy from an unknown source would surge through my body, stressing my ill-prepared nervous system.
>
> Anyway, back to "getting plugged in": Overnight, energy begins to tingle and numb my hands and flow through my body in a way I've never felt before. At times, it comes on without warning. I always get plastered to the bed by the power of this energy, and I'm forced to lie down. I can't move or think. It throws me into a deep trance that I come out of hours later, realizing that my consciousness wasn't with me in this world. These "plug-in sessions" have become a normal daily occurrence that I feel nonchalant about now. This, in itself, seems eerie.

I laugh to read these words, which brings me back to the present moment. I gaze at the manuscript I wrote so many years ago. I remember complaining to Cheyenne about the daily plug-ins disrupting my schedule. Cheyenne, quite upset with me, said, "You should be grateful for this type of support, when others have meditated for years and years to have just one of these experiences."

Until that moment I didn't get that it was such a big deal. I didn't consciously understand the magnitude of these "plug-in" gifts I was blessed with.

I return my attention to the manuscript, immersing myself once again in that less aware, less mature Angelina of the past.

> Cheyenne, believe it or not, but on one occasion, I forced myself to snap out of a "plug-in" session because something just didn't feel right, as if I were floating on water. I opened my eyes to see my bed canopy practically in my face. I was floating in mid air, levitating about three feet above the bed. My shock broke the spell, and I came tumbling onto the mattress. I never spoke to anyone about that. Who would believe me?
>
> Another peculiarity is that if any sensitive person happens to be in close proximity to me during these "plugged-in" sessions, he or she has the same energizing experience. Most times I'm alone, thank God! I intuit that they are intense healing sessions. I believe that something or someone is helping me. Somewhere in the recesses of my soul, it seems intimately familiar to me. But then again, I also feel responsible for these sessions in a way I cannot comprehend.
>
> I know deep down that it ties into my buried memories about past lives and my destiny. Something—a voice inside—keeps whispering messages I've never heard or read about, but I know intimately on a soul level.

RE: Psychic Abilities, Feeling Emotions, Empathy

> Out of the blue, a new psychic ability surfaces and is out of control for days. Then it seems to disappear but is still there, although subtle and more believable. It's as if a switch has been turned on high, and the body needs time to adjust the controls to a moderate output. Every time this happens, I spend days tired and burned out.

The words I read from these manuscripts play out in my mental holograph. A much younger Angelina sits in her studio in the flatlands, listening to the quietness and the chirping birds outside.

The sunrises and the sunsets were amazing in the flatlands. I often sat in the gazebo by the pool, enjoying the openness of this place. The winds could be fierce, though, because all of the tree lines had been sacrificed for a higher crop yield.

I had a small office opening onto the driveway. Opposite, a huge bay window overlooked a young forest beyond the fields. Every once in a while, I could spot a moose or a deer chomping away on Fred's crops.

I contemplated whether to tell Cheyenne about the gift of commanding the elements. I decided to see how Cheyenne would react. And so I wrote,

> One weekend while visiting a dear friend, I discovered I could affect the elements. We sat outside by the river on her deck on a windy day, gazing at the choppy water. I created an energy field and told Joan, "Light a candle, and watch what happens."
>
> She laughed and said, "Angelina, it's way too windy!"
>
> I urged her to try, and, to her consternation, the candle lit and the flame did not move.
>
> Next, I said, "Joan, see how rough the river is and how the winds blow so fiercely today?"
>
> She nodded, and I told her to wait a few minutes. After a short time, I pointed at the river, and the waves had calmed to a smooth mirror near her small beach, though still surrounded by choppy, raging waves.
>
> "Watch now," I said. "The river close to us is going to calm down."
>
> She laughed nervously, and not long after that, the river in front of us had also calmed to a mirror-like surface, while all around it, farther out, were turbulent whitecaps.
>
> By now, she was freaked and asked me, "How are you doing this?"

> I said I didn't know—that I simply commanded it and that it would happen within minutes. These events confused me as much as they did her. I told her I had a hard enough time accepting the reality of the occurrences as they manifested, and no sooner had I settled into acceptance and understanding before a new ability or sensitivity would emerge.
>
> I left her not long afterward, seeing that she felt truly uncomfortable with me and everything that had transpired. She did, however, tell me she wasn't surprised that I could do this stuff.

The holograph of my mind goes blurry for a minute. I lose contact with this past, as the words I once wrote rekindle emotions. When the images fade, I snap back to attention. I bring my energy up, and the scenes of the past once again become clear.

I remember thinking, *Okay, so what next?* I looked for inspiration about what else to share with Cheyenne. Ah, yes, the psychic stuff.

RE: Sam

> I have to censor my outings, and often I can't control the psychic connections I make with people around me. I haven't a clue how I'm doing this—it just happens.
> One day early on, when all of this began, while Daniel and I were working at the shop, his good friend Sam came in. As Sam stood in front of me, I suddenly felt a sharp, stabbing pain in my heart and almost doubled over. I knew this pain wasn't mine; it was his. I felt afraid for him. I had visions of his having a heart attack and dying. But I felt so unsure of myself and didn't want to look like a fool, so I shut my mouth and said nothing. Sam, only forty years old, seemed very healthy, so it just didn't make any sense. I was afraid to say anything.
> When Daniel came to the front desk after Sam had left, I told him, "Daniel, the weirdest thing just

happened. You know how sensitive I've become of late and how my family is like that?"

He looked at me with a perplexed expression.

"You know," I said, "how we have these ways of 'seeing' things that others do not?"

He nodded, but now he had "that look" on his face, a combination of doubt and underlying fear. I told him what I had felt when Sam stopped in. Daniel appeared concerned but sceptical, and we left it at that.

Three days later, we got a phone call that his friend Sam had died of a massive heart attack. When Daniel told me, he was as white as a ghost and looked at me strangely. I began crying from guilt and shame that I hadn't spoken up and given his friend a chance. I had failed, and this would be my karma. I learned a good lesson that day: that if I had a feeling, I had to speak up and not worry what others would think. My pride wasn't worth someone's death.

I wiped a tear as I wrote these words to Cheyenne, still feeling the pain of that loss. Shaking the mood off, I continued to describe my experiences.

RE: Spirits

> My latest phenomenal discovery is "seeing dead people" and such. Something or someone seems to be orchestrating events to coincide with an ability, proving to my sceptic's mind that it is possible. My boundaries between reality and sanity are constantly being challenged.

RE: Cat Drowning

> Last winter I had yet another enlightening day. I failed a test miserably, but I did learn a hard life lesson. Early one morning, I headed out to my studio in the building adjacent to our house in the flatlands. Lost in thought,

I wasn't paying attention to my surroundings when I should have. Regrets get us nowhere, so it's best to make the most of our experiences.

My intuition commanded me to go to the swimming pool, a few hundred feet from the path I walked to my office. On that blustery morning, my little voice kept telling me to come closer and closer and to look over the edge into the pool, but I was so rushed, I pushed it away as nonsense and ignored the little voice of reason.

A few hours later, our dog Spike, in the only language he had, communicated to me that something was in the pool. Finally, I caught on, and, in a panic, I ran to the edge of the deck and looked down into the pool. To my horror, there lay little Kiki, our calico cat, half frozen in water and ice.

The shock sent chills through my body. I couldn't believe this had happened again, because it wasn't the first time we'd lost a cat to drowning in the pool. My sense of intuition had screamed to me that morning. If I had listened earlier, I possibly could've saved her. Even worse, the night before I had dreamed of a red-haired girl drowning in our pool.

My mind goes blank, and I find myself back in my mountain studio, feeling the pain of that memory. Today, I clearly recognize my distracted mental state as being an ungrounded condition, with all of my senses blocked from my awareness and my mind "in the clouds"—dulled to happenings in the physical world around me.

I still deal with the guilt of not listening more closely to my inner voice. It took me forever to tell my daughter, because I waited until she asked about her pet. Another hurtful life experience, and to this day I give thanks to these souls that sacrificed themselves so that I could learn some important lessons. I return my attention to the manuscript, and the past resurfaces.

RE: Cousin from California

On a more positive note, I was intuitively guided to check in on my dear cousin Darren in California, whom I had not heard from in years. I had a feeling that things weren't going well for him. I wrote a brief email, asking how he was. I could feel anxiousness inside him. He soon wrote back, pouring his heart out and asking me how I knew he needed someone to talk to.

I realized that distance didn't affect my clarity in picking up on feelings or intuitions.

And so, as weeks turned into months, adventure upon adventure unravelled the workings of my inner world. From weird dreams to synchronistic incidents, the hidden inner world of spirit gradually revealed itself to me.

Chapter 20

WolfWoman

"The human spirit is stronger than anything that can happen to it."

—C. C. Scott

I remember my first visit from WolfWoman . . .

One cold windy day, with winter on its way, I sat in my studio in the flatlands. I felt much better after taking the micronutrients. My senses had tuned into otherworldly, mysterious places and dimensions.

Through the eerie silence, a mysterious voice called me to come to the back window. In a trancelike state, I got up and slowly moved towards the window, to look out over acres of fields. A glimmer on the horizon caught my eye. I focused on it and sank into a hypnotic altered state. The scene outside suddenly changed to mid winter. At first, I saw only heavy snow buffeting to and fro. Then, in the distance, I could make out a determined figure moving towards me at great speed.

I peered into the blizzard, and as the form got closer, I discerned the build of a man—or was it a woman? No matter, for this person moved with the grace of a woman but the strength of a man. The figure seemed to be garbed from head to toe in leather. I strained my eyes, because I couldn't believe what I saw: wolf skins? Was that a wolf's head on top of the person?

"Yes," I heard a distant voice answer. Then this same voice echoed from within me. I quickly realized it was a spirit, talking to me in the language of the spirit realm. I wanted to reach out and touch the shimmering apparition to be sure it was only a spectre.

I squinted, for wolves seemed to be running by the person's side. Again, from within and from afar, I heard, "Yes, these are my companions!"

"Who are you?" I asked out loud. The power of this spirit overwhelmed me.

The spirit then spoke to me in a riddle, her deep voice echoing through my mind. By now, I could make out the female tone of her voice.

> I am S/He who walks alone;
> S/He who runs with the wolves
> S/He who calls herself WolfWo/man;
> I am leader of this band.
>
> I forever travel the winds of change,
> Winter woman and Gaia at my front and side
> Forever guiding the pack that changes on the wings
> of passing time.
>
> I am S/He,
> An ancient warrior who travels through the ages

I carry a powerful and sacred staff.
I am S/he—male and female perfected.

I stood still, afraid to move, and I strained to hear everything she said. The staff in her hands, its point towering inches above her head, seemed to bear the head of a dragon. It was impressive in size and height, for she herself had to be at least six feet tall. She then whispered in my ear, "You have very few winters to prepare, before the gathering in the spring of that fateful year!"

Her words confused me, for I wasn't sure what she referred to.

Hearing my thoughts, she answered, "Do not fret. As you awaken evermore, all will become clear, and you will heed my council and that of those guided to you."

She paused, then said, "Shape shifters from afar will gather by the campfire at nightfall. The sacred time will be upon you; you are one of the chosen."

She then held up the staff and whispered, "Do you see this?"

I nodded.

"When you find yourself settled in that sacred place, you will be guided by our brother Hawk to this very staff. Pay attention, for one day the ancient ones of this sacred space will show you the way. It will be the sign that it has begun."

In confusion, I asked her, "What has begun?"

She ignored my question.

A melding suddenly occurred, and we were no longer separate but one. I was now part of her. I could see clearly through our eyes, as I looked down to her left leg. Garbed in skins and buckskin pants, she told me that she was once human and lived with the wolves.

Scenes of the past revealed themselves. My first impression of her size was accurate: a big-enough woman, and strong, she knew how to survive in the wild.

She shared memories with me about having to leave her village. Her size and her ability to see the future and talk to the spirit world rivalled that of the medicine man, so one dark cold night she was forced to leave for fear of losing her life. I watched her say farewell to those closest to her, and she slipped off with her small bundle, never to be seen by them again.

WolfWoman told me all of this happened in a time before any white settlers had discovered this continent.

She then permitted me to connect empathically with her, and I felt her essence to the core. I was the watcher but also her, in a peculiar way. She'd learned to live with being lonely at times, for she had become part wild wolf. Early on, a pack had befriended her; hence, she could never live among humans again. The wolves became her family and her true friends.

Through our empathic connection, I could feel her strength and toughness but also her gentleness and sensitivity. With her senses honed, she was part of Mother Earth. The glimmering images before me shifted to scenes of her life when she lived with the wolves. Clearly, she knew their ways well. They travelled together and spent many years as a pack. A lifetime played out before me in mere seconds.

These scenes slowed down, and she showed me her time of passing: when death claimed her physical body, and she decided to accept the gift of becoming a SpiritSoul. I asked her what a SpiritSoul was, and she explained it was when a soul decided to continue its journey on Earth, guiding humans through the spirit world. It was simply another form of experience a soul could decide to live before returning to the Ocean of Souls—a stepping-stone of evolution for souls that developed the ability of passing with consciousness. Scenes of her passing now played out.

One winter, she hobbled slowly towards a rocky cliff and finally fell to all fours. Then she entered a small dark cave. Her wolf pack family surrounded her and kept wild animals at bay. She remained in this cave until she was no more. This took three days and three nights, as was prophesied of all great passings. She hadn't been feeling well and knew it was time to end this chapter of her life and continue serving from another. The wolves protected her, as she curled up in a dark corner of the hidden cavern. Her time finally came, and I was blessed to witness those last moments when she transcended pain and a bright, clear light appeared and surrounded her, embracing her in bliss. Her face lit up with joy, and a painless ascent began. I saw her body from this life slump into a ball, as her soul essence rose and floated upward in a gossamer, whitish, smoky cloud. She turned and looked down at her companions and whispered, "I will be back. Do as I bid you, and in time I will return to you in spirit."

The pack began howling in unison, a serenade of farewell in honour of their friendship. Once she passed on, they devoured her as a final act of love. She had asked the wolves to do this, so that her spirit would stay with them and be pure. Her SoulEssence has been with them ever since, as she wanders through her playground in the spirit world of Earth.

In that moment I knew that she was ancient, and her spirit was old and wise. To this day, the powerful spirit guide named Wolf Wo/man still runs with the wolves. To me, she always appears garbed with a wolf's head attached to the hood of her cloak. This wolf's head hood rests on her back, and she occasionally wears it as a head covering, giving her the look of a fierce wolf warrior. She'd created the wolf-skin cloak only from the strong ones she loved that had passed on, in honour of their strength and courage.

I saw her once again, walking purposefully towards me, as my attention returned to her first visit. She called to me from the world of spirit, walking through a snowy field in a blizzard with her wolf companions by her side. These wolves are spirit wolves—they are snow white, blending in with and then emerging from the blowing tempest. She then picked up her pace to sprint into an outright run, and as they got closer and closer, I heard her whisper, "I will come when you need me."

As they reached the edge of our land, they all suddenly shape-shifted into the wind and the snow. They became one with Winter Woman and Gaia Woman, who suddenly appeared by their side. The scenes before me slowly dissipated, and once again I found myself looking out onto bare fields. WolfWo/man's voice whispered to me from afar that her spirit walks with me and protects me.

I felt a kinship with her, for some strange reason. She and I shared a similar loneliness, tinged with sadness. It tied into this knowing that couldn't be spoken of. It was something that medicine people felt, for the journey that brought this knowledge forever changed us and separated us from others. We understood and accepted and learned to live with it as part of our destiny. In the end we learned it was but an illusion created by the ego. Hence, in time, if we persevered, it would transform us and unite us with our source.

Present Day

This memory brings me back to my mountain studio, and I glance over at the dragon staff propped up in a corner. The natural wooden staff stands over six and a half feet high, topped by a prominent dragon's head formed from a knotted tree limb.

One day, not long after Hubby and I had settled on the mountain, I had been walking with Hubby in the forest around our house, and I heard the voices of forest spirits speak to me. Within minutes, I found myself at a portal in time near a spring, where the veils between dimensions are thin. The spirits told me to stop and look down, and there, on the ground, lay the dragon staff. I recognised it from my visions of WolfWo/man. I hesitated, not quite believing what had happened, for this would also mark the beginning of the end. Could I ignore this quest and pretend this hadn't happened? Deep down, I knew this wasn't feasible. The truth was fast unravelling, and it portended something sacred and important.

As I bent to pick up the staff lying on the fallen leaves, I heard the voice of its previous owner. I looked around to catch a glimpse of WolfWo/man, but she was nowhere to be seen.

> "As I told you years ago, here is the time of reckoning upon mankind. Keep this staff sacred and use it wisely when the time comes. You will be guided in the future on its powers and activation as you come into yours. Oshtalo, my dear—a blessing in the language of our Native ancestors. Oshkiwaanaga, 'you are being called home.' We will meet again soon."

As the years went by, I was guided from mentor to mentor. I learned that WolfWoman truly did act as a guide and a guardian for me, for she once helped me battle the demons that came to destroy me during many long years and not long after I met Cheyenne. Being too busy defending myself, I didn't know she had protected me then. I couldn't recognize her in those times. Her shape-shifting abilities enable her to camouflage herself in the guise of one of her white spirit wolves. But no matter, I now recognize her imprint when she appears and have learned to pay heed.

Since that first visit, she makes herself known to me whenever a sacred event is upon me or when I need to watch my back. She lets me know when I must pay extra attention to events and people. She often prepares me for momentous, life-changing times.

Chapter 21

A Trine Experience— The Power of Three

"When you do things from your soul, you feel a river moving in you, a joy."

—Jalal al-Din Muhammad Rumi

Again, I'm surprised by the innocence of this Angelina, still so unconscious of her destiny. My attention returns to the manuscripts and the years when I described my experiences to Cheyenne.

RE: Entities, Beings from Other Worlds

> I discovered that our world is littered with "beings," besides those that have passed on. Just as people do, some beings have a high vibration, manifest goodwill, and offer us support and aid, appearing as spirit guides and angelic energies. Others, though, have lower

vibrations and are not so good—for example, demons, suckers, and more—and feed off our energy.

I scrolled through the manuscript, noting the dates as the weeks went by, while I continued to share other experiences with Cheyenne.

Good morning, Cheyenne,

I hope this beautiful sunny day finds you well. Yesterday the neighbour's puppy, not understanding the danger of the road, got his hind leg nicked by a truck zipping by. My neighbour Jeannie asked if I could take care of the kids while she ran up to the animal hospital with the dog.

While I waited for her kids to get off the bus, feelings and images of the dog and his pain bombarded me. Suddenly, I felt the prick of a needle in my back. Following the needle prick sensation, my body became numb, and I felt dizzy and sleepy. Jeannie later told me the vet had given the dog a painkiller before setting the broken leg, and we noted that our times for this synchronized. I also intuitively pinpointed the areas of damage, which Jeannie confirmed.

This morning when I went over to the neighbour's to help their cat (see below), that puppy looked me straight in the eye and wouldn't stop staring at me, as if he knew exactly what had transpired the previous day and how I had helped by relieving his pain and anxiety. I confirmed this, as I caught the odd mind picture coming from the dog. I've discovered how to speak telepathically to certain receptive animals by sending mind pictures.

RE: Another Cat Incident

Being such a good friend, my neighbour Jeannie was often instrumental in giving me opportunities to experience my abilities when they surfaced, such as the dowsing. The day after the puppy incident, she called because they'd found their favourite barn cat lying on the floor in shock, and they had no clue what was wrong. I went over to help the cat as best I could.

As I stood over the poor thing, it had no signs of injury but was in obvious pain. I reached out to it and connected to the cat empathically. I laid my hands on the cat and commanded that the life force come forth to help the cat. Within a few minutes, I felt the pain in the cat's hips go numb, as did my own hips.

We later found out the cat was paralyzed. I wondered what had caused such an injury. Cats are normally so agile; it was a mystery to us all. I decided to try something new to see what had happened to the cat.

I sent out the command for pictures, and suddenly they started playing in my mind's eye. I saw the spot where the cat had first been discovered, which Fred later confirmed. Then I saw how everything had happened, in ethereal, wispy visions, as if I were looking through a smoky lens that cleared for brief moments. I could see that the cat had been crossing over to the other side of the barn through two stalls, and a cow had stepped on it by accident. The cat let out a yell and crawled to the place where Fred eventually discovered it.

When I shared this insight with Fred, he said that would make sense, given the type of injury the cat had suffered. The vet later confirmed it when he came to put the cat out of its misery. When I learned that the vet would soon put the cat to sleep, I worried about how this would affect me. I didn't always find it easy to break the empathic connection, which could last for hours and at times days. Luckily, in this instance I broke the connection before he put the cat down. The cat went in a peaceful manner, worthy of the love the neighbours felt for it.

So, Cheyenne, how did I manage to see the past? I'm still confused about this. I simply asked, and it played out in my mind like a memory. I did doubt its veracity, however, until others more or less confirmed it.

RE: Friends in Cincinnati

They say *jamais deux sans trois* ("never two without three"). On the third day, a Monday afternoon, as I went to take my nap, for some reason I thought about our friends in Cincinnati. Daniel's friend Patrick had married Cindy, a Southern beauty, and had settled there, enjoying life in a warmer climate. As I lay in bed, Cindy's image came to mind, and the next thing I knew, I made a connection. As I scanned the insights and feelings coming through, I sensed she was pregnant. From within me, a voice softly echoed, "It's a girl!"

That night I decided to give Cindy a call. When I asked whether she could possibly be pregnant, she was stunned, because for a few days she had suspected she might be. She had avoided thinking about it, because they already had a one-year-old son, Matthew. We began exchanging news, while in the background I heard Matthew crying.

With this in mind, I connected to the baby, and I could feel that he wasn't well. When I inquired, Cindy said that they were waiting for the doctor to call. In the meantime, I decided to tell her everything I felt might be wrong with the child. I sensed a possible ear infection, creating an upset stomach, which made Matthew not want to eat, and the poor kid had a headache from crying. I felt empathy for him, and within moments I had a headache, although Cindy told me Matthew had quieted down.

Not long afterward, the baby had calmly gone to sleep. Obviously, I took something on in that connection, but what and how? I need help in understanding this, Cheyenne. A few days later I received an email from Cindy, telling me that my suspicions about the Matthew's ailments had been confirmed. They thanked me for my intervention and support, because the child had been quiet from the time we hung up until the doctor finally called them back with instructions for proper care.

I didn't feel well for a few days, obviously from taking on Matthew's symptoms. How is this happening and how can I stop it?

RE: Precognition?

The first time I had a conscious precognitive vision, I doubted its validity. I shrugged it off to coincidence and imagination. I figured, *Well, that's what Dad calls "seeing."* Then, more and more often, I became conscious of "seeing things from the future before they happened." They manifested not long afterward in life as I had witnessed them in my mind. That's when I linked this to Dad's stories about our family history and us being "Seers."

Sometimes they came as a dream. My dad called it "the second sight."

I know I inherited this clairvoyant ability from my father's side of the family. Dad has often shared family stories that have precognitive undertones. I later discovered that "the sight" predominates in Celtic cultures. Since Dad has so much Scottish and English blood, mixed with Native, it's no wonder we have these abilities inherent in our DNA.

I remember Dad telling us how Grandpa Howard had foretold his death a few weeks before he died. While sitting in the living room one Sunday, Grandpa Howard yelled out, "Who died?"

Everyone came running, wondering what he was talking about, and he pointed to the road and described all of the people he could see. My dad's people were simple country folk who gathered every Sunday at my grandmother's. As everyone gazed out the living room window, they saw only the empty road. My grandfather went on, describing the whole scene in detail, right up to the horse-drawn buggy with the hearse. Little did Grandpa Howard know he was watching his own funeral, which played out three weeks later (there's that trine again), exactly as he had described, including Aunt so-and-so's clothing and blue hat. My dad has also had some interesting precognitive experiences.

The main issue once again with this latest ability of precognition is that I always feel drained and tired for days afterward.

Present Day

As I read this, I recall a conversation with Cheyenne at a much later time. Cheyenne mentioned that I gave the impression that I wanted things to slow down. If this were true, I had to *intend* them to slow down. My intention to slow my development had to be strong, because my enthusiasm and curiosity fuelled an acceleration of my development. This made it difficult for me to process everything, or so Cheyenne said.

We discussed at length the problems that arose when a person fell into these types of abilities without any prior knowledge. I was told to always remember to maintain my centre and keep myself grounded, at peace. At that time, I didn't realize that most people had no idea what grounded actually meant, except as a loose concept. In later years, I was forced to explore this, in order to truly fulfil my destiny.

I returned to the manuscript and the email to Cheyenne recounting my recent connection to a renowned terrorist. I'd created the connection simply by wondering where he could be one night as I watched the news. At this time, media speculation about his possible whereabouts saturated the airwaves. All of the stations dramatized the recent events, while the hunt for the terrorist continued. At some point, a full picture of the rebel appeared onscreen. In that moment, I let my guard down. Before I realized it, I had reached out and connected to him empathically. Then a holograph opened and scenes started flashing before my mind's eye, bombarding me with disjointed thoughts and physical pains. It lasted only a few minutes, but it took me hours to download all of the information and make any sense of it. The next morning, weeks after our initial communication, I told Cheyenne what had occurred and my impressions of the incident.

I wrote,

> I feel this terrorist has cancer in his gut, and I see clearly where he is at this moment and how he and his army of men have hidden in some type of catacombs in the mountains. They hide their vehicles by camouflaging them with nets. I keep getting the colour of sand here and there.

I saw an arid desert landscape in my mind but had no way of confirming any of it. The terrorist felt nervous and very scared. Trucks and machinery drove into the side of the mountain, which the terrorists had covered with sandy-looking false camouflage walls that looked like the terrain. Not long after I sent this report, Cheyenne emailed me a cautionary response:

> Angelina, stay away from the energy of this terrorist. Again, I say stay away from this energy. You are not ready for this type of challenge. This can be very dangerous, so please heed my advice.
>
> I would like you to restrict your experiments to simply letting yourself feel another's energies, thoughts, and so on. One way to do this is to reach out with your heart to the energy, the tree, the dog, the person, whatever sounds or words you want to use, but I think it'll be clear when you do it.
>
> *Namaste,*
> *Cheyenne*

A few days later, a picture on TV showed where the army suspected the terrorist to be hiding. To my consternation, it was the exact mountain I had visualized a few days earlier and the canyon that the army had to cross to get to the hideout. I knew the catacombs had a back exit in that mountain and that the famous terrorist had escaped from the catacombs and sequestered himself a few miles away, leaving half of his men in the underground caves to act as decoys should they be attacked.

Present Day

Thinking back to that precognitive event, I honestly feel that Cheyenne overreacted to my connection to the terrorist. I recognized a fearful attitude coming from Cheyenne, which surprised me, given Cheyenne's normally grounded sense of right and wrong.

Being an outsider looking in, I clearly saw that something evil surrounded these terrorist events. I intuitively felt that on some level, the terrorist had been made the scapegoat by another entity in a far more dangerous game. When I connected to him, I felt no evil coming from this man but instead a sense that he had been betrayed. In time, I felt sure that the truth about many conspiracies would surface. What the news had reported didn't come close to revealing the reality of the situation. Big Brother had tightened the noose.

Not long after the terrorist incident, I felt a strong need to share another incident with Cheyenne, when one of my parents' closest friends passed away. I wrote,

RE: Elizabeth Connection

> This dead woman's connection with me felt energetically powerful but non-invasive. She wanted to give me messages for her children, whom I had grown up with but had lost touch with once Mom died. The only way she could accomplish this was to come into me to do it, because her communication skills as a spirit were limited. I didn't feel any danger from her, so I permitted her to start easing into me. I felt comfortable with it, and

because she had things to tell me and had no other way to communicate, I let it happen.

I slipped into the strong sensations, which I could handle for only a short time before asking her to back off for a while. She did, without too much coaxing on my part. It had actually been long enough for her telepathic messages to come across to me. She wanted me to tell her two daughters and her son that she loved them and had not suffered. They shouldn't worry, and soon enough they would be together again. Their father had joined her. He was happy and said hi. She promised to watch over them and their children.

She hovered in mid-air for a short time but then left and never came back.

I feel she was a part of me, much as I do when I pick up other people's inner essence from an empathic connection. I experienced the physical pain she felt upon her death, and I later confirmed how she had died. Luckily, her pain was short-lived and transient, as these things usually are.

I remember that when this happened, at one point I suddenly felt as if I couldn't breathe. I panicked for a moment, then realized I was in control. But I didn't step into her energy field; instead, she stepped into mine, and we became one for a brief time.

When these incidents occur, I go to a dark place, similar to when spirits come to us in dreams. They step out of the void of darkness, where the air is thick, dense, heavy, and grey and time, as we know it, does not exist. A deep trance overcomes me. Curiously, it reminds me of the place I escaped to in my years of sickness, when I could no longer bear the mental and emotional turmoil.

Cheyenne suggested that as long as I could get complete imagery and get these experiences verified, I should continue to refine this type of clairvoyance. I should stick with verifiable experiments and see how much detail I could get from them.

This began a training period of three years (there's that trine again) of learning and mastering, as I became aware of my true self and my destiny. Someday the trine enigma will be clarified.

Chapter 22

The Sacred: Initiation

*You are not a drop in the ocean. You
are the entire ocean in a drop.*

—Rumi

Present Day

I open a new manuscript dated a few weeks later than the last one and read,

> Good morning, Cheyenne,
>
> What is happening, exactly, when my awareness shifts, so that I may better deal and adjust?
> Why do I get sick all of the time with each new "ability" that surfaces?

So, everything is energy. We both know that. I sense and feel the areas of pain in living things and the sources. My connections with these "others" relieve their suffering, but at times I "take on" their pain. So, how does this happen? How can I stop it? There has to be a way to manage this.

Cheyenne suggested I get energy sessions and said that "becoming ill immediately after helping someone with these energies is not healthy and must be addressed."

Cheyenne's words reminded me of the most recent happenings, so I wrote,

> I find myself empathically connected with people, and the emotional resonance feels overwhelming, out of control.
>
> For instance, the first time this happened, I had accidently slipped on my neighbour Jeannie's jacket. I immediately fell into a deep trance. I felt all of her anxiety. I felt horrible to be frozen in this numbness, as if I were dying or as if I, Angelina, had disappeared and would not come back. Next, I remember my *SoulEssence* (the energy of the soul) trying to jump out of my body through my head, as if being pushed out by another force. Frightened, I flung the jacket off and dropped to my hands and knees, gasping for breath. This scared the crap out of me!
>
> The other night, while at a rock concert with some friends, I became very uncomfortable as the evening wore on. I felt a steady bombardment of emotions and physical pains from the people around me. I tried to break the connections, but nothing worked. Once I got home, I spent the night vomiting, as my body released the toxins and the emotions I'd ingested.
>
> I'm a veritable magnet, because everything I come in contact with seems to enter my system. How do I trigger

this? It doesn't happen all of the time, so how am I creating these connections?

I now realize that I've connected to everything and everyone empathically and taken things on since I was young, but it's getting worse. I heard that some healers have even died from taking on too many ills from others.

This morning I woke up feeling disconnected from life, as if something in my system had blocked the energy in my neck, and my back felt stiff as a board. Maybe I should undergo that initiation you mentioned?

I know something—a new ability—wants to come through.

I am getting too much too fast and too often, with side effects I can barely handle. I have tried to ask it to slow down, as you suggested, but it isn't working!

I think I need to build up shields or something and learn control over these sensitivities I'm being bombarded with.

A few days passed, and I wondered if what I'd shared with Cheyenne was too overwhelming. On a beautiful, sunny, unusually warm fall day, I decided to do some weeding. I loved the physical demands of tending my gardens, where I often caught glimpses of fairies, spirit guides, and gnomes watching me curiously.

When I finally went up to my studio office and checked my emails, I saw a missive from Cheyenne.

Hi, Angelina,

I have been very busy these last days and wanted to wait to respond at length to your last e-mail. Clearly, after all of these emails describing your experiences, you want my help in sorting them out and preparing for what else may surface. Is this correct?

If so, I feel it is now time for the initiation I spoke to you about. I'll be waiting to hear from you.

Namaste,
Cheyenne

I sat back in my chair, pondering. I looked for that gut feeling that I needed to take this step next. Never one to procrastinate, I immediately typed a reply, telling Cheyenne that doing the initiation felt right. I sent this off and heard the kids getting off the bus. Time to get supper ready. Tomorrow would be soon enough to follow up on Cheyenne's suggestions.

Early the next morning, Cheyenne's reply was in my inbox:

Hi, Angelina,

It's important to keep one thing in mind about all alchemical initiations. Their effects are always appropriate.

I intuitively feel that this initiation will bring welcome and productive peace and order to your current process, while providing a boost to your spiritual development.

I'd wondered whether I could take much more pressure. Almost afraid to believe this was what I'd been looking for, I kept reading.

I feel that our intuitions of it will provide insight into your current processes and will also help us assess your gifts. As we progress forward, I'd like to sort out exactly what happens to you, because I'll also want to objectively verify your various gifts, to the extent that this is possible—no offense intended.

I don't know you very well yet, and I have been around things spiritual and psychic people with all types of energy-healing abilities for some time now.

I threw my head back, laughing, at Cheyenne being so polite and careful.

> I get a good intuitive feeling about us working together. Nothing happens by accident; there are no coincidences.
>
> Opening the spiritual eyes, without proper guidance—and even with it, for that matter—can be a slippery process and full of illusion. I have worked with and been around many people with psychic enfoldments who have had any number of problematic issues regarding these matters, ranging from fear to illusions, delusions, and glamour, all mixed in with some genuine psychic insight.
>
> Unfortunately, a tremendous degree of glamour is associated with psychic ability. In the Buddhist traditions, psychic powers are placed very low on the hierarchy as evidence of spiritual development. In many ways, psychic ability is perhaps one of the most seductive of all forms of glamour. Like all forms of glamour, be it beauty, wealth, intelligence, social status, power, or fame, psychic power can and will serve to feed the ego and is an illusion that masks and impairs true spiritual development.

As Cheyenne had warned, I now had a constant watchdog over my ego and its sneaky ways. I went back to the email.

> This is not to say that spiritually advanced beings are without so-called psychic abilities—quite the contrary. However, the difference is that their psychic abilities are by-products of their spiritual development. They also take them very much for granted as natural human abilities—which is my view as well.
>
> Valid spiritual teachings have been around for thousands of years and in myriad forms. However, there is a lot of bullshit pretending to be valid spiritual teaching, and a lot of the same type of professed teachers.

Let me know what you want to do.

Namaste,
Cheyenne

After digesting Cheyenne's words, I decided to respond while my thoughts were fresh and clear.

Hi, Cheyenne,

I appreciate your honesty. My life has had its fair share of glamour, and I've come to know that the idea is far grander than the reality.

I thought of my years as an entrepreneurial fashion designer. It was such a superficial world. Glamour wasn't what it was cut out to be. It almost killed me, and that, in itself, was a rude awakening.

I have not gone looking for any of these "psychic abilities," but I have no regrets, because all of this stuff has made my life richer.

I'm not looking to prove my abilities to you. I just want to simplify the process, so that I don't get sick or imbalanced. I would like you to help me make these transitions easier to understand and control.

Angelina

The next day I was booked for my first initiation. As the time approached, the butterflies in my stomach turned to a buzzing fanfare. I lay down in a comfortable spot, where I wouldn't be disturbed for about an hour or so. After the remote session, I would type up a report of my impressions and insights and send it out.

I glanced at the clock: 10 am. The energy had built up for the last fifteen minutes. I soon lost consciousness of physical reality. In this dream state, part of me remained completely awake. The next hour passed quickly, with mind pictures and visions flashing before my eyes. When everything had calmed down, I went to my computer and began to type.

Cheyenne, here is an accounting of what I experienced.

I felt the energy, like a heavy pressure, and it lulled me into a quiet, calm state. It reminded me of my afternoon plug-ins.

Transported to another time and place, I saw myself draped in a white dress like an angel with no wings, but I did fly. In my right hand, I held a crystal ball of light. I was waiting for the moment to be right.

A figure with long brown hair, garbed in a cloak, appeared in the distance and floated toward me, to stop only a few feet away. I intuitively called him Jesus. His beautiful serene smile said, "Welcome back." We gazed into each other's eyes, and we exchanged a lot of information, but I'm unable to recall it. In that moment, though, I knew why I had come to Earth and who I was, though I haven't a clue about this now that I'm awake.

Such peace came over me! I sighed in relief, knowing everything would be okay. Jesus reached over, placed his right hand on my forehead, and made the sign of the cross. He kissed me on my third eye and then on my lips, as ethereal music echoed from above.

"We are with you. Seek out the knowledge of who you are, and in this journey of remembrance you will awaken and reunite with us, your family. You are blessed this day. Go forth with my blessings to fulfil your destiny of helping the others recall and come home, as you have."

We seemed to exchange ideas about some kind of mission or destiny. He left by saying, "Thy will be done." Then he turned and went back into the light that had first brought him to me.

Cheyenne, I need to remember something but cannot. Deep down, I know it's very important, but it's just below the surface of my consciousness. It concerns my spiritual purpose. When I asked this Jesus guy for clarity, he simply said, "In time, child, in time." He disappeared into a light so bright and so familiar, I felt as if I had come home.

So many things from the past linked to this vision. I look forward to hearing your impressions. Thank you, Cheyenne, for your support.

Angelina

I sent the email off and kept busy all afternoon. I still felt odd effects from the initiation, which, despite having a calming effect on my nervous system, had energized me somehow. A few hours later, I received a response from Cheyenne.

Hi, Angelina,

Just read your email. Wonderful. One dimension of the initiations is to empower your sense of spiritual purpose. Here are my impressions of what occurred.

I noticed via my third eye vision that Angelina showed surprise and struggled and pressed against—as if trying to escape—a glass tube encasing her, as you would see in images of sleeping beauty when she rested, asleep and oblivious to the truth.

Yet after a bit, all of this settled, and became balanced and in harmony. When the energy I work with first showed up, Angelina seemed to get a bit panicky. I got the intuition that another entity occupied or coexisted with Angelina, and this was what got panicky with my presence, not Angelina.

During the next half hour, Angelina's energies became balanced, stabilized, and activated. All was peaceful.

Suddenly, I observed Angelina being absorbed into the energy of Maitreya (whom some would call Jesus). This persisted for a bit of time. As the initiation came to a close and Maitreya was to leave, He became gigantic and appeared to infuse into the very structure of everything that surrounded Him. Yet still, a large head of Him persisted, as he nodded a Namaste bow to Angelina and then the head expanded, dissolved, and blended into the surrounding cosmos.

I intuit that this was very important to Angelina, quite impactful, and promises well for the future.

Cheyenne

I could see that our reports correlated well with each other. I wrote back,

> About this entity you spoke of, hovering or sharing space around me, is something coexisting with me for some reason?

As I wrote these words, an eerie voice in the background echoed, *"Yesss..."*

I jumped out of my seat, looking around, but the room was empty. Could this voice be linked to the entity Cheyenne had picked up? I finished my email to Cheyenne.

> The session was important and impactful. I thank you for the experience. It has given me a sense of stability and confidence.

Angelina

In the end, Cheyenne never completely answered my questions about this session, except to say not to feel uncomfortable about my Jesus observations. Cheyenne had done a lot of past life work and remembered witnessing the crucifixion. Cheyenne believed that many souls from that time were incarnating now in service to the ascension of the Earth.

Present Day

The breeze tinkling my wind chimes brings me back to the here and now. It must be around noon—time to take a break. Hubby will be home in the late afternoon, and I'd like to finish reading the next few manuscripts before making dinner. I blow out the candles and walk to the house, enjoying the soft wind.

I wonder whether this entity Cheyenne had picked up had been Teacher? Or maybe the part of me that had gone dormant, the inner consciousness that had a life of its own?

And Teacher wasn't saying anything, which was curious. She had been awfully quiet of late.

Chapter 23

The White Place—A World Beyond

"The mind is made of all one learns, one experiences, one's loves and one's remembrances. Therefore man is that which his mind contains. A collection of all he learns and experiences in life."

— Inayat Khan

The next day I'm back at my desk on the mountaintop, anxious to go through my manuscripts. I once again immerse myself in the past—in the time when I learned about the White Place.

After my first initiation, Cheyenne and I decided to address managing my energy field. Why, whenever an ability surfaced or became more pronounced, did I suffer symptoms of my past sickness?

I later realized that these psychic senses ran extraordinary amounts of energy, similar to electrical power, through my nervous system.

During these times, I learned to take extra doses of micronutrients, which seemed to support my nervous system from the added stress the psychic abilities caused when I shifted awareness.

Weeks went by, and I learned the art of healing, as well as how to do this from a distance. As I became more proficient, I could remotely treat a person or an animal at a distance as if they were physically with me. Yet with certain strong connections, I felt sick and drained afterward, to the point of needing to go to sleep. Cheyenne cautioned me not to overdo it until we understood my issues more clearly.

Sometimes I subliminally told individuals to relax, calming them and their pain without experiencing any side effects myself. In many cases, these people said they heard their minds telling them to relax and be calm.

Occasionally, out of the blue, someone would come to mind, and I knew intuitively that the person had thought of me. To test my theory, I called the person on the phone to ask whether he or she had been thinking about me. Most times, the person responded, "Well, yes, I was. How did you know?"

One of my first teachers, Rose, a clairvoyant tarot reader, helped me understand the extent of what I could do with my mind. She and I set up a test, in which I would attempt to bilocate to her.

Without Rose knowing the day or the time I would remotely "pop in," she went about her life as usual. One afternoon, I decided to test my bilocating abilities. I held her mental image in my mind's eye. My body surged with vibrations of higher energy, as my mind travelled through time and space. I saw a light and realized I was floating at the ceiling, looking down on a petite blonde woman sitting in front of her computer.

I recognized Rose and noticed the stripes and the tones of her clothing. I then bonded with her, which allowed me to sense her thoughts and emotions. I knew intuitively that she was writing to a friend of hers. Her striped calico cat lay on the table beside her. Suddenly, she tensed, sensing my presence. She turned and looked me straight in the eye. When we shared our experiences later that day, she confirmed that she'd felt my presence but couldn't see me.

After months of Cheyenne's mentoring, I achieved a degree of self-mastery over my abilities. My shields became stronger, as I unconsciously grounded my energies on the physical plane. One Saturday, I happened to visit a friend who lived in an older century home, and later I told Cheyenne about my strange encounter:

> Hi, Cheyenne,
>
> I would like your advice on something. I think I had a run-in with a poltergeist haunting an old place where my girlfriend lives. This entity came at me again and again while I was visiting, and I put up my shields and sent the energy away. It did back off, exhibiting fear of me. The attacks became less severe, and the next time I went over, the poltergeist ignored my presence completely, steering clear of any room I entered. The entity kept playing games with people's cell phones and equipment, but less often when I came around.

At that, Cheyenne asked me, "Could you please describe in detail the way you see and feel poltergeists?"

My response was,

> Okay. I feel so many different types of energies, and I intuitively know what a lot of them are. A basic ghost is similar to water energy—subtle and pretty harmless. Poltergeists, however, have very strong electrical energy and can move matter. One of my first encounters with this type of entity occurred alongside the river in an old house called the Chenail, which now serves as offices for a tourist centre. While I climbed to the second story, halfway up the stairs I felt a shaking sensation. Suddenly, I got hit by a dense, heavy wall of energy. I felt as if trying to walk through water, as I attempted to climb the stairs. Then it hit me again hard, unexpectedly, and I fell backward from the impact.
>
> Luckily, my girlfriend caught me, just as I tumbled backward into her. She had also felt the force come

through me and hit her. The air looked thick and grey and felt hot and thick.

As I entered the second-floor office where this energy seemed to concentrate, the same heavy, dense energy filled the entire room, swirling like a tornado. This energy seemed alive, with a mind of its own, and I felt its anger. This room had a cluster of electrical components, and I wondered whether, in some strange way, they might be feeding power to this entity.

Later that afternoon at Remy's house, the poltergeist surged at both of us, but together we pushed it off. It had followed us to her home from the tourist centre through our mind thoughts and bound us with it. I cut the connection by strong intent, and off it scurried, back to its lair.

That evening at home, out of the blue, that same energy came at me, battering me and trying to suck the life out of me. It seemed even more aggressive, as if it had prepared for this, building up its power for a strike. It obviously had an ulterior motive in mind. I had an awful sense of it attempting to get inside me, and fighting it off was almost unbearable.

I didn't know what to do, but that little voice inside guided me to turn up my energy and reach my hands into my personal guide's core for extra support. I had never heard of doing this, but I wasn't in a position to ask questions. And guess what? It worked! I felt my shields become stronger as the poltergeist hammered at me, trying to get through. I spent about five minutes telling it to cease and desist, and suddenly it faded away. It had nothing left to attack me with, and it retreated to regenerate its energy forces.

This experience taught me that these poltergeists can strongly implant thoughts in your mind, which most ghosts have difficulty doing, making you think the thoughts are yours. This psychological manipulation, I would think, is very dangerous, especially for those of weak will, and I surmise it's why people fear poltergeists so much.

I figured out that these entities need a power source and feed off underwater or electrical sources. The stronger the source, the more energy at their disposal, to manifest and manipulate the physical world. The old Chenail house, where this particular poltergeist hangs out, sits right beside a river. I've mapped out a few water veins running under that house. The strongest vein passes right through the office with the cluster of electronic equipment where the energy had concentrated during most of the reported paranormal activities.

At mid morning the next day, Cheyenne called on the phone. I was alone and had finished all of my chores for the day. Tired, I had little patience for chitchat.

Cheyenne's first words were, "Good morning, Angelina. I hope I'm not getting you at a bad time."

I said no, that I had a few hours to myself.

Cheyenne continued in a no-nonsense voice: "I'm a bit concerned about these rather frequent attacks or approaches from nonphysical entities. It is very important that you stop deliberately exploring these capabilities that have opened up."

A bit taken aback, I leaned on the counter, trying not to retort. It hadn't been a good day so far, and my nerves were on edge. The kids had fought all morning. There must have been something in the air, because Cheyenne also seemed to be "in a mood."

I answered in frustration, "That's what I've been doing for the last few weeks. I've ignored my psychic abilities, but the damn entities still come. Mind you, it's been rather quiet since my most recent initiation. When you speak of capabilities, do you mean all of them or specific ones?"

Cheyenne asked, "Can you be a bit more precise, Angelina? I'm not sure what you mean by 'specific ones.'"

"Well, I had to do a healing on my dog yesterday when he was sick. Within the hour, he felt much better, and by late day he had flushed out an infection and was eating again and looking great. This I could not avoid," I said in a determined but adamant voice. "So, where do I draw the line? Like, really, which capabilities are safe, if any? And then sometimes it just happens that I pick up things!"

My temper flared, and Cheyenne seemed surprised at my reaction. I took a deep breath and said, "Sorry. It's been a stressful morning. The kids and I are slowly drifting apart. Although we live together, we have completely different realities. At times, I wonder where all of this is going.

"You know, Cheyenne, these abilities have become so much a part of me, it's hard to recognize when it's happening or when I'm doing something out of the ordinary until it's too late."

Cheyenne sighed. "Okay, Angelina, I understand. But when something opens up spontaneously, back off and close down the opening as soon as you can. Your innocence of the dangers involved in these activities, coupled with your enthusiasm and self-confidence, makes me ask you not to take any unnecessary chances."

"I'm surprised that you say this," I retorted, "because I've held back on my enthusiasm, and my self-confidence hasn't been that great! I've been confused lately. In high gear, I'd probably drive you nuts!" I laughed. I always made jokes when I felt nervous or uncomfortable.

Cheyenne sighed again. "I'm not trying to create feelings of fear. Just healthy respect and caution for complex forces that you don't fully understand yet. By the way, are you doing that mudra I taught you—at least ten minutes a day—and are you meditating at least twice a day to produce the stabilizing effects I discussed earlier? These simple, standard but effective practices pay big dividends and rather quickly, if you just keep at them, day after day."

"Yes, I've been doing the mudra but not every day. I'll start to do it every day. I do light meditation many times a day. Is this what you mean when you say meditation twice a day? Just specify exactly what you want, and I'll do it."

In a frustrated voice, Cheyenne said, "If you want to work with me, you'll need to listen to what I say!"

I answered under my breath, "Yes, boss!"

Cheyenne went on with, "We don't need to agree, and we can talk about alternatives, but we do need to address these issues, one way or the other. And don't take this to be an authoritarian type of thing. It is not."

"I understand," I replied, knowing Cheyenne wanted the best for me.

Cheyenne continued, "Your situation is quite complex and needs to be stabilized—the sooner, the better. You seem to have made progress since we began the adjustments, but you need to continue."

We said our good-byes, and the days turned into weeks. Winter settled in, and I put more effort into my daily regimen. Cheyenne seemed happy with my progress. At home, though, everything was falling apart. The more I became comfortable with my new abilities, the less I hid them from my family, and unease often surfaced when I accidentally mentioned something that simply didn't fit into their reality.

And so more time passed, to gradually reveal deeper truths.

* * *

It was early evening, and something told me to check my emails. I normally would have waited till morning, but that inner voice would not leave it alone. And so I left Dad with the kids (he was staying with us for a few days). I entered my studio as the sun began to set. After pressing GET MAIL, I saw a missive from Cheyenne—uncharacteristic for this time of day.

I read,

> Hi, Angelina,
>
> I have a favour to ask of you.
>
> To make a long story short, we have a friend who was hit by a car a week ago Tuesday. He has been in a deep coma ever since, with little other visible physical damage.

Shocked, I could feel the pain Cheyenne must have dealt with this past week, without even once hinting about it in our earlier correspondence.

> I've done quite a bit of distance work on him, part of it attempting to contact him in the spirit realms and determine his needs and intentions.

Contacting a coma patient in the spirit realm? I had never considered where a person went while in a coma. Cheyenne had all of my attention at this point. Cheyenne continued,

> Generally, I've received consistent results; however, certain inconsistencies trouble me.
>
> Would you be able to reach out to him and determine what he wants to do and what he needs from me and from his family, etc.? His name is Mason, and he is forty-four. He is at Hearst University Hospital, downtown. And, please, no matter the news—good or bad—tell me what you arrive at.
>
> Also, I would ask that you make no effort to do any healing—just fact finding, so to speak.

Though stunned at this request, I felt pleased that Cheyenne had asked this favour of me and had such belief in my capabilities.

I pondered the situation, clueless about how to proceed if I attempted to "contact Mason" in the "spiritual realm."

Before I made a hasty decision about whether I could be of help, it would be nice if Cheyenne explained this realm thing in more detail. Cheyenne often warned me about wandering into mysterious dimensions of reality without proper supervision. At times, I attracted lower energies that attached themselves to me. All kinds of health and mental problems could accompany these creatures.

Cheyenne had said,

> These lower heavy energies exist in various realms of reality unknown to the common man, but they are definitely real and can be very dangerous. Our subconscious protects us with tales of demons and horrors shared in whispers and behind closed doors. General society at times calls them ghosts, poltergeists, Earth-bound

spirits, entities, Grim Reapers, suckers, and the list goes on. These lower types of energy interact with the unconscious human being in a bid for power, control, and excitement and to serve their own hidden agendas. They are minions of Lucifer but also creatures of nature participating in the dance of life in an attempt to reach something just beyond their grasp.

With my lack of control over my psychic gifts, I'd recently landed myself in situations I had no experience dealing with. Cheyenne often had the dubious job of coming to my rescue. Cheyenne called it *"cleaning up my messes."* Afterward, I would get a tongue-lashing that had me cringing in my seat. Little did Cheyenne know at the time how well these speeches worked. Being extremely empathic, I "felt" on every level Cheyenne's anger, fear for my safety, and other emotions, in the lengthy, explicit, Cheyenne-ish missives chastising me for my irresponsible behaviour. *I cringe even thinking of them.* Never mincing words, Cheyenne didn't believe in "beating around the bush."

In the most recent explosive email, Cheyenne had said, *"Angelina! Ignorance is no excuse!"*

I remember one incident when I had gotten into deep water using my psychic gifts while trying to help a close friend. I had ventured into an unfamiliar area and had attracted some nasty dark visitors. Cheyenne referred to them as "suckers," for they attached themselves to unsuspecting innocents and drained them of vital energy. They resembled blood-sucking reptiles, with huge mouths and dripping fangs, though I could only see them via my third eye, because they are fifth-dimension creatures. They bit into people's necks and sucked the energy from their nervous systems via the spinal column.

The clock on the computer screen said 8:00 p.m. I decided to send off a brief reply to Cheyenne and then wait 'til morning for a response.

> Cheyenne, I have carefully read your communiqué regarding Mason. Tomorrow morning, I will attempt to do as you request.

Cheyenne always stressed clarity of thought and brevity of words in our communications and said on occasion, "Angelina, simply get to the point so we can address the real issue at hand!"

I pondered why I felt the need to share so much with Cheyenne, and I realized Cheyenne was the only person who understood my world, whom I could be completely open with and hold nothing back.

I continued to write,

> Also, Cheyenne, if I'm able to connect with your friend, what exactly do you want me to tell or ask Mason?
>
> Another thing—I'm occasionally blunt, so don't take what I say personally. I seem to go into a trancelike state, with no frills or emotion involved—straight reporting and fact finding.

Rose had explained to me that compassion and love at all times formed the basis of reading people. One had to consider the person's feelings and the levels of awareness. Any true psychic learned this. One had to use intuition properly and recognize what needed to be said or left unsaid.

I continued to write,

> I'm not sure of the best approach, but I'll try to wing it with the information you've given me. Maybe I could connect to you energetically and travel your emotions for Mason to him. This can work quite well at times. I've never attempted a connection of this type with just a name and a place, but I can try. And thanks for trusting in me enough to ask this favour. I appreciate your confidence.
>
> *Angelina*

I sent my email at 8:20 p.m. A wave of tiredness assailed me, and I gazed out the window. The setting sun bathed the garden in crimson and orange. What a peaceful time of evening in the flatlands!

My eyes lingered on an area of the gardens that had started to bloom. The love I showered on these amazing plant creatures revealed itself in their bountifulness and health. This oasis of beauty and calm had helped me heal on so many levels.

I shut down the computer for the night. I could hear Dad with the kids on the front porch, enjoying a friendly conversation before they went off to bed. We loved these balmy evenings, after such a long, harsh winter.

I made my way to the kitchen, thinking I would join them, and we could all catch the equinox of the evening together. My mind kept turning to Cheyenne's request, but I put these thoughts aside. I started to go out to the front porch, when I felt a rush of energy. I recognized the feeling instantly, excused myself, and hurried back to my office. My kids looked at me strangely but were now used to my odd ways.

I switched on the computer and sat down, feeling another surge of energy. It was already past 9:00 p.m. by now. I logged on, just in time to document what I saw and felt. Despite the late hour, I sank into the sensations coming at me in waves. After a deeper surge of energy, I knew that whether I wanted to or not, for some strange reason I was making a connection with Mason. I went through my breathing exercises, grounded myself, and began to type.

In my mind, I saw black, then a light. I asked to be brought to Mason. The next instant I emerged in a room filled with silvery white light. I couldn't make out a floor or walls, but I sensed they did exist on some level of reality. Not twenty feet from me stood a man whom I intuitively knew was Mason. I then wrote a description of what unfolded in my mind's eye.

> I see Mason standing in a room or a place with no walls, except for white light everywhere. Dressed in a blue hospital gown, he is looking around with a confused expression. He has dark hair, with some greying at the temples. He's a little heavy set, tall or average height, but it's difficult to tell in this space, because there are no boundaries to compare his height with. He seems lost, as if he'd regressed mentally to a childlike state—confused and disoriented, muttering to himself at times, almost like a state of dementia.

> I start to approach him, taking a few tentative steps, though I feel disconnected from any body I have here. He senses me and turns toward me. He stares at me, looking me up and down with an anguished expression. He beseeches me to explain what is going on and where he is. His hands reach out to me, begging for help, but he seems fearful. He obviously sees me but with no indication of what exactly he sees.
>
> I keep my distance from him. I would describe his behaviour as being trapped in limbo, a look of dejectedness on his face.
>
> Now he walks in circles, talking to himself in utter confusion, forgetting my presence, as fear emanates from him in waves. He cycles through these emotions and behaviours, as I stand observing him.

I leaned back in my chair, trying to understand what exactly Mason was going through. Obviously, something wasn't right with him. I wondered how I had connected to him, but the thought soon left me because Mason once again caught my attention.

"Does Mason have a wife and kids?" I decided to ask. I saw flashes on a mind screen around him, like memories circling him.

> I see others on his far side, beckoning to him, but he refuses to go to them. I sense that he knows these others, who are of the spirit world. This crowd of men and women, young and old, could be family and friends who have passed on.
>
> I enter this place at ground level, at the opposite end from the spiritual entities who seem to know Mason. These spirits appear to be floating above an invisible ground surface. Is this a greeting committee?
>
> Though not clearly defined, they are obvious beings of light. Their faces are visible, but with vague features. The light surrounding them also makes up their essence. Though aware of my presence, they ignore me. They centre all of their attention on Mason. All

communication is telepathic, though everyone seems to speak outwardly, much like someone talking in my head.

Some have clear forms, but others are insubstantial and gossamer-like. They beckon for him to come over, but he keeps backing away from them.

He is panicking now and has turned toward me, seeing me once again, reaching out to me in supplication to help him.

I sense that he doesn't know who or what I am, and this creates confusion.

I decide to ease his fears and communicate to him that I'm here to help him, if he so wills it, and that I am a friend of Cheyenne's. This seems to calm him, and he approaches me hesitantly.

I stand still now, not wanting to spook Mason. He reaches out to me, asking me to come and get him.

I softly say, "Not now, but later, after I have spoken to your friend Cheyenne. I am a friend of Cheyenne's."

He now repeats in an excited voice, "Yes, Cheyenne, okay. Okay. Speak to Cheyenne." Now he turns away once again, seemingly oblivious of our recent conversation.

He begins cycling through a more or less normal state of mind to that of a child. His mind and emotions jump all over the place. I empathically feel his extreme, volatile emotions.

In this deep, extremely strong energetic connection with Mason, I'd been transported to a "White Place," as I called it. It seemed like a world I had never experienced before. It resembled the realm others described in near-death experiences—a white tunnel, a place of white light. I felt a pull once again, and my consciousness became fully immersed in this otherworldly white place. I began to write,

> I see thoughts and images, with everything moving so fast, I have difficulty assimilating all of it.

I tried to make sense of the scenes I witnessed and wondered whether they depicted Mason's life. Then I looked at a mirror image that seemed strangely like me. Could it be a reflection of me from Mason's mind? Yes, it was. I felt a bit surprised at how I appeared to Mason.

> Mason has telepathically projected how he sees me. I'm dressed in a long flowing white dress, with long dark wavy hair to my knees, and have a petite build—though I'm tall and attractive, he says, with dark eyes. In fact, this image reminds me of how I looked in the first initiation you gave me.
>
> He wonders whether I am an angel or a she-devil. He doesn't know yet what to make of this or me—and neither do I.
>
> At the same time I'm getting flashes of scenes with Mason, of his life playing out around him. Some type of life review seems to be happening around him. The scenes flash too rapidly for me to comprehend them. Mason has a difficult time assimilating everything, which explains his bouts of confusion and fear.
>
> My mind can't take in the whole experience, and I need time to re-evaluate it.
>
> That's it for now.
>
> *Angelina*

Slowly, I came back to my physical body and breathed a sigh of relief. I pressed the SEND button. I suddenly noticed that Cheyenne had responded earlier, and I decided to take a few minutes to read this most recent email.

> Hi, Angelina,
>
> Thanks for getting back to me so promptly and for your willingness to help Mason and me in this dire situation. He is the divorced father of two kids (a daughter going into college and a son my son's age).

> As I said, ask him what his intentions are and what we can do to help him. Also, you can ask if he has anything that he wants to say to any or all of us (his friends) on this side. I doubt you will have a problem connecting with him.
>
> I would like to coordinate our efforts, if you're willing. I'll join us energetically at a specific time we can determine together, and I will support your efforts. I will accommodate your schedule. Please advise.

Now I understood why I had the strong connection this evening. Cheyenne had probably sensed something was going on and had decided to lend me energetic support. I continued reading.

> Also, there is no real rush. He's in a coma, and he isn't going anywhere. This has more to do with how much I will take command on my end.
>
> You have been asking all along where this goes. Well, this is where it goes.
>
> *Namaste,*
> *Cheyenne*

Chapter 24

Another Reality

Wonders never cease . . .

The next morning, I woke up from a deep, unconscious slumber, still pondering Cheyenne's enigmatic words. I caught a whiff of the fragrance of this turn-of-the-century house that I so loved. Most people thought it peculiar that I wanted this much isolation on a dead-end country road. I had been raised in a small city, with all of the conveniences at hand, but felt the need for privacy and a quiet country life.

Years ago, when Daniel and I first saw this broken-down house, he had misgivings about taking on such a huge project. Yet after a bit of convincing on my part, he eventually agreed. That voice deep inside me had whispered that this was our place, where we needed to be. We were newlyweds then, with our daughter barely a year old and our son on the way. Little did we realize the monumental effort it would take to return the old house to its former glory. Yet in the end, it was well worth it, as I now enjoyed the fruits of our years of labour.

I yawned and stretched languidly, remembering how Daniel used to comment on my long legs and catlike movements. Then he'd wink and say he hadn't married me for my body but for my cooking. That was our private joke. I glanced over at his picture and sent him my love. He had been a very good-looking man and a perfect match to my femininity. His muscular build spoke of strength, and his strong, square jaw defined a sturdy character. His honesty and integrity had always appealed to me.

Yet I never understood his reserve and his quietness. He could go for days without talking when something bothered him, until out of the blue he would explode. I felt his deep scars from a misunderstood childhood. He was a complex man. Though he loved simplicity and wasn't overly demanding, his inner world had been deep and spiritual. He hid this well from most people, but it surfaced easily with the children. He had loved his family so much, and the world obviously recognized this.

The rising sun peeked over the horizon. Its early morning rays reflected promising warmth through the bedroom windows. I loved this time for its peacefulness. I jumped out of bed and grabbed my oldest, comfiest clothes. I tiptoed from the room, so that I didn't disturb the kids, because they had crawled into bed with me—a habit of theirs since Daniel had passed on.

I lazily made my way to the kitchen downstairs. I had about an hour or so to myself before the house stirred with activity. Dad had spent the night while his new house was being built. Remembering the events of last evening, I decided to wait until everyone had left for the day before delving too deeply into Cheyenne's request and what had followed. I needed time alone to review the events of last night.

Today I also had to devote some time to housework, and the perennial and vegetable gardens needed attention.

It was 5 a.m., and as the coffee brewed, I settled in the music room. I lit incense and candles in preparation for my early morning meditation practice.

After an hour or so, I heard everyone waking up. By 8 a.m., Dad and the kids had left, and peace settled over the house. I went online and saw Cheyenne's email:

Hi, Angelina,

I've only just received your report of the connection you had with Mason last night, and it is good news.

If you are able, tell Mason that if he wants to come home (back to his body), we will do all that we can to help him.

Tell him that his brain is damaged, and he will need some rehab. His family and his friends will get him through this, if it is to be...

Tell him how much we love him and want him to come back...

Namaste,
Cheyenne

Cheyenne's comments about Mason's physical and mental state confirmed why Mason had been so agitated, fluctuating from calmness to confusion and even at times regressing to a childlike state. I sent a brief reply to Cheyenne that I would attempt another contact with Mason around 9:00 a.m. or so, and I looked forward to Cheyenne's energetic support. Pressing SEND, I prepared myself for the task ahead.

The clock ticked away the minutes, as I centred myself and prepared for what would come. Without warning, an energetic source surrounded me, and I recognized it as Cheyenne. So it was a go. Great!

It was now 9:00 a.m. Dad would not be home for a few hours, so I had plenty of time. What Cheyenne and I wished to accomplish would require single-minded determination, with no outside disturbances.

I relaxed and sent out the intent to connect with Mason, in the "White Place" where Mason presently resided in spirit. I sank into a void of darkness, losing myself in a deep trance. Sending out the command "Bring me to Mason" went much smoother with Cheyenne's energetic support.

Sitting at my desk, I began typing.

Hi, Cheyenne,

I feel energy coming in, so I guess it's probably you. I am connecting with Mason and will let you know what I get. Off I go.

With those words, I immersed myself in the feelings and images coming in. My body hummed and tingled, as my energy rose higher and my ears rang with the sound of energy coursing through me. My hands became numb, while pressure built between my brows. As the force intensified, I began to disconnect from my body. I sank deeper and deeper and lost complete awareness of my physical body.

My consciousness blacked out for a moment, as a dark void surrounded me. Just as suddenly, I entered the White World. I glanced around but couldn't see Mason. In this eerie but calming place, I tried to locate him. Telepathically calling out his name, I sent out my feeling sense, attempting to position him. Being so empathic, I usually obtained most information on a feeling basis first. I felt as if I became the person I wanted to connect to, like stepping into his or her skin.

I suddenly felt a sharp swoosh, indicating my connection to Mason. I recognized his imprint. I hurriedly wrote,

> I feel anxiousness, erratic breathing, with underlying panic. There is a lot of pressure in my head and at the back of my neck. Remember, when I say "I," I really mean *he*, Mason. My body feels numb. I feel pain similar to last night mid-way down, centred in my back—possibly energetic knots, creating some of the problems in Mason's head. I sense that these knots and his head injury are connected in some way and that the doctors won't be able to recognize this, due to its energy component.
>
> The voice inside me says this blockage in Mason's spine has created his coma state by interrupting the flow of vital energy. I suggest you send energy to his spine and behind his eyes, to his pituitary and pineal glands, and toward the top of his head, because these seem to be the main areas of injury.

I took a deep breath and grounded the first sensations to make room for more information to come through. I could see Mason now as if he were across a room. I brought my attention back to what I felt and continued to report.

> His brow's third eye is throbbing and sore from overuse in the White Place. He needs calming, because he is so afraid and doesn't understand what's happening. He goes in and out of awareness, similar to last night. I sense that he feels my presence. I will approach him and tentatively take his hand and try to bring him to full consciousness.

Now totally immersed in Mason's world, I had lost consciousness of this world. I could type, but as if someone else performed the task for me. In my mind, I now existed as part of Mason's realm. Mason now stood in the middle of the White Place, and I moved closer to him.

I clearly recognized Cheyenne's energetic presence just outside the White Place, hovering along the edges of this realm, but Cheyenne could not enter. Something had stopped Cheyenne with a barrier, much like impenetrable glass encasing us. I became conscious of Cheyenne's need to be pulled in or to pull us out. As this thought crossed my mind, a shimmering holographic cloud with images took form in front of me. The inner voice whispered that I should watch the scenes playing out in the holograph.

I rapidly began typing what I saw.

> I'm being shown a probable future in a window of energy floating before me in this White World. In the images, I'm with Mason, and I see myself reaching upward, out to you, through the barrier encasing us in this world. I grab your hand through the veil of white shimmering mist. This barrier separating you from us has no form or colour but encloses this place. You cannot get through to this world, for some reason. My hand passes through this enclosure to the outside of the white mist, clasping your hand. Mason and I are holding onto each other for dear life, and I tell you in a panicky voice to pull us out, as I clasp your hand tightly. Mason is fearful and hesitant, but I keep telling you to pull.

Something strange had happened. Although I could still see myself in this world with Mason, I saw on the holograph that Cheyenne had pulled us out. I went spiralling with Mason in my arms through an earth tunnel at an indescribable speed. I felt the pull, like a sucking motion. Then the mental image changed.

> I see Mason in a hospital bed, slowly regaining consciousness, but something isn't right. I intuit he may regress unless someone keeps him from sinking back into the coma world. Maybe that's why I'm witnessing this possible outcome ahead of its scheduled linear time—as a warning to prepare.
>
> I feel so frustrated, Cheyenne, not knowing what's actually going on with him in a physical sense while we do this. Anything to give us clues would help, such as twitches or movements.

The holograph dissipated, and I gradually came back to normal consciousness, like waking up from a dream. I had no sense of how much time had elapsed. Glancing over at the clock, I realized only minutes had passed since I'd begun. Frustration set in, along with a feeling of helplessness. Were any of the images I remembered a reality of sorts? This seemed to have been some kind of preview, a view into a probability, but it felt so real.

I finished my correspondence with the following:

> Is there any way for us to do something while we communicate by phone, with you by his side, so we could exchange info as we work? A concerted effort by the two of us might accomplish the job, but we need to see how Mason reacts as we work with him. I realize this might be impossible, but it may be the only way.

Cheyenne's eventual response to my question was:

> Though I think it would be best if we could work on site with Mason, his family isn't aware of my spiritual work and most likely would be uncomfortable with such an

approach so we are left on our own for now. This may change, but...

For right now, Mason's body is in the firm and clumsy hands of Western mechano-medicine.

Overwhelmed, I signed off. I needed to get outside into the fresh air. I felt relieved that Dad still hadn't come back. He would have noticed something was going on with me, with his keen hawk eyes, and I wasn't up to inventing a believable story. I stepped outside and instantly felt more grounded and rejuvenated. Taking a few deep breaths brought my mind back into my body.

After lunch, I emailed some questions to Cheyenne.

Hi, Cheyenne,

I forgot to ask you a few things about your friend Mason.

Is there something in Mason's life he doesn't want to come back to? An emotional issue that's keeping him in the coma? A fear of something or of having to face something that really hurt him and might be influencing his indecision and confusion about where to go next?

I have to stress again that someone needs to exercise his body more, wake him, and play soothing music that will help him wake up. Having a physical connection with him would also help. As he begins to return, these physical contacts will encourage the process and keep him focused on returning and not regressing. He will have to make a huge effort to hold the consciousness he needs to make it back without falling into limbo. If we do this "pulling Mason out" thing, as described in the holograph I witnessed, it may really drain you, so please be prepared.

I also have an odd memory of never leaving Mason's side, and I feel I gained his confidence. I must have still been connected with him and the White Place as I went to sleep.

Let me know what you think about all of this. I need to ground myself better, because I never seem to fully disconnect from the experience, and part of me remains in that White World. Feedback would be appreciated.

Angelina

I pressed the SEND button and made my way to the gardens. My thoughts drifted off, while I mechanically pulled pesky weeds. This repetitive act induced contemplative thinking, and I visualized a snapshot of Mason's children in my mind's eye and how important they were to him. I realized how my children had given me purpose and served as a focus for my nurturing instinct. The inner voice I now know as Teacher began to speak.

> *I always say every woman, if possible, should have the experience of bearing a child. The conventional steps of birthing and then rearing a child are one of the greatest initiations in life a woman will have and can never be replicated in any other way. Children are so important in the experience of both men and women.*
>
> *With childbearing, a girl becomes a nurturing woman and learns all about unconditional love. This also forces her man to let go of ideas that associate her with his mother, for a woman will nurture her man until she has a child; he will then be forced to see her as a woman, full grown, and must release his boyish attitudes about women. He becomes a man, who protects, guards, and provides for his family, as befits the role of father and husband. It brings home the reality of being responsible for another, in ways not easily replicated. Our society has forgotten these important natural roles, in our attempt to become modernized and equal.*

A bird screeching snapped me out of my reverie. I shrugged off the "voice" again as my imagination playing with me. I went indoors to see whether Cheyenne had responded to my e-mails. I soon noticed a response from Cheyenne.

Hi, Angelina,

> On the practical side, I connected and sent you energy today at 9:00 a.m. as planned. It felt successful on my end. I won't comment on the details at this point in time, because I want to keep the field clear and uncluttered.
>
> Suffice it to say that so far, I feel the information you have arrived at is both accurate and helpful. Thanks very much! I do appreciate your help.
>
> I also asked for help from my energy healing teacher Jean—she will look in a bit later today. I'll send you notes on this later.
>
> Nothing else to share, except that I will reaffirm my belief that you need to incorporate yogic stretching (back, in particular) into your daily routine and drink a lot of water. Also, it would be good for you to start doing your meditation with the new techniques I taught you recently.

Let me know how it felt.

Oh, yes, my back. I had a spinal injury as a teenager, and funny how it happened in the area where the energy pooled and surged. I had suffered from back problems, on and off, for years. Cheyenne had astutely picked this up.

> I also sense from the work I did and from your impressions that things went far better than you seem to feel they did.
>
> Please remember not to expect instant results. This is something we need to learn as healers. Also, things are virtually instantaneous on the spiritual planes. They may take some time to translate into the physical.

This was a good reminder. I needed to adapt to a nonlinear way of thinking: everything did not have a past, a present, and a future. Our thinking process was so ingrained in a time format that I'd never considered anything different, until these excursions into other realms of reality beyond the time continuum.

> I don't know where the head injury is. It doesn't matter. The energy tends to draw me to where it is needed. Your guidance as to problem areas seemed very accurate, and I worked accordingly and—I feel—quite potently toward their healing.
>
> I don't know what his emotional issue is. It, too, does not matter.

I disagreed with Cheyenne that the emotions were not an issue. Maybe Cheyenne didn't understand the important role these emotions played in influencing a person's decision. It made me realize that my empathy brought deeper insights than those of most people.

> There is no problem that cannot be surmounted. If you have the opportunity, please check in on Mason from time to time and tell him that I will be available to help him in any and every way that I can.
>
> As an aside of some potential importance, my intuition tells me that Mason and I have a history of past lives together.
>
> Now I am presented with a clear opportunity to repay his selfless, loyal, and excellent service to me during these past lives.
>
> You need to stress two things to him that might help him come around: (1) any problem can be surmounted, and (2) if he wants my help, it is there, without reservation.
>
> Enough.
>
> Also—VERY IMPORTANT—be sure that he is aware of his HIGHEST GOOD and that he is serving HIS HIGHEST GOOD, right here, right now.
>
> If he wants to go home, and he knows this is in the highest good of all those concerned, he has my blessing, and I will do everything I can to get him home (as in the

Celestial Realms). However, and it is a big however, if he needs to keep on working here on the Earth plane, then we will do everything we can to facilitate this as well.

Is all of this clear?

Remember, if you need to take a stronger hand in this, MAKE SURE it is in the service of the HIGHEST GOOD OF ALL THOSE CONCERNED. Otherwise, do nothing.

I laughed, always curious at how our exchanges bore the mark of a face-to-face conversation between two people. In my mind, I answered, "Clear, boss!" Cheyenne was obviously used to a leadership role. But then again, so was I.

Chapter 25

Memories Surface—Laughter and Longing

Within our hearts we all have a dream. Some say without
dreams we are doomed.
Many dreams seem unrealistic, but all realizations do begin with a dream.

—Michèle C. St.Amour

The Following Morning...

It was still early, and I had time to kill before checking in to see if Cheyenne had sent me any news on Mason. I glanced at the calendar—late spring already, with the anniversary of Daniel's passing only weeks away. I missed his company and having someone I could laugh with, be intimate with, and share a world that few understood. I guess I felt lonely. The kids, being teenagers, were gone most of the time. Dad would soon move into his new home, so days went by when I was left to my own devices.

I thought of my son's little "episode" of the previous night. He now had girlfriends and was at the age of sowing his wild oats. I couldn't always get him to be mindful, without a man's constant influence on him. I worried when he didn't come home on time or call to tell me his whereabouts. So many teens took drugs and engaged in other regretful activities that whenever he came home late, I feared the worst. Last night he had me in a fit of temper.

At two hours past his curfew, I finally decided I'd had enough. I went looking for him, in the best way I knew how.

After a few centring exercises, I went into an altered state of consciousness, with the sole mission of finding my son. I settled my emotions, then remotely flew through the dark night to a destination only my spirit knew. I loved the freedom of spirit flight, which had become easier as the months went by.

With my attention suddenly in front of me, I descended to a dimly lit bedroom on the upper floor of a house I didn't recognize. The setting sun cast long shadows everywhere. Standing at ground level of the room, I looked around and saw two figures intertwined on a bed.

I approached softly, though I needn't have feared, because I was in spirit, but habit made me cautious. As I got close enough, I saw my son sound asleep with his latest girlfriend snuggled up against him. Little did I know that this dark beauty would one day become his wife. Thank God, they had their clothes on, though it wouldn't have surprised me if they'd been in the buff, for my son was as virile as his father had been. Though our son was seventeen, he had a strict weekday curfew. School wasn't his favourite activity, and he needed time to put his nose to the grindstone with homework.

I noticed that the room was prettily decorated, with a rose lace coverlet and a delicate shaded lamp on a night stand. My son groaned and began talking, as he tends to do in his sleep. This gave me an idea, for people are more susceptible to spirit or telepathic communication when asleep. And since he had been born with exceptional psychic gifts, I decided to try to get through to him.

I approached him, leaned close to his ear, and whispered, "Come home!" in a loud, clear etheric voice. After a few tries, I almost gave up, but he suddenly seemed to stir, so I tried again. I bent over one last time and whispered as loud as I could, "Come home!"

He jerked and suddenly woke up, yelling, "I have to go home!"

His startled girlfriend, Isabelle, awoke in a panic, asking what was wrong.

As he got fully dressed, he kept repeating, "I have to go home. My mother is calling me."

Thirty minutes later, he pulled into the yard on his motorbike. With a sheepish look, he walked into the kitchen, and I couldn't resist. "So you heard me!"

He stopped in his tracks, stunned. At this point, I still felt upset and didn't really think of the ramifications of what I had done.

"You're lucky you were sleeping, which made it easier for me to get you home! But you scared the heck out of your girlfriend when you woke up yelling, 'I have to get home. My mother is calling me!'"

I laughed at the funny expression on his face. He just stood there in shock.

"Mom, are you kidding me? I was in a deep sleep, and suddenly there you were, yelling at me to get home."

I nodded with a grin, shrugging. "Qué seras, seras . . . Sorry, dear, but you had me worried. You were more than two hours late, and it's not the first time you did this. I wanted you home, and I wanted to make sure you were safe."

His response was, "This can't be true. This is a joke, right?"

"No, it's not. Your girlfriend has a nice rose and lacy bedroom, by the way. You left the bedside lamp on, and I could see around a bit. I hope you're using condoms?"

By then, he knew I had been there in spirit, and it was just too much for him. He turned and stomped up to his room, mumbling that he was going to take a shower. The next day he told me never to do that again, that I had invaded his privacy. I said that if he chose to worry me, then I would use everything in my power to have peace of mind. We didn't talk about this again for quite a few years.

It was still dark outside.

As I sat, not thinking of anything in particular, I recalled another unusual experience from my past. One night, a spirit, a woman, came to me in my dreams. A man stood behind her, as she explained something to me, but when I woke up, I couldn't remember it. Then that little voice inside told me to sketch her, and I drew her likeness in only five minutes. The sketch matched my memory, bang on, and I really captured her eyes.

Later that day I had a meeting with a woman to discuss a manifestation or "haunting," as some called it, in a house she had just bought. That little voice inside told me to bring the sketch.

When I showed the woman the sketch, she almost fell over in shock and asked me, "Where did you get this?" She said it was the spitting image of her sister but in thirty years' time.

I described the woman's colouring and character, which confirmed to us that this portrayed a probable future of her sister in her later years.

We decided that the man with her sister, whom I described and later sketched, was her brother-in-law but older and more mature than at present. The woman and her sister had bought a 125-year-old house together and had experienced ghosts and manifestations since they'd moved in. The big old mansion had lots of eerie feelings attached to it. We realized that a time warp portal of sorts ran through the house and that she was witnessing the future of the house, after her sister passed on. Her sister felt very attached to her possessions, so it seemed unsurprising that she would then haunt the place.

We left it at that, and I went home with many questions. Yet I knew that, as in all things, I would get those answers only when ready to understand them. This had been one of my first experiences in traveling the threads of time and weaving strands of raw magic. This entire experience with Mason, pre-viewing his return before it happened, reminded me of the incident with the woman and her sister. It had the same feeling, of a circular time continuum.

As similar memories surfaced, I recalled that these experiences eventually led me to know I was born a weaver and, as such, I had the gift. A weaver, said to be rare, is born with the ability to command all of the five elements of creation. Hence, after mastering these elements, the individual becomes known as a Master Weaver. My aboriginal Elder had spoken of this during his visits, but I hadn't understood the ramifications of his words until later. The gift of weaving that I learned allows a weaver to pull strands of magic from the Web of Light, the world of Grandmother Spider. The weaver's hands weave patterns that release power and often transform into other things, such as art created of magic. This power would lie deep within me until my ignorance dissipated.

A memory surfaced, and an ancient script with odd writing appeared before me. I began to read,

> The prophecy: *"A long time ago in ages forgotten, it is said a day will come known to only a very few. Called the Day of Gathering, on this a day all of those with the gift of weaving magic will gather in a valley that lies between seven mountains. All races, from man to elementals, elves, dwarves, and others, will unite. They will build a temple that they will name the Temple of Weaving . . . to protect their magic. The five Master Weavers (elements of life) have created the 'Great Protector,' a barrier that no being could ever cross with malcontent."*

The scene before me changed once again, and I found myself back in time with Daniel, on one of my first weaving experiences. One summer night he had gone to a boxing match in the city with his father and some friends. I decided to "check in" on him and did my tuning-in act. In seconds, I found myself floating below the ceiling, looking down on hundreds of people sitting around a boxing arena. I asked to be shown Daniel, and my vision fell on him sitting in a front-row seat, across from where I floated.

I looked around, taking note of what was going on, to confirm it with him later. He and his friends sat in plush burgundy seats, watching the two fighters in the ring. One, a Caucasian, wore boxers emblazoned with the American flag, and the other had very dark skin. Daniel did love his beer and had caught a buzz that I could feel, with my empathic link to him. An entire night of information came to me in only minutes of observation, testimony to the magic power of weaving.

The next day when I told him what I'd done, he was speechless. He couldn't deny the truth of the details I'd provided, and because I never made things up, he had no choice but to open his mind and take me seriously. In time, I understood that this ability arose from my Weaver's bloodline. I also realized that this same ability had played out in my visits with Mason, in some strange way.

Realizing I'd been lost in thought, I brought myself back to the present and checked my emails. Cheyenne had sent me another email late last evening, after I had gone to bed.

> Hi, Angelina,
>
> You should find this of interest...
>   This is from Jane, of the energy institute where I told you I'd studied. I'd asked for her impressions on Mason's condition—she's a very accurate, clear channel. I have complete confidence in her perceptions. She received these impressions when she "checked in" on Mason.
>
> **To: Cheyenne—Original Message—From: Jane**
> **Re: A friend in need... Importance: High**
>
> Hi, Cheyenne,
>
> I "tuned in" for your friend Mason this morning. I quickly got approval to connect into his energies, and his Higher Self seemed very open, with no blocking of information. The coma has allowed him time to review his life and whether he wanted to stay or not. He was shown future scenarios, and he reviewed them to see whether he wanted to "play" in that arena.

I sat back, taking a minute to digest Jane's words. This was exciting. Jane's letter gave the whole experience with Mason another dimension of reality. I read on.

> (So when you checked in earlier—he was "wobbling"... deciding whether to stay or not.) According to what I got this morning, he wants to stay. (Now we all know that with free will, there can always be a change of mind. But at the time I checked in, he had decided to stay.) There seemed to be a bond between you, him, and, curiously,

another was with him I couldn't recognize. Is anyone else involved that you know of, who might be having a positive influence on Mason?

I grinned at this, knowing Cheyenne hadn't told Jane of my involvement but that she'd picked up my presence. This was getting more interesting.

I didn't check in any further, as I didn't want to intrude on his energies. I ended with sending him love and Light. I also saw Archangel Raphael standing behind him, closely watching over him—as a family member or a friend would do when a loved one is in a serious condition.

I will continue to send my prayers and intentions for his highest good and the highest good of all involved to be served.

Sending you ... Love & Light & Prayers,
Jane

I noticed that Cheyenne had added a response,

—Original Message—From: Cheyenne

To: Jane

RE: A friend in need ...

Thanks so very much for your kindness and help.

Do you remember my super-psychic client/student (I discussed her with Jason some time back)? She has also taken a look, and her insights are consistent with your comments.

Namaste,
Cheyenne

I felt compelled to ask Cheyenne more about Jane, because she seemed to really know her stuff. I wrote,

> Cheyenne, I have some questions about Jane's way of seeing. She speaks of Mason's reviewing his life, and this is consistent with what I saw going on with him. I noticed a settling in him, which conforms with what she states. Also, the communication I had with him recently dealt with his deciding to stay. He realized it wouldn't be easy, but he had decided at this point to make the leap.
>
> I must say, though, her human perception of events and her seeing Raphael standing over him seem a little weird. How does she know it is *this* angel and not a figment of her imagination?
>
> I'm curious, because when I work with the other dimensions it isn't so "cut and dried." Then again, I'm inexperienced. Yet up to now, everything I've witnessed is so different from our folklore and paranormal accountings, written beliefs, and human perception of these things, so her use of these common terms has me confused.
>
> She does sound like a caring and put-together person, and what she says seems consistent with what we both gathered.

Cheyenne shared the following,

> For your information, Jane has channelled a number of other archangels, along with five different variations of certain initiatory energetic procedures. Jane is quite familiar, comfortable, and experienced with these various spiritual beings.
>
> In addition, Jane requested healing assistance from Archangel Raphael for Mason.
>
> To your question, "Can it be so 'cut and dried' with perception in the etheric realms?" Well, yes, it can, once we have mastered our talents through years of training and practice and explored these landscapes in great detail for many years (as Jane has done). I've told you this from the beginning. Even with your broad-based,

effective talents now, you are still just at the beginning. I'm relatively sure that you've started from such an advanced point with these gifts because of past life training.

Jane is as humble, generous, patient, loyal, and sincere as one can be. She is the "real deal."

I wrote back,

Thank you for clarifying her position.

By the way, Cheyenne, before I went to Mason on our last attempt, I flew in on you to see if you were ready for what turned out to be a practice run.

Did you feel my presence in any way?

I hovered above you to your front right-hand side. You appeared ready, so then I went off to Mason. I just wondered if you picked up on this or perceived me in any way?

Cheyenne responded,

About your "fly in"—no, I wasn't aware of you in a visual sense, but I perceived a certain sense of "urgency," shall we say, and proceeded accordingly.

By the way, if I neglected to tell you, my apologies—Mason's paralysis is temporary and drug-induced by the doctors to keep his blood pressure and brain pressure down. You don't need to attempt to heal this, because there is nothing to heal. He has no paralysis from the accident. If anything, just remind him—as I did—that he needs to relax, heal, and come back comfortably.

In answer to my question:

What am I becoming, Cheyenne? I'm a bit freaked out at the things I'm doing and with Jane's confirming all of this. Where is this going?

Cheyenne's response was,

> Regarding your question "What am I becoming?" that whole way of looking at it is wrong. We—all of us—are already perfect gods—all powerful, and so forth, and so on.
>
> We have just forgotten this "little fact." Awakening is not becoming—it is remembering—and getting rid of all that crap in us that blinds us to our true nature. The biggest load of crap that blinds us consists of the ego games. As a matter of fact, it is the ego's job to blind us to our true nature. Keep that in mind.
>
> Now getting back to Mason. On a practical note, I suspect it's best to just let Mason rest now. If you want to be more proactive, send him distant healing energy, as I taught you to do.
>
> Let's give him a few days before we decide to take further action.
>
> Please be so kind as to take a peek once a day, and let me know briefly what you see. I believe Mason may be on his way back, and we need to give him the space to do it in his own time. If there has been no change by the end of the week, I will suggest we attempt to contact him and extract him, as you visualized on our last attempt, if this is his wish.
>
> Gentle energy healing and an occasional hug of encouragement would be appropriate and helpful at this time.
>
> I still haven't heard anything from my contacts for Mason, on how he is doing, but I'll let you know as soon as I do.
>
> Have a wonderful weekend and trust that all is well...
> Be at peace.
>
> *Namaste,*
> *Cheyenne*

Lately, I'd been so preoccupied with Mason that I'd neglected friends and potential clients. My reputation for helping people gain insight into mysterious happenings had begun to spread.

I spent the rest of the day answering emails and getting ready for weekend activities with the kids. I also had a class on Merlin magic that night, so I had no time to waste. Every once in a while, a nagging sense of Mason calling out to me disturbed my concentration, but I shrugged it off.

The kids came home, and once they settled in with my dad for movie night, I headed off to town. I'd begun to study high magic a few years ago, right before Daniel had died. I needed to know more about things happening in my life that conventional society couldn't address. A friend had introduced me to Anne, a teacher of Merlin's high magic. The minute I met her, I knew she had some answers I'd been looking for. Now, after a few years of studying the occult and the ways of this feared path, I found the Friday night classes fun and so eye opening.

Tonight we would explore meditation and open our centres up to other dimensions of reality. I still hadn't told Cheyenne about this course, for I feared it would be greatly frowned upon.

I arrived a bit early, so Anne and I had some time alone. Not long after we sat down with our coffee, I felt an uncomfortable pressure coming at me and didn't know what to make of it.

After ten minutes of this, she asked, "Are my guides bothering you?"

I felt a bit taken aback, for what she described as "bothering me," I would have defined as a "psychic attack." I took a moment to roll around the idea that her guides would be inclined to attack me and that she didn't seem to think it out of the ordinary and in fact was acceptable.

I looked at her strangely and for the first time began to question the wisdom of taking this course. Or was it creating more problems than I realized? Maybe I wasn't aware of the dangers involved.

I frowned in annoyance, not wanting to follow this train of thought, because I enjoyed these Friday classes. Yet I made a point of not letting my guard down, as I had in the past.

I asked her, " Now, why would your guides feel the need to attack me?"

Anne paused for what seemed an eternity, simply looking at me. I held my ground, wanting an answer. She suddenly turned her gaze away, mumbling a noncommittal response, and I knew that she felt intimidated by me and by what I could sense and see. I got the odd impression that soon it might be time for me to move on. Maybe my skills and needs had outgrown my teacher's.

My fellow students arrived, and class began. We always started with a guided meditation that created the mood and the space for what would come. That night, though, the teacher instructed that we remain in our states of altered consciousness and ask to be given a message. All seemed pretty normal until I suddenly felt myself sinking deeply and, just as abruptly, leaving all sense of my body, that time, and that place.

My mind went blank and then black. My mind's eye played out millions of little white-lighted stars zinging past me, while far away a single point ahead became brighter and larger as it approached. It turned into the eye of God, as I came to know it, and then I was hurled into a time and a place centuries earlier.

I stood in a cold, damp room, surrounded by rock walls hung with tapestries depicting scenes of times past. I looked around curiously and spotted a harp in the corner, as well as what seemed to be day-to-day signs of living. I glanced down to see myself garbed in a gold velvet dress that reached the floor. Beautiful lace edged its ample sleeves, and gold-embroidered designs of exotic birds and Celtic symbols adorned its bodice. I felt like a princess, and as I gazed at my surroundings, I realized I *was* a princess, witnessing a life in my past.

As questions arose, I once again moved through a vortex of time. A holograph of events played out before me, of a past life with Daniel, in which he was sent off to war. A knight, everyone knew him for his bravery and courage. Scenes of our courtship flashed by, and I watched as we fell in love. Unlike most princesses of those times, I loved my knight, and we planned to wed on his return.

I then witnessed a scene on the day he left, as I handed him my scarf to wear for good luck, as was the custom in those times. I watched as days of loneliness went by. Then, months later, the scene played out of someone returning this scarf to me with news that my beloved, a hero, had been killed while saving many lives. In that moment, my world fell apart, and I felt the stabbing pain of loss once again in my heart. I knew this feeling so well. *Would it ever end?* I asked myself. *When does the pain of loving and loss ever go away?*

I broke down, never to be the same again. Days stretched into years, as I mourned the loss of my lover. I filled my time by painting images of angels that resembled him and playing melancholic songs on the harp, as I attempted to soothe the scars on my soul.

Again I felt the pain of the woman I once was, and this time the stabbing in my heart brought me back to the present moment. Before my awareness became anchored once again, I wanted to know what this was all about. Why was I being shown this past now? In answer to my inner questioning, I heard that voice inside me whisper from far away, "You and Daniel earned this present life together to finish what you began in this past. Daniel also earned himself a golden angel at his back for the deeds of bravery he once gave his life to. Look to your past paintings and your present interests for the truth of these words. This angel of gold, a protector of the brave and honest of heart, walks beside those who would protect you and yours during your quests. This angel is with you to this day, protecting you, as is destined."

This reminded me that one day I'd observed a godlike angel with a mane of golden hair and dressed in gold warrior attire, standing behind Daniel. As I'd questioned my sanity, the angel turned to me and looked me directly in the eyes. He said Daniel had earned his protection and that because of what I had come to do, everything would come together in this life. As this last thought surfaced, I wondered when the puzzle of my life would ever be complete.

* * *

The next day, I found an email from Cheyenne in my inbox. It read,

> Hi, Angelina and Jane,
>
> I finally got some news on Mason. I spoke to his son, Steve, today at our community fundraiser. When I asked him how his Dad was doing, he answered as only a teenage boy could: "Better, he is doing better."

At the end of the day, I pressed him for some details. He said his dad was doing a lot more on his own (I presume the physical problems are tapering off) and that he is no longer technically in a coma, because he is responding, but apparently he hasn't opened his eyes or spoken yet. I guess he still isn't entirely out of the forest, but it's looking good.

Thank you so much for your help.

I will continue to send healing on a daily basis and keep you informed as I get updates. You both should feel great to know that you played a part in what is starting to look like a "miracle." I'm absolutely delighted for Mason and his family. Another one for the "good guys"!

Namaste,
Cheyenne

Chapter 26

Other Worlds, Other Realities, Other Truths

If both the past and the external world exist only in the mind, and if the mind itself is controllable — what then?

—George Orwell, 1984

A few days went by. That weekend, I'd been busy with the kids, so I didn't have time to check in on Mason. When I downloaded my emails, I noticed that Cheyenne had written.

Hi, Angelina,

Have you had a chance to look in on Mason lately? Feels peaceful to me . . . but . . .

How are you doing with all of your various issues? It might be time to think about booking your next initiation. Let me know if this feels right for you.

Namaste,
Cheyenne

That was curious. The "but" got my attention. I hadn't thought of Mason all weekend, except for the odd feeling that I'd never really gone far from him. Part of me never seemed to be here completely. I suspected that part might be with Mason. Maybe that was why I forgot to look in on him these last few days.

And so, feeling guilty, I planned to check in on Mason tomorrow, due to the lateness of the day. That would give me time to report my findings to Cheyenne by afternoon and respond to the recent invitation for my next initiation, which I did feel might be due. I'd experienced the usual signs that foretold something on a higher plane getting ready for a physical and spiritual shift—headaches, symptoms of my past illnesses, old fears rising to the surface, and general aches and pains. I should have figured out that an initiation waited in the wings, but, being so busy, I'd had no time to dwell on these things.

I felt more preoccupied at this point with Cheyenne's "but . . . ," which nagged at me as I fell asleep that night.

As I floated, in limbo; darkness surrounded me. I felt the soft mattress beneath me as I lay in bed, half asleep. A bright light, which at first I thought was the full moon, caught my attention, and I groaned at the discomfort of sensing it. I brought my awareness to my surroundings and realized I had come to the White Place. Aware that I was sleeping, I shrugged this off to dreaming and let it unfold.

I looked down and saw that I wore that lacy white cotton dress I loved. My hair, silky and loose, fell to my knees. I felt so light and so free. I had seen Mason here the last time I visited. The place seemed empty, though. I called out to Mason, wondering about the mysteries of this White Place.

The last time, he had stood in this room of white light, wearing a blue hospital gown and looking around in confusion. I recalled his dark hair, with some greying at the temples giving away his age, and that he appeared a little heavyset, of average height. Where were all of the other spirit forms that had beckoned for him to come with them? I now knew they were deceased family members, as I'd first suspected. The place seemed eerily empty.

My inner voice guided me to walk to my left, to another room lit with an odd red glow. Though it was still a very white place, a burning haze hung in the air and vibrated in earthen reds and browns. As I gazed into its depths, I could see Mason, sitting and talking to someone or something invisible to my eyes. I strained my ears and could just make out that the discussion concerned his past deeds. This appeared to be a form of judgment day for him.

I intuitively knew that every soul went through this here, reviewing its life and deciding whether it needed to be purged for a time before moving on. From here, many souls would choose to sojourn in what we humans called *purgatory*, so that the dross of misdeeds and ill faith would burn away in purification. Because feelings, as we humans knew them, didn't exist at these levels, all of the unsubstantiated fears humans had about going to hell were simply based on ignorance of the true nature of purgatory.

I decided to grant Mason his privacy, so I stepped out of the area and found myself once again in the White Place.

A noise made me turn around, and there stood Mason, now dressed in white garb, much as I was. He silently stared at me in a lucid, speculative way.

"Weren't you just over there in the purgatory life review room, Mason?" I asked him.

He didn't answer right away but looked me up and down. Then he spoke softly, "Yes, I was there, and a part of me still is. In this world we can be in many places at once, and so the injured, bedevilled part of me remains in that place, reviewing, and then will go to be purged, in order to support my decision to go back. I have been shown all probabilities if I decide to stay and move into the spirit world, as well as what waits for me if I decide to return to my earthly life."

Mason paused, looking away. "I've decided that I wish to return, but this will require me to become as I was the first time you visited me. Who you see now is my Higher Self, my soul consciousness. I will once again become that fearful, confused man. Are you willing and able to aid me in my quest to return?"

Without hesitation, I nodded that I would.

"This may ask more of you than you realize," Mason said, "so be sure it is what you desire. I must now leave, for my time in this state has ended, and Mason of Earth must now come forth and finish what he began."

He began to turn away but suddenly stopped and said, "Good luck, and we will meet again."

With those words, the Mason garbed in white disappeared, to be replaced with Mason in a hospital gown.

This Mason I was familiar with, and he seemed less fearful and less confused. To my surprise, he looked at me as if he knew me. As I stood there quietly observing him, he spoke.

"So, there you are. I wondered where you had gone. I'm feeling much better now, and your constant company has helped me tremendously."

On hearing these words, I realized my suspicions were confirmed that I'd never gone far away from this place. Something had kept me bound to Mason. I definitely would need to discuss it with Cheyenne, for this simply would not do.

"Hi, Mason. So, you're saying I've been here with you most of the time?"

He nodded yes. No wonder I hadn't been sleeping well and felt so tired.

"How do you feel, Mason, about your decision to come back?"

"I am fearful, Angel Lady. I'm still not sure if I can do this thing. Will I be able to do this? Are you going to help me through this? Can you?"

Suddenly, he became bewildered and began mumbling in fear. After what seemed like minutes but was merely seconds, he calmed down and became coherent again.

I took a moment to answer but said, "I'll be here for you and do whatever it takes to get you back, Mason, if this is your wish. I promise, and your friend Cheyenne is also here to help. We will all do this together, okay?"

Mason nodded, and, as I watched, he regressed back to his previous state of confusion, with all memory of his life review and his Higher Self now dormant in his subconscious.

He began pacing and mumbling in a deranged manner, almost like a crazy person. I felt surprised at how quickly he had transformed. He turned and came to me like a child, wanting me to hold his hand. This seemed to calm him, so I sat with him, holding him and rocking him, which appeased his anxiety, and his confusion lessened.

Suddenly, I felt his energy shift, and in the next instant he became a man in my arms. His thoughts were not those of a child but of a man who felt love and desire. I realized that during all of these days, we had built a rapport I'd been unaware of and that Mason was falling in love with the one he called his White Angel.

I froze, unsure what to do. But how could I push him away now, if he needed this innocent affection to find the courage to come back? Was it really a problem? It wasn't as if this were the physical world. What harm could it bring? And anyway, I was dreaming, so what the heck! It had been so long since I'd taken comfort in the arms of a man that I found myself easily settling in. It felt more like a nurturing moment than anything else, and so I let it be.

"If this is all it takes to support his return, then how can I push him away?" I reasoned.

I decided nothing harmful would come of this. After the night passed and he rested like a child in slumber, I slipped away in the early morning hours to return to my sleeping body.

The next morning I woke up late, with my body stiff. I looked at the clock, and despite the late hour, I felt as if I hadn't slept all night. Sluggish, I got up and made my way to the washroom, wondering why I felt so tired. As I gazed at my dishevelled state in the mirror, last night's memories surfaced, and I gasped in shock.

Oh, my God! I thought. *I've been spending all of my time with Mason, and what am I going to say to Cheyenne about all of this?* The fact that I knew Mason would return and would need our help confounded the whole situation. I decided to wait and see what happened before I told Cheyenne.

Hadn't Cheyenne said that all was well? Maybe it was all a dream and my imagination?

"Yeah, right!" I said to myself. Time would tell. I ate breakfast, and when I sat down at my computer, I saw an email from Cheyenne.

Hi, Angelina,

Apparently, I may have been misinformed about Mason. Although he is apparently better (doing more on his own), he is technically still in a coma (this is as of Saturday).

Can you check in on Mason and let me know your findings, if possible? I know this is draining for you, and you have your own issues, so please don't overdo it . . .

If we need a big energy "push" again, let me supply the needed energy . . .

Namaste,
Cheyenne

P.S. Just so you do know, your visuals and my intuition have a lot of parallels. I will share later. This is all very real . . . and, of course, just really interesting.

I decided to ask Cheyenne about the possibility of romantic involvement in this White World place before I went back in. I suspected that Mason might have a crush on his Angel Lady. I told Cheyenne what I remembered, holding back only the more personal details. I also wanted to know more about Mason as a person.

Cheyenne responded immediately, which had me curious.

Hi, Angelina,

Yes, romantic attractions are quite real in these realms. After all, we are still just people. Energy work is uniquely intimate, with souls touching souls and hearts touching hearts through unconditional love.

Because many people feel confused about all of this to begin with, a taste of unconditional love (which most people never get anyway from their friends, mates, peers, etc.) can be quite intoxicating and muddled up with romantic and sexual feelings.

So, it's all the more important to maintain focus and clear intent while doing this work—in both the physical and the etheric realms.

I sighed, knowing that my impressions of Mason's feelings towards me were quite true. I would have to pay extra attention not to do anything to encourage his feelings to become deeper.

To answer your questions about Mason: He is a very kind, energetic, outgoing, gregarious kind of a guy, with a rather high moral tone. I have never heard Mason say anything negative about anyone.

All that being said, Mason (long divorced) seems to be in the mode of actively seeking a romantic mate.

Combine Mason's current state (where I'm sure he is lonely, confused, depressed, and scared) with the above, and there can certainly be a tendency to "latch on."

It's very important that we don't let Mason "latch on" to either of us, because this will just get in the way of his full recovery. He needs to learn to stand on his own two feet. And I suspect this was an issue with Mason before all of this, as well.

Also, make sure that you keep this connection to Mason on a high spiritual plane. He is not attached romantically. The last thing we need now is to have a connection of this sort forming.

Don't worry about what happens when Mason comes out of his coma. If some kind of issue arises then, and I doubt it will, we will address it at that point.

In the meantime, behave towards Mason as a healing angel, offering unconditional love and light and encouragement, but keep it on that level. If you feel that he attempts to cross a line, be firm and gentle, as you would with a child.

Let me know if this answers all of your questions. We will continue with distant healing support and comforting and reassuring.

I will let you know if we should do anything differently. Thanks again for your help.

Namaste,
Cheyenne

I hit REPLY and typed the following, because I didn't want Cheyenne to think I'd become in the least involved romantically with Mason.

Hi, Cheyenne,

I have no problem keeping my intent clear and romantically uninvolved with Mason. My main concern is for Mason. I treated him at the time as I do in this realm, and it worked quite well. But thanks for your concern and for handling this issue with kid gloves. This could be a little disconcerting or awkward, couldn't it? LOL! My awful sense of humour again, but hey, if you can't laugh, what is the sense to life?

I'll keep checking and reporting on Mason. I think you may be on to something about a lack of resolve on his part.

A few days went by, and I popped in on Mason every once in awhile. What I encountered one day had me worried, so I wrote to Cheyenne right away. I suggested we might want to take action, for Mason seemed to want to come back but needed our help.

I reported,

The last few days, before Mason went off on his emotional and visionary tangents, he appeared coherent for a bit but then regressed to a lack of concentration. I had to figure out how to get his full attention and keep it, to find out whether he wanted our help, and he did finally confirm this.

As of early this morning, I felt a calming of his inner self, but I fear that a sleep state is setting in. He has gone off elsewhere since then, and I've spent quite a while this morning searching for him and calling to him through myriad labyrinths in the White Place. I think his adult consciousness in that world went to sleep, and his child self is off wandering, lost and searching for something. I might have finally located him and will know only later today when I attempt to contact him again.

I think he is trying to come back but is stumbling around, lost in this White Place, which has so many dimensions. He might get lost for good and, if so, won't be able to return. I suggest we do something soon. Let me know.

I waited anxiously for a response from Cheyenne. I felt a new sense of fear coming from Mason. Time now seemed of the essence. If we wanted to help Mason, it had to be very soon, or we might lose him completely.

Within the hour, I received a reply from Cheyenne.

I will be brief. I checked in on Mason, and it is as you said. I intuit that we need to consciously make an attempt to extract him. I am waiting to hear from you and am ready whenever you are. Time, as you say, is of the essence now, if we wish to support Mason's return.

I answered,

I can be ready to go in, in half an hour, which will be 2:00 pm. It is now 1:30 pm on my clock.

Cheyenne's response was fast in coming.

Thank you, Angelina, for being so open and available to do this. The issues you suggested are very relevant, and all is now clear for us to help Mason find his way back. I feel that since he has not left us, he is meant to come back, but it is ultimately his decision, as you state. Yet we will do everything in our power to help. Remember, I will link you, Mason, and me, as well as a number of spiritual light entities. Then, reach out to him. I will do what I do, based on what I see.

I will connect with you just prior to 2:00 pm. Since I have never done anything quite like this either, I'm not sure how I will pull you out, as you put it. I am just sure THAT I WILL. Fear not. You do what you must, and when you feel it is time, I will expect you to telepathically yell, "Pull!" I hope I'll get the message. I feel confident that I will.

I replied,

I will start going into a trancelike state around 1:30 pm. This will take me a while, to allow for meditation and sinking into it. If you can aid me in any way around 1:50, it would be appreciated. I figure once I'm in and in contact, it will take me about fifteen minutes to get Mason ready to exit, but wait for the call because I'm not sure. When I yell, "Pull!" try to mentally picture your arms grabbing me and pulling Mason and me through the labyrinth that I described to you. Hold on tight, and if you feel the urge to grasp him, please do, because my hold on him may weaken. You have quite a task ahead of you, because you have to support both of us.

Cheyenne wrote.

Okay, after we are done, we should communicate via email or telephone and report what has occurred. I figure anywhere around 2:30 to 2:45 should be about right. I am going now to prepare, and good luck to us all. God speed, Angelina!!!

I got comfortable and turned off my phone. Before long, I felt a buzzing, humming energy surround me, of Cheyenne connecting us together. I sank fast into a deep trance. I found myself entering a south gate of the White Place, contrary to all of the other times when I entered on the northern side. I walked through a labyrinth of tunnels into a silvery white light place, which I now know exists between the worlds of spirit and Earth. This is the place described by many people who have near-death experiences.

Mason had been sleeping, and when I appeared, he awoke and knew exactly what was happening. He asked, "May I have time to say goodbye to my friends and this place of light?"

I told him, "I'll be back shortly. Cheyenne and I need more time to get ready."

I returned to see Mason sitting in a field on top of a mountain with birds and butterflies and animals, listening to the sounds and watching the sun come up, as if remembering Earth. I so loved this aspect of the White Place: it had numerous worlds in one. This stage set of Earth seemed to strengthen Mason's resolve to come back, so, seeing his courage swell, I told him it was time.

We then found ourselves again standing in the original White Place. I looked into Mason's eyes, and he seemed calm and resigned. This live soul retrieval, as I would come to know it, was very different than the enactment a few weeks ago.

Taking a deep breath, I felt the high energy. A pulling suction sensation attempted to draw us up towards a northern doorway that I sensed but could not see. I told Mason to take my hand, look into my eyes, and not let go.

"This won't be easy, Mason, and you'll have to find the strength to come through with me. Cheyenne is here supporting us."

We began hovering above ground, and right before we reached the point of extraction, I reached out through the white mist and grabbed Cheyenne's arm. I pulled a part of Cheyenne down through an opening, so that the three of us could stand in a circle. For the first time, Cheyenne was allowed admittance into the White Place to determine that Mason wanted to come back. We then explained our plan to Mason. When we finished, Cheyenne was forcefully ejected from the White Place. I felt Mason and myself losing ground, because I didn't have the strength to uphold us both energetically.

I felt a need to be pulled, and on cue, I yelled, "PULL!" Cheyenne heard me clearly, and a surge of energy lifted Mason and me upward. Our feet hovered more than six feet above the ground. Suddenly, fear entered Mason's eyes, and he hesitated, floundering in his resolve. I grabbed his arms and told him to hold on tight to me, and he wrapped his arms around me, as a child would with a parent.

I once again yelled, "PULL!" and in moments, we found ourselves being sucked through that earth tunnel at the speed of light. The reality had a much more profound effect than the dream vision. Lights and time zipped by, and Mason buried his face in the space between us, whimpering and crying. Cheyenne turned up the energy to a tremendous magnitude. Mason and I experienced phenomenal feelings, being sucked upward and through the bubble of the White World. Our intense emotions had us crying, and we travelled through the tunnels at a speed so fast, I felt amazed that we didn't get pulled apart.

What seemed like minutes must have been only seconds, before we were hovering at the ceiling over a hospital bed. I slowly glided down with Mason, now lying inert and unconscious in my arms. Because energy had no mass, I could easily support him in this way. As a mother would her child, I gently lay him down into his physical body, prone on the hospital bed. His energy body, a glimmering shroud of multi-coloured lights, glided in smoothly.

Next, his soul, a white gossamer cloud, followed and settled down into his body. I told him to rest and take his time, however much he needed to come back to full consciousness. I remember floating above Mason's body in the hospital and seeing him lying there with his eyes closed. I told him I would be there for him, if he needed me, and not to be afraid.

As I hovered above his body, I saw his features clearly and how restful he now seemed. I looked around and realized we were not alone. A young man sat by Mason's side, with his head cradled in his forearms, leaning on the side of the bed. This must have been Mason's son. On the other side sat an older woman—either a sister or a friend. Fidgeting, she didn't seem pleased to be there. With worry and exhaustion apparent on her features, her skin kept stretching into odd expressions.

I wondered whether they had any sense of what had happened, and at that instant the young man looked up and straight at me. I jumped back, wondering whether he could see me, but then he shook his head and laid his head back on the bed.

I glided back up to the ceiling, and, with one last glance below, I commanded to be brought home.

In seconds, I found myself looking around my studio. I felt numb and dizzy. I slowly stood up and stretched, trying to get my bearings. I glanced at the clock, and only twenty minutes had gone by. I hurriedly sat before my computer and began typing, not wanting to lose any details.

I wrote,

> I must congratulate you on your work and abilities, but I hadn't worried in the least that you wouldn't come through, Cheyenne. I'm curious how much of what I visualized has paralleled your thoughts and so on.
>
> I'm still digesting this. I feel great but tired and will send you a full report once I have rested. I will check in on Mason and keep you posted. I'm looking forward to reading about your impressions. I am off to rest.
>
> *Angelina*

I took a nap and woke up only when the kids got home from school. The balance of the evening had me making dinner and spending time with the kids, so I didn't get back to my computer until early next morning. I decided to look in on Mason before starting an email exchange with Cheyenne.

I wrote,

> Good morning, Cheyenne,
>
> I just checked in on Mason, and the pressure in his head has receded, but I'm under the impression that he hasn't regained consciousness yet.
>
> I contacted Mason easily. He is scared and in a dark place just below consciousness. He has been looking for us, and because I've not contacted him directly, he felt abandoned. I just eased his fears. I sent him healing energy and feel a lessening of his anxiety, as well as the

heart pressure. When I spoke to him, all I could see was Mason lying in the dark.

I'll wait for your direction. All seems fine for now. By the way, since the extraction, my abilities have strengthened, and I'm really affected by everyone around me. It seems the work we have been doing is in some way responsible, almost as if it were an initiation, up and above the norm, but I AM COMING UP SHORT OF SOMETHING. Until I learn to adapt and block this new receptivity, it's driving me bonkers. I feel everyone's physical and mental pains literally, especially my kids'. I've been getting migraines and such, but the same old pattern. I will adjust and learn to block and use my gifts only when needed. Any feedback would be appreciated.

Angelina

Cheyenne responded, "Thanks for the update on Mason. Let's just wait a few days and see. I feel it's time that we book your next initiation. Would tomorrow afternoon work for you?"

I answered yes, and so I began to understand the cycles of transformation. Healing often brought uncomfortable experiences and physical ills not generally associated with it. Healing might demand more effort on my part than I ever could have imagined.

The next day I felt a bit nervous. With these new senses surfacing, I didn't know what to expect from this latest initiation.

Healing, self-realization, and self-mastery were much more complicated than described in books. Those books didn't mention the heartache and the suffering that come with higher awareness. No wonder people preferred to pop a pill and cry wolf than to face the reality of what they created. I began to grasp that whether I liked it or not, I was the one fully responsible for my choices. I had created the foundation for my ills, and only I had the power to change them.

As I prepared for this next initiate experience, I relaxed, and the energy surged. I sank into an abyss of darkness. My body disappeared, and I travelled into another dimension, far from this one.

I later reported,

> Cheyenne, I think I have finally lost it. I'm almost embarrassed to share this with you. But here it goes...
>
> The initiation brought a series of visions to me, as I travelled to a planet very far from here. I emerged on its surface and noticed this planet had two moons, which I found curious and quite beautiful. People who looked very humanoid were going about their business. No one seemed to notice my presence, and I stood watching the amazing brilliance and clarity of this world. I'd obviously ended up on a planet in another galaxy, and these people belonged to a race similar to our own. I heard the thoughts of many people discussing issues among themselves, and I realized they had the gift of telepathy. These highly evolved beings had unparalleled psychic gifts and understanding of higher worlds. Shocked, I felt as if I were home, finally.
>
> Then I was transported to a gathering hall in the White Place. I witnessed a debate between all kinds of funny-looking creatures, mixed with other human-looking and acting ones. A voice told me this was the Galactic Confederation, though I haven't a clue what that is. I sensed it is a governing body of the universe. The discussion concerned the fact that this world I had been on would self-destruct internally in the next five hundred years, and those who had gathered had to find a place to relocate the planet's inhabitants within that time but in secrecy, because of a Reptilian race that threatened harm to them.
>
> These people seemed capable of creating a psychic shield with their minds to protect their home planet. Once they boarded the spaceships for relocation, however, these shields would not be functional, because the people used the natural magnetic energies of the

planet to create them. The members of this peace-loving species had no will to go to war and no ability to fight.

If I haven't lost you by now, then here it goes.

The hunt for a planet that these Star People—as I discovered they're called—could move to finally succeeded. A primitive race with DNA very similar to that of the Star People inhabited this planet. They would have to relocate secretly, to avoid alerting the Reptilians, who repeatedly sought ways to enslave and mate with the Star People. The Reptilians had discovered that they could gain the healing abilities and psychic powers of this race by blending their DNA with the Star People's DNA when they took on physical form.

The planet they discovered, as you may have guessed, was Earth, and for the next few centuries the Star People gradually relocated on the planet. As foreseen by these people, their home planet underwent natural combustion and exploded into a million stars in outer space. By then, the Star People, as Earthlings called them, had been dropped off in groups all over our world and had settled in. They lived for many millennia before the Reptilian race discovered their location. I was told that to this day, the Reptilians, who are fourth- and fifth-dimensional beings, search and travel our world, seeking the purest Star People who still exist, which would allow them to tap into these people's special abilities. The Reptilians take on humanoid forms but still have reptilian features and mannerisms. They can be very cruel and self-serving. Much as we have a soul in a physical body, so do the Reptilians, and they must forget their origins, guided only by the essence of their soul being, which is dark and manipulative. Over the millennia, the Star People have mated with Earthlings, so their once-pure DNA has been watered down. Even now, the Reptilians seek the purebloods, the royal blood of scriptures, to mate with, if possible, and take their gifts, in order to be powerful and rule the universe. This Reptilian race would take from the Star People the light and power of their essence.

I then wondered whether I should share the following vision, knowing how absurd it sounded. Yet I knew it was real in another dimension called *soul*.

So, here I was, being shown all of this, and then I felt myself coming back to my body. Just before I gained consciousness, I stood in the White Place, all alone. Suddenly, something burned into my back. I turned abruptly to behold a manlike figure sitting before me, with arms and legs crossed in a nonchalant way, gazing at me with a smirk on his scaled face. Grey, red, and green scales covered the entire body of this giant lizard man. Though shocked, I didn't feel that the being was threatening, except for his smug, knowing look.

I simply stood there, staring, in the deafening silence. Just when I thought I would scream and demand an answer, the lizard creature spoke in my mind.

"So, here you are. We have been searching for you for quite a time now."

The hairs on my back went up, as a chill ran down my spine. I realized the Reptilian had adopted a casual stance to throw me off. I recognized my mistake in allowing myself to think this being was no threat to me. My shields automatically went up, but it was too late, for the Reptilian man had entered my mind and had a hold of me, energetically.

He rose and glided toward me, his movements graceful and hypnotic. I stood frozen in fright, realizing I was at his mercy. He circled me, bending into me, for he was much taller than I. I felt him at my back, looking me up and down, as he bent over to smell my neck. I jerked away, and he laughed.

He lifted my hair and seemed to enjoy its silkiness. I could see he wished to have a piece of me, but I wasn't sure what that meant in his world, and I didn't want to find out. I swung around, finally able to break his hold on me, and he stepped back, surprised.

"Ah... You are so much stronger than we anticipated! This cat-and-mouse game will be very interesting in the years to come."

His presence brought memories of when I'd felt this invasive dark force around me in the past, but now I could put a face on its source. I asked what this was all about, and, in answer, images began playing out in my mind.

The story of how they'd discovered that the Star People had not perished when the planet exploded but instead had relocated in secrecy had the Reptilians scouring the universe for centuries, searching for clues about where the Star People had gone. The Reptilians needed only a slip of the tongue from a Galactic Confederation official, and soon they had located the Star People on Earth. Their search had ended in vain, though, because the blood of the Star People had become so diluted with time and marriage that it would be difficult to find any of pure blood, if they still existed. As the Reptilians observed and infiltrated Earth's society, they realized that people with developed psychic powers potentially had the purest blood of the Star People, *sang royale/royal blood*, so a new mission of search and capture began. This was about the time that human beings began reporting UFO sightings and abductions.

The images faded, and I felt myself slip away. I heard the Reptilian's words clearly, though: "We are watching you and waiting. Beware, for one day I will have you. You are mine, and I will win."

Next thing, I'm awake here and wondering whether I have gone bonkers.

So, I will understand, Cheyenne, if you want to have nothing to do with me, because this is quite clearly a

> delusional episode, and the fact that I even thought to share it and give it truth is bad enough. I am sending this email before I lose my nerve. I await your impressions.

I pressed the SEND button with misgivings but shrugged and realized that nothing in my life these last few years could be classified as "normal" or sane.

Within half an hour, I had a response.

> Angelina, please don't worry, for this is not new to me. Many people have shared experiences such as yours, so there is a whole body of truth supporting the probability that these Reptilians do exist, and much of what you shared can verily be true.
>
> Now, I do have concerns about what this Reptilian said to you, and if ever you should encounter him or any of his kind again, please take it as a serious threat and be vigilant. I really do not feel that this is safe, and I have a gut sense that much of what he said has truth. Please keep me informed about any future dealings with these creatures. You know I am sworn to protect you and will as best I can.

With that, Cheyenne said goodbye and that we could connect in the morning concerning Mason.

I sat back, when a realization began to surface. That awful dark force emanating from the Reptilian WAS THE SAME darkness I often felt around my Merlin teacher, Anne. Finally, I had answers, and I decided to henceforth curb my curiosity about esoteric practices and Celtic rituals.

I hurriedly drafted a letter to my Merlin teacher, explaining that I could no longer attend her classes for a while. I sent it off, hoping this would not draw any bad feelings to me, for I knew she was a Reptilian. I could now see the reptilian in her features and mannerisms. I shivered, shaking off any fear, for I would not give this any more power. Time would tell whether the truth came close to what I had witnessed.

Chapter 27

Bridging the Worlds: Two Worlds Become One

"Two worlds are but one reality."

—Michèle C. St.Amour

During the next few days, I often "popped in" to check on Mason. Though still in a coma, he had been brought back on some level. Yet his consciousness lingered just below the surface, lost in a void of silence. I couldn't fathom why he didn't wake up. With permission from Cheyenne, I decided to contact Mason, because I didn't like what I'd picked up clairvoyantly. And so I travelled into the void.

As I centred myself and asked to be brought to Mason, I glided to a place just beyond waking consciousness, a dimension that people woke up to when they opened their spiritual eyes. Unlike previous times when I'd found Mason in the White Place, I'd now landed in an extremely dark, eerily quiet realm. I held my hand up to my eyes but saw nothing. I merely sensed my arm in front of me.

In this all-encompassing darkness, I would have to rely on my subtle senses. I sent out my sensory field and felt my way around, surprised by the cold and the sense of peace in this place. I felt cocooned in a womb of outer space. Could this be the void of creation we read about in spiritual books? From far within my mind, I heard an echo: *"Yesssss."*

Hesitantly, I glided a few steps, feeling emptiness below my feet. I wondered, *How can I locate Mason when I cannot see? Is Mason even here?*

Again, that familiar voice from within whispered, *"He is here."*

I sent out an echo of sound, calling to Mason. Quietness met my call.

I contemplated what to do next. Something moved not far from me, and the hairs stood up on the back of my neck. A chill ran down my spine. I turned and sensed nothing more. I shook away my nightmares of dark places, for my apprehension would draw such experiences to me. In this place, anything could manifest simply with a thought. In this soul of creation, all possibilities reigned but a thought away.

I called out to Mason again but more resolutely. I stood still, about to give up, when I heard a rustle to my left and a tiny childlike voice.

I reached out, sending the command to bring me forth, and swirled through the abyss. The tiny voice grew clearer and louder in my mind. It dawned on me that this had also happened when I looked for Mason in the White Place, and he remained stuck in a childlike state, lost.

I again commanded to be brought to Mason immediately. I whirled ahead and found myself standing face-to-face with him. He appeared relieved. I didn't question the fact that I could now see him.

"Where have you been?" he cried, wrapping me in a big brotherly bear hug.

He felt confused by this new place since arriving here. Panic had set in these last few days. I explained that he had left the coma world, though he still remained in an unconscious mental state.

"You simply have to resolve to wake up," I told him.

"I can hear you, Angel Lady, but I cannot see you clearly, except as a dim memory."

"You are in the void of unconsciousness," I explained. "It has no light, because this is the place before anything has manifested."

He nodded.

"Mason, you must rouse yourself and not worry. I am here with you, though you cannot see me."

I wondered why I could see him, though.

The inner voice answered my silent query: *"Your mind's eye is seeing with your unique subtle sense of clairvoyance."*

I nodded in understanding.

Mason thanked me and said he would awaken shortly. I sent out a hug and wished him all the best. I intuited that his memories of this would be buried so deep in his subconscious, he would probably attribute them to a dream.

I commanded to be brought back and instantly returned my familiar world. I immediately reported everything to Cheyenne.

> I contacted Mason, and he is scared and in a dark place just below consciousness. The pressure in his head has receded. He felt abandoned and afraid, because he hadn't heard from us. I told him we have been with him and not to fret. I then sent him healing energy and felt his tenseness and anxiety easing. I could see through his eyes that he is in complete darkness, and this disconcerts him. I told him to simply will himself to wake up.

I paused in my writing, with my gut screaming that Mason would wake by early evening, and 8 pm kept popping into my head. Yet I doubted my intuition, so I played it safe.

> Another thing—I sense he will emerge within the next twenty-four hours. Please keep me tuned in.

Cheyenne's response came a few hours later.

> I worked with Mason at a distance for forty minutes this A.M. What I intuited is consistent with what you got, although less on the confusion/fear factor. It's more a reluctance to face the work he needs to do. Strangely, I'm able to get to him now, whereas I couldn't enter the White

Place. I felt my work was effective. We need to wait and see.

Namaste,
Cheyenne

I sighed, impatient that this had dragged on. I needed to get back to my normal routine and let the Creator do the work. I decided to have some friends over for a gathering to dispel my obsession with Mason. I got on the phone, and by end of day I'd organized everything.

I had invited twenty friends over for a full moon gathering. I felt good to be socializing, as in the past. I'd cut out so many activities while studying with Cheyenne. I needed to re-enter society.

We began the evening's activities with a healing circle, followed by a meditation. Quite an assortment of personalities had gathered, and I sensed that something was up. I tingled all over, and the energy seemed unusually high, even for a full moon night. My sensory antennae stayed on high alert, a sign to pay heed to the invisible world.

The kids stayed in the house, doing their thing, while I held the gathering in the upstairs studio of my shop.

We all caught up on our news before beginning the ceremonies. I knew not to go too deep during the meditation, for who knew what could occur with the places I travelled to these days? Most people at the gathering didn't have the awareness or the ability to handle this.

As I sat down, I sent out word to my guides to keep us all safe and blessed.

Sitting on the floor cross-legged and facing one another, the twenty-one women circled an array of candles on a silver tray that reflected their radiance. I went into a light state of meditation. Everyone was very serious, and the music in the background created a lovely atmosphere, with more than fifty candles illuminating the room. I'd opened the windows because of the mild weather and the candles emitting so much heat. I felt the energy surge in me and that "plugged in" sensation swirled and rose from the base of my spine, wanting to snake upward. I held it back, feeling this wasn't the place for it.

All remained quiet, as each woman became lost in her inner world. An inner fire built in me, unlike anything I'd ever felt before. I wondered whether I could manage the depth of trance these powerful energies created. At these thoughts, my inner voice directed me into a deeper state of meditation. I obeyed without question.

A consciousness inside directed me to let the energy build within my womb and hold it to a specific feeling of fullness. I couldn't have stopped it, even if I'd wanted to. Just when I thought I'd explode, the inner voice told me to release the force from my heart centre. I did so, while on some level I felt so familiar with this, as if I had done it many times in the past.

As the energy surged forth from my upper chest, I experienced an inexplicable feeling of pure love, founded on indescribable bliss. A sharp, heavy pain in my chest followed this. I saw via my subtle eyes a beam of crystal white light emerge from my heart centre. This pure light reached out to touch each person in the circle, directly at her heart centre, causing everyone to feel a sudden jolt. As if a star had burst from my breasts, its rays had landed in the hearts of all of those gathered. I sat stunned, questioning what I'd witnessed.

At that instant, numerous women in the circle felt simultaneous emotional releases, and everyone snapped out of the meditation. Stunned, I wondered whether the light from my heart had caused the sudden release people experienced.

In her usual dramatic way, Josie excitedly told us she had seen an angel of white light appear in the centre of the circle. Her unruly blonde locks bounced as she bobbed up and down, telling her tale. Two others agreed that they had also seen a form silhouetted in white light. I remained silent. A sinking feeling came over me, as they continued to describe what sounded an awful lot like my Higher Self. The magnitude of what had just happened hit me.

Tracy sat in silence directly across from me, with confusion on her face and a question in her eyes. I looked away, refusing even to contemplate that this event had not been my imagination. I spoke of it to no one, not even my good friend Jeannie. I didn't want to deal with the consequences if I did, for egos abounded in this circle. In these gatherings, I decided to keep my awareness of other dimensions to myself.

Let's just say, the experience made their night, and many shared their phenomenal healing clearings for days to come.

We closed the circle, and everyone went off, still talking about what had occurred. I kept my silence, but Tracy looked at me strangely as she left and mentioned that we had an appointment in the morning.

The next morning I awoke, remembering that Tracy was due to come in for an energy healing session. When she arrived, we sat down with a cup of tea. She looked at me and suddenly asked me what I had done last night. Surprised by the question, I didn't immediately remember the heart energy burst, having pushed it to the back of my mind. Seeing the puzzled expression on my face, she explained how she had witnessed the events of the previous night. While we were all meditating, suddenly her gaze had been drawn to me. She saw a bolt of white light emerge from my heart and hit everyone in the heart, including her. She felt a jolt and a huge release of emotions and witnessed the same effect on others, as some cried openly and others sat silently. She once again asked what I had done.

I sat stunned, as it sank in that this had happened as I'd envisioned it. Spirit had confirmed it. I needed a few minutes to regain my equilibrium. Then I told her about my experience and my doubts of its validity. I thanked her for sharing. Now I had to deal with yet another new phenomena.

* * *

Later that day, I checked my emails and noticed another one from Cheyenne. This was unusual, because we tended to communicate only in the mornings.

> Hi, Angelina,
>
> *Mason has emerged from his coma!* He opened his eyes last night around 8 p.m.
> I have included a copy of an email that I sent to some of Mason's friends with the details.

I sat back in shock, wondering if it was finally over. I felt sad that it had ended, mixed with a sense of wonder and accomplishment. *Now what?* I thought. *What would come of this?* I hurriedly skimmed through the entire missive.

Hello, Friends,

I am delighted to be able to share some VERY wonderful news about Mason—he has emerged from his coma! I got this from Holly, a close friend of Mason's, who went to visit him this A.M. Last night Mason opened his eyes. Someone then came in and did some tests with Mason, all of which he apparently passed.

That he can respond to verbal instruction is a very good sign.

Incidentally, Holly also said that he looked great, with good colouring, and he was doing more physical things on his own as well.

This is really wonderful news!

Please be so kind as to keep Mason in your thoughts and prayers, for now he has a challenging road to recovery. I am absolutely delighted that Mason has finally emerged.

Regards,
Cheyenne

In an aside, Cheyenne told me,

Angelina, I suggest that you back off a little with your spirit visitations and focus on sending healing energy, love, and light. This energy will be very much needed. I will go down to see him this weekend.

Congratulations on a job well done! I knew you were a quick study, and this is a good demonstration of it. Thanks again!

I immediately wrote back to Cheyenne.

> Well, I'm floored! So my sense yesterday that Mason might emerge was right on. I'm so glad for you and his family! It's so nice for people to have friends like you guys. Congratulations!

Cheyenne responded:

> Well, after you get up off the floor, give yourself a good pat on the back for a job well done. As for me and my role, after all, what are friends for?
>
> However, as I said before, I felt that Mason and I have roots that go back prior to this life. To some extent, I feel that the events that unfolded tend to verify this. Keep in touch. I am off and running for an evening celebration.
>
> *Namaste,*
> *Cheyenne*

I replied a few hours later, once it all had settled in.

> WELL! Well! I'm still on the floor, Cheyenne. I think that about says it all!!!
>
> The enormity of everything has sunk the ship; the passengers are coming up for air . . . LOL!!!!
>
> Your emails have brought home what we accomplished. I didn't even dwell on how having proof of any kind would change everything. Since the retrieval, I knew deep down what we had done, but until you told me that Mason actually came out of the coma, it hadn't really sunk in. I felt him emerging and knew it would be that night, but I played it safe and phrased it casually in my email to you. Now all of my self-doubt has evaporated, and the truth of it has swooped in and knocked me off my feet. And, as you state, the responsibility brings home the seriousness of what we discovered about alternate realities.
>
> This clinched it, because you do not praise lightly or unless you have concrete proof.

Anyway, my stomach butterflies will pass, and all will soon return to normal.

So what now? After this, the normal routine will seem pretty boring! LOL! I'm incorrigible!

Good luck with seeing Mason, and you do realize he won't volunteer any info unless you bring it up? Yet I realize you can't broach the subject until he's well.

If you see Mason, let me know ALL the details, please! This is simply fascinating.

The only thing left to top our cake would be for him in the future to actually have visuals or impressions of what we attempted.

Angelina

Cheyenne responded,

And yes, it would be absolutely wonderful if Mason has memories of this, because, if he does, you can rest assured that this story will be published.

Doubting your capacities at this stage in your development is perfectly normal. However, just remember, if I had doubted them, I wouldn't have asked for your help.

But remember, with power comes great responsibility.

And after all, it wasn't us, as in the little "I"—it was us as a conduit for Spirit.

I'm sure this type of work will just get more and more interesting, so stay tuned...

Have a wonderful evening!

Namaste,
Cheyenne

I sat back in my chair, wondering where this would take me. My life had been turned upside-down. My head began aching, and, with the headache, a memory surfaced. I decided it was time to write to Cheyenne about something that had plagued me since we began the visits to Mason.

> I've noticed that when I'm around people, my empathic nature has me connecting me to them on such deep levels that I take on their personalities and feelings and lose myself in their emotions and sensations.
>
> I only became conscious of this new level of invasiveness last week at a gathering I hosted. Once I noticed that my behaviour and the associated emotions and thoughts were not of my choosing or in fact mine at all, I would disconnect from the person in a conscious way, as you taught me. But by then it was too late. Their energy had "invaded" me.
>
> Can you clarify what is happening, and how can I stop it?
>
> I never know what is "mine," with these subtle, all-encompassing events.

Cheyenne could not help me and suggested that I maintain a log. In time, the problem might be clarified. I wrote.

> This new level of empathy will obviously allow me to relate to others at even deeper depths, which means I will judge less and empathize at deeper levels than before. God help me! LOL!

With this new development, some strange things had occurred.

* * *

Months ago, I started having severe headaches, followed by visions or indications that something, some information, wanted to come through. The most recent time I'd been plagued by a headache, I picked up my friend Fran on her lunch break from work, and we drove to the marina by the river to enjoy coffee and a chat. Fran had the gift of sight, and Spirit often used her to pass me messages.

That particular day, we talked about generalities, catching up on the few months since our last time together. Fran suddenly got "plugged in," as we call having a vision, for she was as psychic as I. I asked her what was up. She told me to keep talking and wait. After a few minutes, she stated that she saw something from another reality, another dimension, and felt a bit freaked by it.

She saw a gold feather being swiped across my forehead. As she told me this, I felt the pressure in my head recede a bit. She described a band of white light appearing across and around my head, and she had no clue what this meant. At this point, my headache more or less left, and I kind of felt something there, but I wasn't sure what.

She said that when we'd first parked, she tried to connect to me energetically to help relieve my headache, because she was also a healer—but she couldn't. Something had blocked her before these visions began. We made light of it, and I forgot about the incident.

That same evening I sat on the front porch, listening to the silence. Out of the blue, a being appeared on my left. I thought I was hallucinating, because the being appeared so solid and spoke so plainly and concisely. A voice whispered that he belonged to a special committee or was sanctioned by them or worked in conjunction with them. White light surrounded him, and everything around us looked like the White Place.

The being wore a robe similar to those in ancient Rome, in an electric blue colour, shimmering with the light of that world. He had shoulder-length hair, curly and golden brown. His energy felt loving and accepting. A band of white light circled his head on a level with the third, fourth, and fifth eye. It brought to mind the white band Fran had seen around my head earlier that day.

He telepathically communicated the following to me:

You are being shown and asked to remember the planet of many moons. Some of us were birthed from this place, and we are being asked to help others transition into a higher consciousness that will unite mankind as one. We lived fully, with all seven senses, in this home we originated from. But many have forgotten, as it was destined to be.

Now is the time of remembrance.

Many have scattered and must be brought together, if humanity's destiny will be fulfilled.

As suddenly as he had appeared, he was gone, and I remained sitting in the dark night.

Yet another being had talked of destiny and saving the world! I felt confused by so many visions and unclear messages. I shrugged and decided to put this one on the shelf with the others, until I'd solved the puzzle of my life. I couldn't force these things—everything came in its own time.

The next morning, I met with Rose, my first teacher. I asked her what she could see around me, and she said my crown was wide open and beaming upward and outward. She saw wings at my back and got the word *initiation*.

I told her about the being in the electric-blue robe the previous night, as well as what Fran had seen.

I wanted to know about the golden feather. I sensed that it meant a graduation of some sort to higher wisdom, like a ceremony to open a door. Surprisingly, a few days earlier, she had read about the symbolism of the golden feather. She said she would dig it out for me.

Rose also had the sight, though not nearly as developed as Fran's or mine. Yet she could often tap into clear ideas in a very grounded way. Her intuition told her that my teachings would now come from a higher dimension and that I was one of the first and would learn more about it in time. She felt that this being I'd described had very high energy and was innately good and that I had been blessed in some way.

This being came to see me three more times. I told him he had better be very clear and concise, if they wanted me to do anything, or else I would simply ignore them.

The next instant I saw a group of others similar to the Roman guy in that "White Place," laughing and saying I would never change, and they understood.

I began to call this being "Roma." He came into my sight on my left side and had substance and clarity not normally associated with spirits. Spirits didn't usually appear like this, and the left-side approach differed from my usual way of seeing. His communications also seemed more earthly. He simply popped up, in my mind's eye, and his clear, precise way of speaking made me suspect my mind had played tricks on me.

I suddenly heard that inner voice say, "*No, not your imagination. He is very real, and pay him and the others heed!*"

I nodded, because I couldn't have created this being. I decided not to tell Cheyenne about Roma just yet.

The next day I received this from Cheyenne:

> Hi, Angelina,
>
> RE: Mason update—he is in rehab now. He is speaking—a bit slower than usual, but pretty much the way he always has. He has full movement, but he can't walk on his own as of yet—not sure why. It may have to do with the problem you felt in his lower back.
>
> You had said the doctors might not pick up on it, and you were right. You pinpointed it as an energy blockage, perhaps having to do with home issues and the associated emotions. This seems to prove your intuitions were correct, so bravo once again!
>
> My family thinks a miracle has happened, and they are grateful for all that we did.
>
> Let me know if you have any questions.

I answered,

> My intuition tells me he remembers "stuff," but it's all muddled, like a dream. How much his conscious mind is willing to accept will be based on his will to heal.
>
> If he can do this, he will definitely remember a lot of it in time. If I'm right, you will have to keep him from shouting it to the world. You will have your hands full, once word in your community gets out. Then the responsibility issue will hit us right between the eyes. You'll also have to figure out the best way to handle everything, in everyone's best interest.

Michèle C. St.Amour

These are just my thoughts of what might come, but it's all still up in the air, and everything depends on Mason.

Namaste,
Angelina

So that was the end of that.

Chapter 28

Endings and New Beginnings

"There will come a time when you believe everything is finished.
That will be the beginning."

—Louis L'Amour

A Few Months Later . . .

My energy had shifted once again.

The previous initiation had caused my empathy to temporarily lose the ability to maintain boundaries. Cheyenne felt perplexed by this roller-coaster ride, as did I.

Each initiation created a similar experience. By virtue of repetition, I continued to learn about laws governing the world of subtle energy and initiation.

"*The science of transformation* . . . ," said that inner voice.

I hoped this latest "spirit infusion" settled soon, because I always felt "buzzed" from its intensity. My nervous system had taken a beating. My adrenals were out of whack. My adrenaline high made sleep almost impossible. I asked my guides for breaks, and I got moments of intermittent peace, but I would be relieved if this settled into a more "normal" state.

I laughed out loud at that. *Normal* no longer existed in my world, and did I really want normal?

I'd discovered the power of the words I chose and how they told a hidden tale about my subconscious reasoning. I learned about the polarity of words. Each word carried a vibration that either uplifted you or fed off you, just as some people energized, while others depressed.

Present Day

I come back to the present moment. I stand up to get my circulation going and to ground myself, because all of this jumping back and forth in time can be so confusing. Yet it does teach me to "let go" and blend my energies, my female (yin) and male (yang), into one cohesive whole. I'm beginning to understand that Teacher is far wiser than I could have imagined. This time jumping indirectly "trains my brain" to consciously accept intuitive information in a logical sequence simultaneously. Interesting, indeed . . .

Tracy's words at the full moon gathering still echo in my mind. How did that blast of white light emanate from my chest?

As I sit back down at my desk, pondering, Teacher makes herself heard.

> *Angelina, listen closely, for this is very important.*
>
> *When a person comes into emotional, psychological, and spiritual balance at high-energy frequencies, the seat of the soul heart opens up. It is something to aspire to, but few ever find the guidance and proper mentorship to "walk the heart to light," which means following the path of Truth.*

I nod, but my attention begins to wander.

You have come to set straight misguided ideas about things, so pay attention while I share these truths with you.

I feel a cold breeze blow past me, like a slap on the face. It brings me swiftly back.

Each soul has come to live an experience unique to that person and his or her karmic deeds. Few are able to move above spiritual egotism. Fame and glory surround the spiritual path, and many false impressions and ideas abound.

As your new friend Lynne wisely said, "Everyone wants to be an elder but they haven't a clue what it implies. They want the idea of it but not the work or discipline of it; now, the heart thing, as you call it.

I nod, because recently I was introduced to a community of spiritual followers, who all had such ungrounded notions about spirituality. People don't realize that everything isn't bliss and love when one becomes "realized." One, in fact, becomes "more human," more *pied à terre*, as we say in French.

Remember, Angelina, when your heart is open, you experience the beauty of your divinity.

Look to the prophecy for guidance and direction. Unravel within its symbolism the hidden truths in your visions woven by Grandmother Spider.

The Sacred Heart energy can be likened to a powerful vortex generating a field of free-flowing immeasurable energy. It comes directly through to you from the Cosmic Source of Divine Love energy. It can destroy, as it can create. This energy is healing, initiative, of the sacred, a beacon of light a person emanates from the heart core. You may recall what this looks like from pictures of saints and wise men.

It is the sign of the sacred within a mystic.

That catches my attention. A mystic? Did she call me a mystic? To me, mystics epitomize suffering, martyrdom, going without, saintly smiles and countenances, and the list can go on. No way will I ever walk that road! I enjoy shopping and beauty too much to find happiness in living a mystic's life!

I hear laughter, then it rumbles in an outright roar. Is that Teacher?

> *You all have such out-dated ideas, my dear, about masters and mastering the spiritual life. The Creator does not want you to suffer, and this is where you made most of your mistakes in the past. Beauty is of the Creator, so it is fine to want beauty in and around you.*
>
> *It is not about going without but, in fact, about not needing. That is the secret to Remembering!*

The heart light recently blasted from my chest again—yet another mystery to unravel. What triggered it and what should I do with it? How do I turn it on or off or keep it from exploding outright? Teacher, reading my thoughts, continues,

> *The Sacred Heart—which you call the "white light heart"—is used to heal, protect, and initiate others into the sacred. It is a sign of a realized mystic.*
>
> *You and I walked this path of awakening a long time ago, and I never thought to walk it with you again.*
>
> *It is unheard of that one should return to such ignorance but retain such power. But, of course, I should not be surprised, knowing the soul group you are part of. You all have such intriguing, unconventional soul paths, this forever keeps us "Planners" on our toes.*

This heart light talk triggers a recollection of my early teen years. Teacher stops, as the memory in me surfaces. Tears well up in my eyes.

The holograph of time opens, and I see myself as an impressionable pre-teen, tall and gangly with long hair, on the brink of life-changing events. Because I'd forgotten who I was, normality coloured my life until puberty beckoned, and the time to resurrect the old began.

The scene before me took place during Lent, right before Mom's cancer diagnosis, when life would forever change.

I gravitated to the only source of spiritual nourishment I knew at that age: my Christian upbringing. I felt so at home in the energies of the church and in the kind teachings of a benevolent and loving Jesus.

Mom always dragged me with her to Sunday morning mass, which I didn't mind at all. I loved catechism, a subject we visited every day at school with spellbinding stories. Our Jesus loved us, because the wrathful, angry God of my mother's upbringing had been laid to rest.

To this day, every time I set foot in a lofty church, I'm overcome with a feeling of something out of time. People designed the architecture of churches specifically to enhance yin energy, drawing a vortex of feminine energy that connected us to the Cosmic Source.

That year, I had decided that every day during Lent, I would go and pray for contact with that which I knew not but felt from deep within.

"I will pray to Jesus, and He will come," I said to myself. "He is resurrected, so that means He isn't dead. And if He isn't dead, then if I pray hard enough, He will come to me as He has come to others!"

For three weeks, I faithfully went to church, praying, then pleading for a sign, but nothing manifested. My faith was strong. I knew that Jesus was real, and I trusted the feeling that filled me with such hope. Maybe I hadn't done it right?

So I worked harder at it and stayed longer in prayer, in supplication. I knew Jesus was my friend. I had such faith in His existence.

Nothing happened. No answers came to my questions. I wanted to give up. I felt the same disillusionment as when my parents had explained that Santa Claus wasn't real. I'd felt pain on learning this, as if a knife had run through my heart. In that moment, magic had been stamped out of my life. This revelation crushed my childhood faith in the unseen. At that moment, at the age of seven, something inside me had died.

Even now, I can bring forth that pain of crushed dreams and dashed hopes about something existing behind the palpable. My parents had lied to me in such a cruel manner. How could loving parents let me believe in something so deeply, in this jovial man they called Santa, and not know how much pain I'd feel to learn the truth?

This same pain almost surfaced because of my deep feelings for Jesus, a longing for divine, unconditional, all-encompassing love. Yet I refused to give in. Something deep inside urged me to have faith, an unspoken voice I felt but could not hear. I decided to go back to church one last time, though I felt angry and tormented.

When I arrived at the empty church, I sat on a bench, halfway from the front. I knelt and began to pray.

This day seemed different, because of my anger and hurt feelings. My prayers were not thankful and loving but condescending and wrathful, full of disillusionment and questions. Lost in thought and in agony, I didn't notice the light until it surrounded and infused me.

I looked up in surprise. White light with rays of gold filled the room. Its brightness hurt my eyes. As my eyes adjusted, I made out a figure before me, floating a few feet above the floor, with a loving, welcoming smile. It was Jesus Himself, in His full glory. I couldn't believe my eyes. All of my anger dissipated. The warmth from his eyes melted away my doubts and the pain in my heart.

Filled with love energy, I thought I would explode into a million stars. I had a sensation of expansion and floating upward. My heart swelled and then burst from my chest, as a light so white and bright surged forth to join His. Time stood still, and I found myself in another dimension of reality. We glowed, fused, and looked deeply into each other's souls. In that moment, I knew and remembered everything. I felt peace. I was home, the only home I had ever known, before I had asked to forget.

Ah, this was what I had missed and searched for so desperately. Here lay the foundation of my deep sadness. Jesus smiled again, and I noticed the presence of many souls from my group who had always supported me.

I then knew the true meaning of taking the Eucharist, ingesting the real presence of Christ, incarnated through God's Son, Jesus. Faith in life and in myself resurfaced. Jesus telepathically sent me a message to let me know He and the others were with me, of me, and guiding me. Even if I didn't see them, the Christ was in me, within me, and of me. I nodded in loving understanding. Slowly, his image faded and disappeared.

I sat in quietness, absorbing the truth of who I was and why I had once again come to Earth. I looked around to see if others had witnessed this. Though a few souls had come in during this mystical encounter, no one seemed to have noticed anything untoward. Still infused with loving bliss, I decided to walk the path of crucifixion, remembering its true symbolism. One day I would share this with the world. As I reached the image, I gazed at Jesus on the cross, bleeding and offering His suffering for the salvation of humanity in retribution for all sins. The hidden symbolism remained lost to man, but I would bring it forth in time, so man could be freed. Those first minutes reunited me with my soul and my soul purpose. I renewed my vow to God the Creator and to myself, knowing that everything had a purpose.

I left the church, but by the time I got home, I'd convinced myself the vision had been my imagination. Still, a sense of peace and purpose had replaced my anxiety and empty heart.

This experience eventually receded into my subconscious, because I wasn't meant to fully remember it yet. Yet a remnant of the love and dreamlike awareness of its source supported me to this day. The wreath of thorns around my heart, symbolizing suffering, had been removed on that encounter—a sign that my awakening would begin, as preordained. This, my first experience of the white heart light, happened at barely ten years of age. Within weeks of that encounter, I began my menses, and so childhood ended.

Remote Viewing with Cheyenne

The holograph closes on this memory of my youth, but, in a breath, another opens in a cloud of swirling energy. I feel confused as images surface, and I wonder where I'm now being guided. I recognize a time when Cheyenne asked me to help solve an ongoing murder spree in the States. I focus my eyes and become immersed in yet another memory.

As I remember, it began with me staring at the computer screen, hypnotized by inner thoughts. An email came through with a resounding "ding."

Startled, I jumped. It was from Cheyenne. I decided to open it. Our correspondence had been less frequent lately, because Cheyenne could no longer answer many of my questions. I'd begun to look to other avenues for answers. I once again read the signs that foretold I might soon say goodbye to one mentor and move on to another.

Something else bothered me about Cheyenne, but I couldn't put my finger on it. Something nagged at me about certain aspects of our association that made me uncomfortable.

I began reading the email.

> Hi, Angelina,
>
> A recent event portrayed on the news has caught my curiosity, and I'm being guided to ask if you would like to collaborate with me and see what details we can dig up via remote viewing?

Remote viewing? I asked myself. *What exactly is this?* I vaguely remembered something to do with astral-projecting to locations to use one's clairvoyant abilities to obtain information. When I asked for more details regarding RV (short for "remote viewing"), Cheyenne told me,

> It's a form of gathering information that uses scientific protocols to develop and extend these abilities. I would, of course, familiarize you with said case, if you agree to this experiment.
>
> A bit later, I'll send you a book on it, written by one of the leading authorities and developers of the RV protocols. He spent many years in the CSL (Cognitive Sciences Lab) in the United States, as one of the main developers and researchers of remote-viewing protocols. He was also an active researcher and subject of the highly secretive STARGATE project of the U.S. government, which trained remote viewers for the army to gather intelligence information during the Cold War.

This was getting interesting, and I wondered what Cheyenne wanted us to "remote view."

> A series of killings in the area has officials perplexed, and I wonder if you would be willing to "go in" and have a look? If your findings are coherent and efficient, I do have the ability to bring them to light to the proper

personnel and departments. Let me know if this type of case working appeals to you.

Namaste,
Cheyenne

I sat back, wondering whether I wanted to do this. I took but a second to decide. Of course, I did!

I felt a stirring of excitement and anticipation. I sent off an email, and in no time Cheyenne instructed me not to research any details online about the case and to avoid any newscasts concerning this, so as not to influence my information gathering. I agreed, and because I didn't watch the news or much television, this wouldn't be a problem.

Shortly after that, Cheyenne sent me a brief email with vague details and told me to "go in" and report my findings immediately afterward. The email read,

> A rash of murders has occurred in the area, with no clues about the suspect or motivation. To date, six people have been killed.

I sat back and let out a breath, releasing any uncertainty about being able to do this. Of course, I could, and so I began setting the stage.

I asked to be brought to the culprits who had been responsible for the murders and found myself in a dark void with thousands of lights zipping by. I ended up in a night-time location. I couldn't make out anything except a streetlight ahead, reflecting off the pavement and showing a parked car in front of a three-story brick building. The trees had an abundance of fall foliage, indicating a location south of me.

I saw no people around. My inner eyes approached a brown car that looked like a Chevy. I flew past it and noticed it appeared to be lived in. Before I could take a closer look, I flew up the stairs of the building to an upper floor and through a door to an apartment.

What had seemed to be an apartment was in fact a room for rent, I later learned. I heard two male voices discussing something. One sounded older and mature, while the other seemed much younger and juvenile. I asked to be brought to the voices, and with this thought, I stood before two black men, a teenage boy and an older man with an African American hairdo. The older dark-skinned man had a flat thick nose and did most of the talking. They kept their heated conversation to low whispers. The younger man didn't feel right about what the older man wanted to do, but he feared voicing his thoughts. A sinister air hung over the two, and both wore matching brown leather bomber jackets.

Empty takeout containers littered the place. I just knew these men were the murderers and that this was far from over. I listened to them plan and discuss their next shootings. They would hit again the next day, targeting a white woman in a nearby mall. I felt horrified at the rancour and hate emanating from these two. Their auras appeared very dark, with a greyish glow that spoke of evil and vindictiveness.

I found myself back in my body, and, before I forgot, I sat down to type all of the details I had seen. I included a composite sketch of the two. I sent it off immediately to Cheyenne, who said to email any more details that might surface. I had a habit of reviewing and seeing more details at a later time.

Cheyenne told me that no one had reported anything like what I'd seen and that the investigators suspected the shooter would be a white middle-aged male. This was a far cry from my observations.

The next day I got an email from Cheyenne, stating that as I had predicted, a woman had been shot in the parking lot of a mall that morning, and that, all things considered, my intel about the culprits might just be right. Would I be willing to go in again and see what else I could dig up? Of course, I said yes—but not until the next day, because the kids had just come home.

The following morning, my remote viewing brought me to that same Chevy car, though its colour had changed to sky blue. It was parked outside a white trailer house with a grassy yard during daylight hours. I couldn't see anyone but felt that the murderers lived here or had come from this house. I got a few numbers but could not get a name.

Cheyenne told me,

Numbers and names are difficult or practically impossible to obtain, in most psychic-related phenomena, so don't worry that you haven't received these details.

Cheyenne said that in time and with practice, I might develop this ability. But now, without any concrete clues, nothing much could be done, except for me to continue to view and see what appeared.

I stayed away from the news to avoid influencing my viewing, and during the next week Cheyenne reported a series of shootings. The last one, of an FBI agent, created quite a stir. We decided I should go in one more time.

My last attempt had been more than a week ago, and as I searched, I couldn't get anything. I seemed to have reached a dead end. Maybe I'd tried too hard or knew too much about the case now, because, like it or not, this had become international news. I had heard the odd report, which might have influenced my ideas. I had taken in too much information and couldn't make my mind blank. My mind wanted to take off with its own ideas. Imagination could be so dangerous. I couldn't always separate my ideas from what came in.

Then I got the idea of going to the White Place to contact the murder victims and get information from them. Since I had managed to contact Mason there, I might as well try.

I felt myself flying in a sky of bright clouds, and though I was in the White World, I had never visited this part of it. I had no vision of the earth or the sky above, but the sun and misty clouds surrounded me.

Suddenly, I broke through the clouds and appeared in the White Place. Before me stood a group of people I presumed were some of the sniper victims. They dispersed in confusion soon after I began looking for answers and were unable to communicate with me—all except one.

A woman of average build with dark hair approached and stared at me. She understood why I had come and telepathically agreed to help me. I held her hand, and we travelled down into the past, for I needed to know more about her and how I could help her.

I found myself in a middle-class neighbourhood with beautiful houses on well-manicured lawns lining both sides of a street. She obviously knew this place well. I got the impression that she'd lived in this neighbourhood, and she wanted me to say goodbye to her loved ones and tell them she was okay and had not suffered. She showed me a funeral and pointed out the people whom she knew and who grieved for her. I nodded, not making any promises but letting her know I would do my best.

A holograph opened before us. She grabbed my hand and jumped into the time portal, dragging me with her, before I could protest or even think about it. She took me through a vortex of time and showed me how everything had happened, clearly identifying the same two black men I had seen earlier.

We found ourselves—as ghosts—observing the events surrounding her death.

I must say, this is eerie, I thought. Yet a part of me knew this world well and didn't react at all. I would have to revisit this strange sense of déjà vu later.

She walked out of a building, and in slow motion a car drove by. As it passed, shots rang out from behind the car, like backfire from the exhaust. I knew it was a rifle, though, because my ears and eyes had been educated by years of target shooting with Dad. I saw the woman fall down, and people screamed and yelled as they ran for cover. The car drove away, spinning its wheels—that same blue Chevy, though the colour fluctuated from brown to blue. I clearly made out the dark older man behind the wheel, as he sped off. I could see his mouth moving as if he were speaking to someone—I guessed it must be the other younger black man.

Then we spun out of time, and an inner voice told me to watch the next scene, because it revealed the future. We found ourselves in an area south of the other murders. I could see a restaurant in a district of shopping malls, located not far off a highway. An off ramp led into the parking lot. I got the feeling the killers would hit here next. I asked for a name or an address, but nothing came forth, except images of the future shooting. I saw a man fall down outside the restaurant, which looked like a popular steakhouse.

I felt a tug and came back to my body, as if nothing had occurred. Dazed, I quickly typed the details before I forgot them and sent the email off to Cheyenne.

Cheyenne responded,

> Did you get any sense of a name or numbers? Without this, we cannot feasibly go to the authorities but will simply have to wait and see. I know it's frustrating, but that's typical, especially when we use this unconventional method of gathering information. Few believe, and the rare people who do are not willing to put their careers in jeopardy, unless the intel is concrete and provable. I'll keep you posted on the developments.

Three days later, a TV news report said that a man had been shot by someone presumed to be the sniper at a restaurant south of the other murders, as I'd predicted. I recognized the area from my RV session and felt overcome by frustration. I wondered why I could see these things but couldn't use them to help.

Two days later, yet another victim was shot, and though I tried to get more information, nothing would come forth. I shrugged it off and waited.

Another few days went by, while I was busy with the kids. That night I had a party to go to, but I noticed an email from Cheyenne and opened it before heading off.

> Hi, Angelina,
>
> Good news: it seems that your remote viewing skills have proved to be efficient and reliable. The authorities have captured the shooters, and, as you said, the two men exactly fit your description. They drove a blue Chevy, and their last known address shows a trailer house and a place very similar to what you spoke of. They had rigged a hole near the license plate, to fire shots from inside the vehicle as they drove by. Obviously, from the reports coming in, they lived pretty much in that car.
>
> Congratulations on your accuracy and precise fact finding!

I foresee a bright future for you in this arena, if you practice and so wish it. Your ability to time-travel and see so clearly, at such an untrained level, is astounding, to say the least, and, as I said before, most probably due to your past life training. Time will tell what this is all about, so be patient and enjoy the ride!

You once asked me where this could lead? This is one direction it could go and where you could help. Namaste.

I felt unsure about all of this—discouraged to be so close to helping, yet so far from providing concrete evidence. Cheyenne had me work on several more cases during the next few months. As each one progressed, I became better at targeting specific information, and although numbers and names still eluded me, the details and the facts became much clearer.

Chapter 29

And So the Mysteries of the Subtle Worlds Unravel

*"It is only by grounding our awareness
in the living sensation of our bodies
that the 'I Am,' our real presence, can awaken."*

—G. I. Gurdjieff

One night, a few months after that sniper case, I found myself watching the end of the news. The broadcaster announced that a woman had gone missing and that if anyone had any information, would they please call the number on the screen?

Immediately, I felt plugged in and got carried away to the White Place, without a sign of why. I looked around, dazed, and before me stood a woman dressed in a white tracksuit. I had learned that when I did remote viewing, certain codes conveyed specific meanings. For example, if a person was a victim, he or she always wore white and had crossed over to the spirit world.

The lovely woman before me had long dark hair and wore a white ensemble, sprayed with blood. Although she couldn't speak, her eyes pleaded with me to help her. She held an infant in her arms, and it, too, now existed in the afterlife.

Then the scene changed, and I saw her in the early morning light, jogging along a path in a park. A dark brown SUV pulled up beside her. She trotted to the vehicle with a smile of recognition. A man dressed in brown pants and a brown bomber jacket—which I later discovered was my code for "the culprit"—suddenly hit her over the head with a tire iron and shoved her into the back of the all-terrain vehicle, looking around to make sure no one had seen.

Next, I saw the young woman all tied up in a boat on an expanse of water. By this time, she was dead. The boat stopped, and the man threw her overboard, weighed down by a cement block. She was visibly pregnant, and I heard the foetus scream in agony, as it shuddered in its last death throes, to finally sink into peaceful sleep. This snapped me out of it fast, but not before I was shown the bay and the general area where she had been dumped.

I came to and wrote down all of the details. Then I sent this off to Cheyenne. Yet with this unconventional way of solving cases, our hands were once again tied. Many months after the murder, the police arrested the husband as the culprit. They found the victims on the shore along a bay, much as I had described. The man was convicted of the murder of his wife and child. In the end, justice was served.

By now, I had accumulated quite a pile of case studies, as we called them. Some I did on my own and others with the help of Cheyenne.

My life became more public. I began going on more outings and receiving clients for intuitive readings, healing sessions, and teachings. My senses expanded and developed at a rate neither Cheyenne nor I could keep up with. The search for more answers ensued, and Cheyenne would begin to exit my life, as I had foreseen not long ago—and as had most of my teachers, once we accomplished what we'd soul-contracted ourselves to do.

Yet I had a few more questions, the most important being: by remote viewing something, did I in any way feed a probable occurrence or help the details to manifest more easily? Quantum physics reported that energy went wherever attention went. I needed to research this subject.

The distance between Cheyenne and me had been triggered on Halloween, while I got ready to go to a party. I dressed up as a witch, black cat and all. I laughed at my reflection, and the kids screeched at how realistic my costume looked.

I checked my emails one last time, in case the party plans had changed. I noticed an email from Cheyenne with a link to a site selling sound-wave products. The email encouraged me to go see them and to buy all of this company's New Age products. I found this, in itself, very odd, and my psychic antennas went on high alert.

What was this all about? It seemed uncharacteristic of Cheyenne, which piqued my curiosity.

I had a half-hour to kill, so I followed the link. At first, I noticed nothing, but then I felt giddy while surfing the site. I decided to dig deeper.

Something wasn't right with this website. I picked up entities and hypnotic spells wound into its program to make people buy the company's product. My recognition of these entities caused an aggressive energy to hurtle toward me and hit me in the gut. I was being attacked. A sucker flew at me, screeching and screaming, with great claws and teeth that could shred me alive.

I immediately shut down the computer, but not before the sucker had a go at me. I doubled over, and it took me a few minutes to catch my breath. These were obviously powerful people, with spells of equal power, but how had Cheyenne gotten pulled into this spell without seeing it?

I checked the time. I had to go to the party, but I would look into this later.

I got home late and waited until the next morning to revisit the website—though I'd prepared this time. I opened the site with my guard up, which protected me as I snooped around and confirmed what I'd suspected earlier.

I found it so unlike Cheyenne to get pulled into this kind of ruse. I had decided to email Cheyenne first thing this morning about what had occurred and my impressions of spells and bindings. I received a reply saying that Cheyenne hadn't felt or seen anything untoward and considered the music quite refreshing and unique. In the words and the energy of the correspondence, I felt the spell, but Cheyenne clearly remained unaware of it, so I made light of it and said I wasn't interested.

Why couldn't Cheyenne see the obvious, coming from this site? What had happened to Cheyenne that now made me wary of our association? Maybe I should go check the site again? Possibly I'd misunderstood or misinterpreted something?

I would give Cheyenne the benefit of the doubt and revisit the site to see. The inner voice of Teacher remained uncharacteristically quiet, which also caught my attention.

I logged on and got onto the site. All seemed fine and quiet. Maybe I had just imagined a freak incident?

Then, surprised by my uncharacteristic doubt, I asked myself why I'd questioned what I knew was true? Why did I try to excuse Cheyenne's lack of insight?

I decided to snoop around once more and see what I could find. All seemed quiet, but I picked up something familiar from a past I knew well. That alone made me dig deeper.

My thoughts wandered to the fact that the website now made me question whether I needed to close another door. All of the signs pointed to it. Had I once again surpassed another teacher? If my intuition and gut feeling proved true about this site, then how could I trust that Cheyenne still had the ability to safely guide me? How would I know if Cheyenne missed something crucial?

To be honest, my real fear was, where would I go next? Could I find someone else to help me, as Cheyenne had?

With that thought, I felt a past binding come to the surface of my mind and wondered about it. This had occurred once before, indicating a connection to a past I had yet to remember. Why here and why now?

The minute I asked, a holograph opened, and flashes of scenes from the Dark Ages fast-forwarded before my eyes, but I couldn't grab hold of them. No matter how hard I tried, nothing made any sense. Frustrated, I commanded the holograph to close.

My thoughts had me distracted, and in that moment I became vulnerable. The attack came from everywhere, and not one but dozens of creatures came at me from the screen, howling and screeching, as they tore at my etheric field with their teeth and long claws. In minutes, I was down and felt as if I would faint. I barely had time to shield myself and turn off the computer. I remember thinking, *What the hell was that?* Then I passed out from the depletion of energy, due to the wounds I'd sustained.

I woke up hours later, weak and very sick. I crawled to the phone and dialled my new friend Samantha's number, because I couldn't trust Cheyenne at this point. Samantha had an interest in energy work, and people in the area knew her as a good person. Her phone rang, and she picked up. In a trembling voice, I explained what had happened. She immediately told me to lie down and said she would come to me astrally to see what was going on. A half hour later, she rang me back to report that my auric field was in shreds and that I had been bleeding life force all over the place. It was a wonder I'd survived.

"What the heck did you do for this to happen, Angelina?" she asked.

I told her what had brought it on, and she suggested I might think about cutting my ties with Cheyenne for a while. Something about the relationship had obviously become dangerous. After much thought and many feelings of regret, I realized this would be the smart thing to do, but why did I keep looking for excuses not to do it? I felt as if I had lost my will and didn't have the strength to fight this or take action—as if I were bound in some way. Yet hadn't I felt this before with others? I stopped musing, because each question made me lose my resolve to do what was healthy. I agreed with Samantha.

The next morning I wrote a lengthy letter, thanking Cheyenne for all of the support, but I said it was time for me to take a break. I purposely kept it light, saying that we would keep in touch. Cheyenne did not react, remaining uncharacteristically quiet about everything. I breathed a sigh of relief, and that alone should have been my warning. Yet it would take years before I could piece together this life experience into a coherent picture, so I didn't want to dwell on it right then.

I needed more than a month of licking my wounds and self-healing to fully recover from the website attack. I knew then that spellbinding and black magic were not restricted to objects and could travel the Net, as did all information.

As the days and weeks went by, my life took another turn. Other events resulting from my new senses made it obvious that some of my previous beliefs might not be true. Samantha had come along when I needed someone to help me unravel the next step of self-development. I discovered that I had touched only the tip of the iceberg, in terms of teachings.

Samantha and I became the best of friends, as we explored and travelled the world of energy and the subtle senses. Our first meeting had occurred shortly before I called it quits with Cheyenne.

She had invited me to a party of local holistic practitioners who performed alternative healing, to be held on a secluded property near the water. I had been guided to connect with her by phone. This would be our first in-person meeting. Would the party be yet another gathering of "wannna be's," seeking thrills? I felt disillusioned by all of the people out there masquerading as teachers, who refused to accept that they had no extraordinary powers or knowledge.

> *Now, now, Angelina, be nice . . . is this how one who needs to cultivate compassion and understanding should be thinking? Shame, dear.*

I shook off Teacher's voice. I didn't want to hear this. I felt a pinch and I squealed, then reluctantly agreed to work at being less condescending and more humble.

We had an early spring that year, with unseasonably warm weather. I got lost driving around, trying to find the party, and when I finally located it, cars packed the driveway. I slipped my jeep into a space on the side of the road, grabbed a basket of giveaways I'd brought for everyone, as was my custom, and walked hesitantly to the house. I tended to act reserved when I felt uncomfortable, and I began to have second thoughts about being there.

About to turn away, I saw the woman I would come to know as Samantha. She walked slowly toward, me, sensing my skittishness.

She had a genuine loving smile and long, naturally grey hair—quite stunning, though an odd contrast to her youthful features. I couldn't have guessed the age of this pretty woman, who had obviously been a beauty in her youth. She had dressed plainly in jeans and a sweatshirt, and I looked down at what I wore, feeling a bit overdressed. My designer days still heavily influenced my choice of clothing, and I rarely went out without the designer warrior gear.

Samantha later told me that I was quite intimidating in the way I dressed, with my naturally dark, beautiful looks. She herself had felt underdressed every time we got together. I felt surprised to hear this, because I didn't see myself in that light, and she always seemed so confident. We both laughed at ourselves.

She extended her arms in greeting and wrapped me gently in a welcoming hug.

She noticed my stiffening up and stated, "I greet everyone this way, so you'd better get used to it!"

All of my misgivings slipped away. I forced a smile of acceptance, humouring her, because she did seem nice and genuinely happy to see me. My walls came down a notch but went up immediately as I glanced over her shoulder and caught three witches staring me up and down, with frowns of displeasure. Samantha felt this and turned with a smile to introduce me to her friends.

They reluctantly smiled back, as she told them, "Now behave, you three. Please come and meet Angelina and make her feel welcome."

The smallest one, whom I would later call Little Suzy, came forward first. With crossed fingers—to ward off evil spirits and witches—which I immediately noticed, she smiled and said welcome. Next came Brigitte, whom I later discovered was her best friend—these two rarely spent any time apart. Last, but not least, came Johanna—an ungrounded but gifted woman who never knew how to be tactful.

She immediately said, "So this is the super-psychic witch you told us about. Doesn't seem so special to me!"

At this, the other two snickered and Samantha frowned, a reprimand to them. She told me not to pay them any mind, that they were harmless and quite nice once you got to know them. I forced a smile, but I would definitely not let down my guard with those three around. Brigitte had a dark cloud hanging around her that I planned to check out later.

Let the games begin! I silently told myself and felt surprised to hear a response coming from the woman I thought might be Little Suzy: *And so they have...*

Ah! I thought, *There is more to this little one than I would have guessed.*

I smiled back at her and caught Brigitte watching our silent exchange with a thunderous frown marring her face. Just when I thought she would explode from holding her anger in, she grabbed Little Suzy's arm and said she needed help in the kitchen.

I sighed, relieved to be set free from that none-too-friendly greeting. Someone called Samantha over to another group and she excused herself, telling me to sit down and make myself comfortable. I spotted a chair on the outer edge of the gathering in a secluded spot along the water and decided that would suit me fine. With my back facing the water, I smelled the new-growth scent of sweetgrass and wondered whether it grew in abundance there, because the conditions seemed perfect for it.

I looked up, into a more or less clear sky, as the sun beat down on my head. It was unseasonably warm, and I wished I had brought a hat. Minutes ticked away, and low conversations hummed all around me. I got lost in daydreaming and found myself inadvertently calling in the clouds to cool things off. No sooner had I sent out the command than the wind came up and clouds appeared, which created a nice shelter from the heat. I smiled in satisfaction, knowing that the aboriginal Elder's mentorship had served me well.

"Well, well, our little witch does have powers! And not your run-of-the-mill ones, either! Be careful who sees you playing, for some would envy and covet."

I nearly jumped out of my skin! Little Suzy had crept up beside me without my sensing her approach. She was good. About to bring up all of my shields, I saw her friendly smile and realized she didn't intend to attack or be mean. Stunned, I had to shift gears fast and answer with my own genuine smile.

At that, reading each other's thoughts, we both started laughing until tears fell down our faces. I liked Little Suzy and felt I might get to know her well in time.

Our hysterics caught the attention of Samantha, and she came over, asking, "What's so funny, you two? I see you have discovered something in common? Should I be surprised, Little Suzy? Didn't I tell you, you two would get along just fine?"

Little Suzy nodded in agreement, abashed at her earlier air of confrontation.

"We'll begin our healing sessions shortly, but you two can keep getting acquainted till then. Little Suzy, please tell Angelina how all of this works."

Little Suzy nodded and then explained the proceedings to me. She said that Brigitte had stayed away because she was afraid of me. That didn't surprise me.

The afternoon became a pleasant outing. I refused to participate in the group energy healings and opted to observe. I noticed that Brigitte had dark masses in her that I suspected could be cancer. I didn't want to presume anything, so I kept it to myself, until Little Suzy, in her nosy way, caught the tail end of my thoughts as I was leaving.

Her last words to me were, "There is much more to you than you would have us believe, and I'm determined to get to the bottom of the mystery that cloaks you, sweetie. Be warned—many here envy you already, so don't let their friendly overtures fool you. Call me, and we'll talk. I think you have something to share concerning Brigitte?"

With that, she turned away, and I was off. What a curious person! Indeed, we would talk.

Chapter 30

At a Crossroads

"In the place of stillness, rises potential.
From the place of potential, emerges possibility.
Where there is possibility, there is choice.
And where there is choice, there is freedom!"

—Gabrielle Goddard

The next day Little Suzy phoned, wondering whether I had time for tea. She obviously wanted some answers, and this was her way of opening the door. I agreed to meet her at a local teahouse.

Feeling unsure what to wear, with the weather so changeable, I chose something stylish but muted. That way, I could blend into my surroundings. Of late, I had gained quite a reputation and had drawn unwanted attention from certain people and organized groups. Tales of a witch, a charlatan, a healer, and—the most common—a psychic medium were being whispered.

I arrived a few minutes late and noticed Little Suzy strategically sitting in the far corner with her back to the wall. Many holistic and health-conscious locals frequented this teahouse. It served an amazing menu of homemade organic food, bought locally. The deeper I delved into altered states of consciousness and higher energies, the stricter I had to be about what I ingested.

As I approached, she wore a welcoming smile and invited me to sit in the other chair with its back to the wall. I nodded my thanks, for it was respectful and precautionary not to expose our backs to a room. My first impression that she knew her stuff proved to be accurate.

"I hope you don't mind, but I asked Samantha to join us."

I nodded that it was fine.

"Samantha will be interested in hearing what you say about Brigitte, because she has put a lot of energy into helping Brigitte overcome a cancer she contracted a few years ago."

Her words confirmed my impression that Brigitte was no stranger to disease. I really liked Little Suzy, a gal after my own heart. With her no-nonsense attitude, she didn't believe in beating around the bush.

I smiled, then heard a voice in my head answer, "You are so right. No time for running around in circles. Life is way too short for those political games!"

I jumped, my head snapping up to stare her directly in the eyes. Had my imagination played tricks on me, or could she really have such telepathic clarity? She smiled back innocently.

Samantha arrived as the waitress appeared, and we soon settled in with scones and tea.

I got right to the point. "As you both suspect, I picked up something in Brigitte yesterday. Because she has such an aversion to me, it's best I go through you two, and you can decide what to do with the information."

They both nodded, eager to hear what I had seen. They said they felt much too close to Brigitte to have an unbiased view. They would share what I said with Brigitte. She could see the powerful witch in me, and it scared her. I decided to do my best in the future to allay Brigitte's fears and gain her trust.

"I picked up that Brigitte has cancer in her gut."

They simply stared at me, not the least bit surprised.

"Old stuff, behaviours, and ways of thinking that she refuses to shift are tied to this cancer. Her fear has her gut frozen in it. Her cells cannot breathe and have weakened, and, in consequence, she has contracted this cancer. I also feel that she knows, but her dread makes her purposely avoid getting checked."

Samantha suggested that I come the following week to a gathering at her house, where a group would exchange energy work. Brigitte would be there. Maybe I could gain more insight into the situation. I agreed, and we said our goodbyes.

The week sped by, with more and more people calling me for appointments. The upper floor of my studio served well as an office, and this guaranteed that I could work odd hours without disturbing the kids.

People asked me to do all kinds of things now, from foretelling the sex of an unborn child to divining and treating the karmic nature of an illness a person suffered from. The inner voice of Teacher continued to guide me and spirits spoke to me in much the same manner, with slight differences in nuance and quality. Samantha sent people my way, and word spread that I had unusual abilities.

I diligently practiced my daily regimen, including the heart mudra, and I wondered how Cheyenne was. Memories surfaced about the day I'd been taught this amazing technique. It helped me feel grounded, centred, and at peace. I told myself that Cheyenne and I had just naturally stopped writing, and that was okay.

The day of the gathering soon came, and I found myself among the first people to arrive at Samantha's. She lived alone, about thirty minutes from me in a quaint French colonial–style house on a country road. This was my first visit to her home, and I deposited my basket of giveaways as a thank-you for being a part of this day. This Native American tradition had etched itself deeply in my soul, as the right thing to do when gathering.

Samantha found it highly unusual and said that the picture I created, so fashionably dressed and carrying my traditional basket, was always a surprise and a joy.

Once everyone arrived, we paired up in groups. I joined Brigitte and Samantha. She had therapy beds set up in various rooms. We would take the spare room setup. I volunteered to get on the table first, so that Brigitte would feel in control and would trust that I wasn't dangerous.

I lay on my back on the table, and Brigitte began energetically working at my abdomen, as Samantha stood at my feet.

Not long after she started, Brigitte doubled over and had to lie down on the bed beside me. Samantha later told me that she'd been guided to treat both of us, for we had become one person in the energy. She had never witnessed anything like this. She could see that I had taken on Brigitte. I only remember no longer being myself—Brigitte and I had melded into one person.

Brigitte and I held hands, as Samantha worked on the healing. I heaved and contorted the whole time, trying to birth something from down in my gut out through my mouth. I suspected it was the tumour I had seen in Brigitte at our last meeting. She now lay quietly beside me, as if in a trance. Little Suzy had been in the kitchen and, when this started to happen, her psychic antennas picked up something unusual going on, and she came running to support Samantha.

Little Suzy and Samantha, one at my head and the other at my feet, worked and encouraged me, as I felt this thing inside me, fighting me. I felt agonizing pain in my gut, from this living thing that contorted my insides. At one point I felt the energetic presence of Cheyenne. Samantha also later commented on Cheyenne's presence. How did Cheyenne know I needed help? What kind of binding did we have for this to happen? I didn't like this one bit and felt determined to find out how it could occur.

I got whatever I'd tried to heave up only as far as my throat. I felt exhausted and told them I couldn't handle any more. Samantha closed the session, and Brigitte sat up, not knowing what to make of it all. This would be the calm before the storm.

Brigitte felt freaked out, and Samantha blamed Little Suzy, thinking she had created this in some way, because Little Suzy often triggered powerful healing. Little Suzy denied having conjured anything up, so Samantha gave her the benefit of the doubt.

When Brigitte had first arrived, I'd immediately picked up that she wasn't well. She had told us she didn't feel well but didn't think more of it than that.

After this latest "taking on" scenario, I decided to tell Samantha and Little Suzy my concerns about Brigitte, but neither of them took me seriously. They hadn't had much experience with that side of me, or maybe they didn't want to believe I was never far off the mark in my predictions. I kept my silence, not wanting to divulge anything more of my abilities.

As the weeks went by, Brigitte developed many health issues. Samantha once again supported her by giving her weekly energy treatments. Brigitte still refused to get the proper diagnostic tests done.

One day while I visited Samantha, my ride to get home never showed up. I'd left my own car at the garage, to be repaired. Brigitte arrived for her weekly treatment with Samantha. By this time, she was less fearful of me, so she agreed that I could support Samantha as a second during her energy therapy.

Brigitte lay down on the therapy table. I took her energy readings, which absolutely told all. I saw that she would leave soon; her spirit was being choked out of her.

"Samantha," I said, "Brigitte should have gone to the doctor months ago, but I feel that now it's too late. Expect a call soon about Brigitte going to the hospital. I picked up energetically that her lungs are not right. A lot of heat has also accumulated in her head. Her legs have no circulation, and she feels intense pain. This started with her self-doubt and fears, which she can't overcome."

When will people realize that most disease and sickness are by-products of how they think and the choices they make? When adults become ill and want to heal, they first have to become accountable for their choices and, second, have to accept responsibility for creating the inner conditions for the illnesses to develop. Most illness is curable; one only needs to choose a healthier lifestyle and outlook on life. Some ideas and thoughts feed us energy, and others take energy from us—energy that would normally keep us healthy and youthful. I felt so sad to see someone like Brigitte, who knew all of this and still couldn't overcome those obstacles.

As I'd predicted, Samantha received a call from Little Suzy one evening, saying that Brigitte had lost consciousness and was taken to the hospital in an ambulance. Tests discovered cancer in her lungs, her gut, and her kidneys and a tumour on the right side of her head.

Little Suzy told us that Brigitte wanted to fight it, but we all knew it was too late.

The next week Samantha and I went to visit Brigitte in the hospital. By that time, I had begun communicating with Brigitte by spirit.

We arrived just after lunch. As we stepped out of the elevator, we were both hit by a field of energy so strong, we almost fell to our knees. I looked at Samantha, and we both had the same question in our minds: *What the heck was that?* It was like walking through soup, and I really had to work at bringing up my shields. I realized this ward specialized in palliative care, so that explained the thick, disruptive energy. As we walked down the hall, I glanced into the rooms and glimpsed all sorts of spirit beings hanging around. I felt awed by the ethereal quality of this space.

We had a nice visit, as the energies settled. I felt very much at peace and knew Brigitte would soon pass, but Samantha and Little Suzy hadn't accepted it, so I didn't say much. Samantha began sending Brigitte healing energy, then sat down. I took Brigitte's hand and told her softly that all would be well and that I would be with her. Brigitte later told Little Suzy that I had brought such a sense of deep inner peace to her, and it never left after that.

When Little Suzy told me this, I realized my state of peace was abnormal for the circumstances. I later came to understand why.

From that visit on, my Higher Self had stayed with Brigitte, and it drained me. My exhaustion lasted a surprisingly long time. I felt sure Brigitte's time to pass on had arrived, but then it dawned on the three of us that we felt inordinately tired all of the time. The inner voice told me that Brigitte had been feeding off us, to hold off the inevitable. When I shared this with Samantha and Little Suzy, they first felt stunned, then shocked, but they knew it was true.

We decided to create energy boundaries, which immediately put a stop to the energetic feeding frenzy that Brigitte had engaged in, out of her desperation to avoid death.

A few weeks passed, and we heard reports from both Brigitte and Little Suzy that I always remained there, helping via my HS (Higher Self). Brigitte's health had been touch and go since we broke off her constant siphoning of our energies. At that time, we directed the Divine Source to bring her what she needed, in place of what she wanted.

Another few weeks passed before we got news that Brigitte was in fact dying. Today we had medical confirmation of this fact, and so we all dealt with this sad news in our own unique ways.

Last week, Little Suzy had called and wanted to know certain things about dying and what I got from my connections with Brigitte. After I hung up the phone, I decided to check energetically on Brigitte. I suddenly found myself so easily in the White Place that I doubted that it had happened, because my family and I had been sitting in front of the TV at the time.

I blinked, and my vision cleared. I noticed a zombie image of Brigitte, standing in a white nightgown, as if waiting for something, in a daze. She floated in the White Place, and then another Brigitte, a double of herself but as we once knew her, appeared. This other Brigitte and I sat down, and she leaned an arm on her knee and rubbed her face. She mentioned the summer when I had shared my impressions with her about the cancer and what she had to do.

She said, "I know you told me, and I didn't listen."

I nodded, recognizing her need to bare her soul.

I, in turn, told her what she would experience when she crossed, because I'd done this crossing with others in the past. I told her about the fear one feels when the ego makes a final attempt to survive and said that I would walk with her as she crossed—that she should reach out to me. I had asked my spirit guides to make sure I remained conscious of what went on as she passed.

I told her not to be afraid. We had a nice talk. Then I found myself back in my chair at home.

The next day on the phone, I told Samantha the details of my etheric visit with Brigitte. Samantha then said that prior to my call, she'd just hung up the phone with Little Suzy, who had told her about everything I'd just said, nearly word for word. Little Suzy now spent all of her time with Brigitte at the hospital. They had seen me floating around the hospital room the night before and that Brigitte and I had engaged in a deep conversation. Little Suzy's phone call to Samantha proved the truth and validity of this work. It took me by surprise, being yet another confirmation of the workings of my Higher Self. What a great gift Brigitte and Little Suzy had given all of us!

Brigitte and I became very close in the etheric realm. Little Suzy reported that Brigitte often cried out to me to take away the pain, and that I did. She told Little Suzy that I always stayed with her, and she now loved me and no longer feared me. She said Samantha also remained there, rubbing her feet.

I felt that I needed to give Brigitte something to take with her, but I didn't know what. I thought it should be an object, but, of course, she couldn't bring anything physical with her once she passed on. I asked Spirit for guidance.

One night I found myself crying, as my emotional shields came down, and I felt a deep abiding affection for Brigitte I couldn't explain. We had never been close in real life, yet this went very deep, as if we were old friends. Maybe it stemmed from another life? It confused me.

I then had a vision that I could take the cancer from Brigitte. This seemed impossible, merely my ego playing with me. Maybe I didn't accept death on some level. Yet if I could take away her cancer, it would demolish what we believe about normal reality.

> *Do not be so sure, Angelina. Do not scoff at what you hear. There is much truth to what you intuit.*

I looked up, cocking an eyebrow. Like, really Teacher, curing cancer? Then why did Mom suffer so much, for so many years, if I could have healed her? Teacher once again spoke up.

> *Have you never asked yourself why your mother lasted all of those years with such a deadly disease and how your not feeling well began when she got sick and lasted only until just after she passed? A convenient coincidence or something else? You might want to think about that one in the future. All is not always as it seems.*

Yet I did know we had far more abilities than we thought. I shrugged this off. *And anyway, if that were the case, how come I didn't cure Brigitte? Ha! Explain that one, my dear Teacher.* Silence answered me.

Two days later, Little Suzy called and said that some of Brigitte's grown children had brought a lot of disruptive negativity into the room, and it upset Brigitte. On hearing this, I felt guided to build a shield of protection around Brigitte and her room.

I went to my studio and began by creating a healing and protective circle: gold sand, for love energy, and blue sand, for healing and protection. Then I put the proper medicines in all of the directions. In the centre, I placed items that would complete my magic circle. I activated with intent and a drumming sequence of vibrations that attuned the circle to Brigitte. I intended to create a shield around Brigitte that only heart-based love could enter.

I added that all who entered in negativity would be purified and turned to love or else made to exit the shield. I also wove a web of protection around Brigitte and Little Suzy, with their permission.

Without divulging what I had done, I then asked Samantha to astrally go and see Brigitte and scan her room. Samantha reported that she felt a shield of sorts and saw gold light. She felt peace and calm within a circle in Brigitte's room. When I bilocated to check on my work, a bright white light emanating from Brigitte nearly blinded me. This made me think she might almost be ready to go. Samantha's words satisfied me that the shield was in place and functioning as I'd intended.

Three days went by.

The fourth day I felt very tired, and I napped that morning. All morning I felt energetically plugged in, reminding me of an initiation ceremony, and I awoke to visions. Spirit guided me to connect to Brigitte, and I went to her room, where white light surrounded us. I looked at the clock, and it said 1:04 am, but then at a later point it said 12:00 noon, which didn't make sense.

A voice told me to cut off all blood flow to the cancer cells and to gently blow Brigitte's light out with a white light coming from my heart. I knew that this act would liberate her in a kind, gentle way, allowing her to cross over.

I proceeded to help her cross over, while showing her what to expect.

As I floated in mid air, I could see Little Suzy bent over Brigitte's prostrate form, crying and upset at her friend leaving. Three guides—people once very close to Little Suzy—encircled her. I heard "Grandmother" and then the names of two men whom Little Suzy later confirmed she knew well.

I then noticed Brigitte lifting out of her physical body, as a white gossamer etheric double of her disconnected. This was the soul of her life. It rose and exited through the top of her head, where the crown accessed the higher dimensions of the self. Her etheric double stayed behind for a last farewell. Brigitte had now left her body and stood by her friend's side, feeling sad for her friend's loss.

She then turned to me with a smile, as I explained all would be well, and we needed to go now. I knew her soul self could not get too far ahead of her, or she could become Earthbound for centuries to come.

She telepathically told me that she wanted to walk through the corridors and say goodbye to all of the beings and thank them for their support. I agreed with a nod, and we glided out of the room. Many higher beings, as well as spirits, worked in places such as this, to help the sick. As we passed the various rooms, glances came our way, and I even spotted a few angelic beings.

I heard faint celestial music from above and knew the time had come. I pointed to the white light that shone over us, and I told Brigitte to take my hand, for I would fly in it with her. She felt afraid and didn't want to leave, but I assured her I would stay with her. I took her hand and brought her up, as I'd done with Mason, and we suddenly emerged in the White Place. I instructed her to go to the centre, and we sat, as I explained how this worked.

She would spend three Earth days here, reviewing her life. When she felt ready, others she had once known and loved here on Earth would greet her. I would be close but not with her, because she had to do this alone. I would come in and out, checking up on her, and I would see her often, for she would visit in spirit.

She felt confused but sat and waited.

As I exited, the life review began, and she was in the zone, so I came back. Before leaving, I pointed out to her the spirit of her mother, standing not far away, waiting for the time when Suzy would cross completely. I told her I would see her once more, before she took that step, and to call me if she needed me.

I came back to normal consciousness at exactly noon. Spirit told me to dismantle the shield, for Brigitte no longer needed it.

I called the hospital and spoke to both Brigitte and Little Suzy. Brigitte felt much better, for some reason, and sounded coherent, so what had my vision been about? Could this be the break before crossing, when a person suddenly becomes lucid, as Mom had the day before she passed?

Or maybe this was a miracle healing? Time would tell.

My gut feeling said that Brigitte would soon cross over. Maybe I'd seen the probable future? It seemed to be mid day when we did this, based on the light from the windows in her room, unless the white light in the vision had brightened the room. I then recalled seeing a different time than when I came back.

I wrote down other details of this experience, with my mind still fresh. I saw myself from a vantage point, watching as she and I interacted. I had my HS (Higher Self) appearance—long, dark, wavy hair, and I wore dark pants and an embroidered blouse. I seemed denser, compared to some around me, and my colours more vivid than Brigitte's, which indicated a lower vibration, or maybe my physical connection to Earth had caused this?

The other beings were made up of translucent light, with less vibrant, more muted colours. Brigitte looked a bit like me but with slightly less vibrant colour.

From the outside, I watched Brigitte and myself. Who was watching? How could this possibly be?

In my last recollection, we stood by her deathbed. I could see her dead body on the bed, as Little Suzy cried, grief stricken. I stood with Brigitte, looking at her body, an empty shell of who she used to be. She had such sadness and regret in her eyes. She knew deep down she could have saved herself, if only she had found the courage to let go of her fears.

The next day at noon I got a call from Samantha, telling me that Brigitte had passed on early that morning at 1:04 am. And that was that.

* * *

The following day dawned bright, and my cousin Debbie called. I hadn't seen her in years, but she'd recently re-entered my life.

"Hi, Angelina. Can you talk?"

Without a pause, she went on, taking it for granted I had nothing else to do, which was so like Debbie. "I want you to meet my teacher Cindy. She talks just like you, and I think you two need to connect."

Debbie, enrolled in a nurse's aid training course, had always been intuitive by nature.

This phone call had followed our most recent conversation, which had me depressed and crying on her shoulder about my situation. I'd broken down and spilled my guts, ending with how I felt lost. I'd wondered where to go next for help and direction, because so few people could relate to me these days. I explained that I had some new friends, but they really couldn't help me. I felt tired of being alone, and I needed answers. I agreed to come to lunch the next day and meet her teacher Cindy.

I arrived at the old medical centre in the heart of town, where Debbie took her course. This turn-of-the-century home had been renovated for training sessions such as this. I made my way to the basement, the location of the training facility. As I stepped into the reception area, a peculiar sense of walking through a shield assailed me.

It being lunchtime, the students had scattered about, talking and relaxed. No one paid me any mind but for the odd glance. Debbie, close by, spotted me within minutes, before I could get my bearings. Something here felt off energetically, but I couldn't put my finger on it.

"Angelina, you're just in time. Cindy is very anxious to meet you." She turned, as a woman of mid height with short dark hair approached.

I couldn't have guessed her age, for she seemed ageless. She had such a look and feeling of youth but was obviously a mature woman, based on the aura she exuded. She calmly extended her hand in greeting, and as my hand touched hers, an electric shock wave of energy passed through me that I wouldn't have expected in a million years. My eyes were glued to hers. Her knowing smile made me feel as if she could see my soul, and I felt okay about it. A shiver ran down my spine, and somewhere deep inside I recognized that I knew this woman and knew her well. She nodded, as if answering my unvoiced question.

"Angelina, is it?" she asked. I nodded, as she continued, "You and I need to talk, but first we're going to get rid of some baggage that's attached to you."

She ignored my perplexed look and literally dragged me to a back room and shut the door. It was just her and me, and we stood face-to-face, sizing each other up. The hair went up on the back of my neck, as the silence stretched out between us. I almost looked away, but her words snapped me back to attention.

"Who is that person who has you so bound up that you do not even know yourself anymore?"

I stared at her, perplexed by her question, and she clearly saw that I hadn't a clue what she meant. A flash of Cheyenne came to my mind, but I shrugged this off as nonsense. I hadn't heard from Cheyenne in weeks.

"You have been working with someone for quite a while now in the energies, and that person has you so bound with energy cords and is siphoning your energy, as well as using your abilities for his or her own. I see all of these cords binding you to this other person and more. We must first free you, before we can talk. I'm amazed that you made it here and that these bindings didn't stop you from coming here, knowing I would free you."

At this point, I felt completely confused, for the idea of bindings seemed strange and alien to me. I *had* experienced difficulty getting there, however, because at first my car wouldn't start for no reason, and then the phone wouldn't stop ringing until I finally decided to ignore it and let it go to voicemail. I hit every red light possible, and fear of this meeting, bordering on a panic attack—which I hadn't suffered for a long time—began to surge, as I arrived in town after my forty-minute drive. I'd begun to look for excuses to miss this meeting, and now I realized all of this could be linked to what she'd told me. Could energy bindings really have this much power over a person?

Before I could ask any more questions, she stood beside me and ran me through an exercise. I acted like a puppet, not questioning and simply doing as she asked. As we progressed, I recognized she mainly concentrated on the use of love energy at all times, as the driving force and the deciding factor. I felt a freedom of spirit and a flow of energy come back that I hadn't experienced for a long time.

What was this amazing technique she had me doing? It resembled no previous exercises I'd ever heard about or explored. And the way she called on this love energy and directed it with specific words and precise gestures was eye opening.

By now, she had my undivided attention, as she performed a series of movements from head to foot. She was obviously doing something energetically to me, and I didn't stop her, because I felt frozen in time and space. I doubt I could have moved or spoken, even if I had wanted to. Yet I felt no fear or anxiety, but instead safe and protected. She finished by sealing me from head to foot. I felt as if I had been cocooned in a warm blanket. What an odd sensation and one I had never felt after such work!

When she had finished, she said, "Okay. That should do it for now. What you felt is the closing of your sheath."

I'd just had confirmation that she could read my thoughts, and this didn't surprise me in the least. What impressed me more was that I felt more than okay with all of it, because she hadn't been intrusive or disrespectful. Everything just seemed so matter-of-fact with her.

"Now, explain to me what the hell you have been up to, to have such powerful energies binding you and a very powerful person holding these. If I'm not mistaken, this same person has also interacted with you in unethical ways, without your awareness."

Not knowing what she referred to, I explained the previous years to her, and she nodded every once in a while. She understood everything I spoke about, which surprised me. She realized that possibly more than one person could be involved in these bindings, because I'd had many teachers in the past, but time would tell. Nothing I shared threw her off. This, out of everything, caught my attention.

Then a thought crossed my mind, and I wondered whether I could talk about some of the recent events that had me so confused. I had kept them private so far. I had no idea how to explain the "visitations" I'd experienced. At first, I had put them down to dreaming, because in the past I had been a vivid sleepwalker and talker. Yet I began to wonder as these "visitations" intensified and even occurred when I was fully awake.

I'd felt vulnerable, confused, and at times violated in an oddly familiar way. It brought to mind the incidents with our school principal, who had taken unacceptable liberties with our gymnastic team when I was barely in puberty. I pushed those memories deeper into my subconscious, refusing to open that keg of worms, especially with a woman I'd only just met.

As I brought my attention back to her, she quietly gazed at me. Her intense look felt comforting and motherly. I wanted to be held by her, so that I could cry out all of my woes and confusion. Her tone softened, as she recognized I was on the verge of losing my self-control.

"We will talk of that another time," she said.

I knew she had picked up some of my confusion but, out of respect, had decided to let me lead. She gently asked me to stand up, about ten feet away from her, and took out a wand, similar to the water divining rods used by the dowser our neighbour had hired. He had two rods, however, while she had only one. She told me to stand still, as she checked my energy. Her hemming and hawing aroused my curiosity.

Noting my interest, she told me never to attempt this on anyone, unless I'd been trained for it, because it could be very dangerous. Great and, at times, deadly karmic repercussions could result from undoing a person's energetic field. This field she called the Chakaura™ was more complex than anyone realized, and it took years of training to understand all of its protocols.

Undoing a person? Chakaura™? Did she mean an energy structure? Her language mystified me.

My silent query made her respond, "People don't realize that the energy field I call the Chakaura™ is a living and breathing organism, quite sensitive to any foreign objects. I trained for years in a closed initiate school, which taught us that the chakras and the aura are not separate. One is simply the result and the emanation of the other, hence Chakaura™: chakra, aura. When someone purposely enters into another's Chakaura™ field, something occurs on another level. It's like cutting open the skin to get access to the organs within. These become one hundred times more sensitive to movement or disruption, because this purposeful action of 'going into' a person's energy removes his or her natural protective sheath, which protects and holds together the unified fields in daily activities. So we must be that much more cautious and respectful. Similar to the way that doctors must perform operations with slow movements and cautionary procedures, it's the same in energy work or when a person opens you up. Specific protocols must be adhered to, which are practically non-existent in today's public healing methods.

"One such is that we never go into a person's field with objects or tools or with open hands."

Before I could get a word in, she asked me to sit down. My mind reeled at what she'd told me, because I had taken chakra readings of people with a pendulum for months now, never realizing this could be unhealthy and even dangerous. And what about that sweeping motion some healers did during a session? Now I recognized why I never felt quite right after an energy session when someone did this to me.

When I asked Cindy about this, she responded, "Well, think about it. You have all of these sensitive energies of light beaming from your inner core outward that are easily influenced, because they are even lighter than air. A person purposely, with intent, cuts you open with her hands, so now you have no more shielding sheath holding everything in its place. If a person comes in with something as solid and powerful as a hand and begins sweeping through these sensitive fields, it mixes up the fields. Healers must respect the natural anatomy of energy and its healthy state. The people who practice these techniques are ignorant of the true laws governing anatomy and energy work. Pay heed and learn. Stay away from any courses or workshops that guarantee you'll be a healer or a practitioner in a weekend or in a few courses. That is hogwash, wishful thinking, and anyone with half a brain sees that—or should, anyway!"

I nodded, liking this woman more and more. Her no-nonsense attitude was contagious and exactly what I needed right now.

I felt horrified at my own healing practices and wondered how many of my personal tragedies and even small accidents might have been linked to the karmic repercussions of the energy techniques I'd practiced? How, in fact, would I know? I hadn't a clue about how this karma would be created.

"All of this is created by energy bindings, which are the highways of communication and an exchange of our emotions and thoughts. This is the world few understand or really know. And you now need to master this world, for your path demands it. Even worse is that you're not in the least aware of grounding as the foundation to self-mastery."

My frown prompted her to explain: "I have yet to meet anyone who truly gets grounding, and it's no wonder, because its true nature has been kept secret within the walls of our school and within the teachings of the Royal Way." She stepped back, looking me up and down.

"It is why you were brought to me."

Everything she had spoken of seemed much more complex than anything I had read about. I needed to find out more. Where had she learned all of this?

She had gone back to looking at my field, which she obviously could clearly see. "With all that you have lived through and experienced, I didn't expect your field to be in such a perfect state of balance. This is highly irregular. I thought I'd have to perform a 'Chakaura™ balancing,' and this isn't the case at all."

Before I could ask about a "Chakaura™ balancing," she continued, "Okay. I want you to go see this woman, Lionesse. Call her and tell her I sent you and that she is to take care of you. She runs a very special school for the gifted, an initiate school that is where you need to go. Your path now lies in this school, Angelina, and it is your destiny unfolding. Do not ask questions, and simply do what I ask, if you wish to find what you seek. In time, all will be revealed. Tell Lionesse I sent you, and she will understand."

With that, she said her goodbyes and told me I could call her any time. Now she had to get back to class, for lunchtime had ended.

I left in a daze, not understanding what had just happened but holding the card with Lionesse's name and phone number tightly in my hand. Strangely, I knew that this would begin another chapter in my life. I felt thrilled but also afraid. I knew deep down that I had no choice and that, as Cindy had said, this was my destiny unfolding.

I decided to sit on this for a time, and when it felt right, I would call this Lionesse woman. What was the rush anyway? I conveniently put the card inside my purse and went on my way. It would be months before it resurfaced, and I felt ready to take this step. But I eventually *did* take the step.

Present Day

I bring my awareness back from the manuscripts I've read and see that hours have gone by.

Nostalgic, I realize that we all see a certain way, but it is far from the true reality of our existence. I accept that something more is out there, grander than anyone can imagine. The subtle world has a science of its own, with its own set of laws, beyond anything our society may be ready to accept. I will continue to seek and purvey truth, as best I can.

I realize why this consciousness unravelled so late in my life. This way, I wouldn't have as many ideas or as much programming to get rid of, compared to people who were aware all of their lives. Forgetting has saved me and has been the key to my "remembering." My rebirth when I crashed turned out to be my greatest test, to make me what I am today.

I see and accept, as well as understand, my destiny in this life. Where it leads me in the coming years will not matter in the end. My true destiny is to find and share the light of love, help others awaken, guide them to their full potential, and become more enlightened in spirit.

This life, only one of many I've lived, is a gift I inherited.

My remembering started on the day of my birth and will continue until I die.

This begins my adventure, and many more adventures await me. The way serves merely as a means to an end.

The sun is about to set, and it's time to think about preparing dinner for Hubby and myself.

My life-changing meeting with Cindy made an auspicious ending for the book.

I type THE END. Sadness comes over me, as I wonder whether the book will be everything I want it to be. Will it stir profound memories in others? Will it spark them to awaken? Will it encourage them to listen to their inner Teacher?

> *Angelina, be peaceful. This is but the first book of many, and it will be as it should . . .*
>
> *Go make dinner for Hubby.*

Giving Thanks

Thank you, Creator, for sustaining me through all of
these years.
Thank you, Teacher and mentors, for
your guidance and great wisdom!

Thank you, dear husband, for your belief in me and your
continued support,
for without you, none of this would have come to be!
You are and always will be
the love of my life. It was destined that we finish what
we started so many lifetimes ago,
and finished it well we have.
I love you for your amazing self-discipline, your
honesty,
your values and ethics, which are so rare these days.
I love you for so many reasons.

To my children, my beautiful children, who have had to
deal with a mother
who was never very conventional. I love you dearly for
exactly who you are.
You are unique because of it and will find your way
back, as I have.
To my beautiful grandchild, who will carry on the family
traditions
in his own unique way. What a gift!

To my family, I love you all and wish you all the best that
life can bring.
To my only sister, a very special thanks for those years

Michèle C. St.Amour

when I was at my lowest
and you were there every day, supporting and helping me heal.
You don't know how that became my saving grace. Love you, Sis . . .
Love you, Dad and Mom—you forsake a life so we could all grow into our own.
Please know you are very special to us all.

To the friends who have come and gone along this path.
I will love you always
for the roles you have played. To all of the others who have come and are still with me.
You know who you are, thank you.
Words are not enough.

And last but not least, to all of my readers and especially my students—
without you, this work would never have come to be.

Oshtalo

About the Author

Michèle Cleveland St.Amour was born in Kingston, Ontario. When she was very young, her family moved to Cornwall, where she grew up in a Franco-American community. To this day, it greatly influences her work and her unique expression.

Dedicated to a life of service, Michèle offers methods of self-transformation based on ancient wisdom teachings from many sources, including her Aboriginal elders. Not anchored in any belief system, she believes that health is a continual process of staying strong spiritually, mentally, and physically and that we must remain in harmony with ourselves, other people, our natural environment, and our Creator.

Michèle's passion for life and high energy touch everyone she encounters. Her keen mind and balanced heart help people overcome boundaries that no longer serve their highest good.

In her early thirties, Michèle went through a spiritual awakening often referred to as the "dark night of the soul." Her many years of physical, mental, and emotional healing forced her to delve deeply into her inner world and her unconventional experiences and states of being. Similar to the paths of other mystics and seekers, her quest enabled her to understand the esoteric meaning of our human journey.

Michèle's novel *Chakaura: Awakening the Muse* parallels her own awakening and tells the story of a young woman's daredevil attitude when faced with altered realities and the moment of enlightenment that changed her forever.

Michèle C. St.Amour

My goal in this book is to offer a different view of the world of spirit through a grounded science. In sharing Angelina's journey of awakening, I aim to de-mystify the path of remembering, which ultimately leads to enlightenment.

—Michèle

Michèle lives simply in a solar-powered house in the mountains, growing a good amount of her own food and implementing a sustainable lifestyle as much as possible in our modern world. She also gathers wild herbs and always plants a wide selection in her garden for various medicinal remedies, in keeping with her Native heritage.

Michèle, a highly intuitive and gifted individual, mentors and guides countless people to self-realization at the **Chakaura™ Institute of Soul**, a clinical and educational centre teaching the principles of natural health. (www.chakaura.ca) Her specialty is knowing the soul, its role, and how to bring soul consciousness to your life experience.

At her centre, Michèle provides programs, workshops, retreats, and seminars to those guided to her. When requested, she will travel to other locations to offer programs and seminars.

To learn more about Michèle and her activities, go to:
www.michelestamour.com

We Welcome You to the

Chakaura™ Institute of SOUL

The Science of Transformation
Body, Mind, Soul & Spirit as One...

"*Yes, it does really exist!*"

We are a wellness centre educating people
on the principles of natural health!

We offer support, knowledge, and simple tools to guide you on your path to self-realization and fulfilling your life's purpose.

Michèle C. St.Amour

The Science of Transformation
Body, Mind, Soul & Spirit as One...

The Chakaura™ School offers:

~ Conferences, Seminars & Workshops

~ Retreats

- At Chakaura™ or on location. We offer 2- to 14-day retreats tailored to your specific needs.
- We travel. We will come to you for a retreat. Contact us for details about hosting the Chakaura™ team in your area.
- In other locations, we organize throughout the year around the world. Check out our events page.

~ Self-Development Programs ~ Introductory and Intensive

- Michèle's Popular "**Journey of Self-Discovery® Program Series**"
- **Advanced Self-Development Programs**
- **NEP** Professional Training for career-oriented individuals wishing accreditation as **Chakaura™ Practitioners** (**NEP Program**) and more.

~ Our Acclaimed

- "Chakaura™ Structural-Balancing" Therapy Training

And more...

The Science of Transformation
Body, Mind, Soul & Spirit as One...

The Chakaura™ Clinic

Chakaura™ Clinic is a centre offering personalized holistic naturopathic energy medicine support. We tailor a plan for your specific needs.

The naturopathic philosophy advocates stimulating the healing power of the body and helping you better manage the underlying causes of stress and ill health. Everyone has a personal signature, so no two plans are ever the same.

Symptoms of stress-related issues are warning signs of improper functioning of the body and harmful lifestyle habits.

Naturopathic energy support is chosen based on the individual's physiological, structural, social, and spiritual environment and his or her lifestyle factors.

Chakaura™ offers:

- **Clinical Services** in Chakaura™ therapies and naturopathic modalities
- **Consultations** for perfect health!
- Our renowned **"Chakaura™ Structural-Balancing" Therapy**
- Other **Chakaura™ Therapies** tailored for your needs
- **Chakaura™ Micronutrient** Support & Program
- And more

NEW

- Our **Chakaura™ Travelling Clinic**

    We come to you with our team of experts. Host us for a weekend conference, followed by a day or more of clinical services. Please contact us for the details.

Visit us at: www.chakaura.ca

Lightning Source UK Ltd.
Milton Keynes UK
UKHW022342100719
345919UK00006B/1432/P